5.

BUCKINGHAM PALACE

09.

87

37

R15

BUCKINGHAM PALACE

The Place and the People

ROY NASH

Macdonald
Macdonald Futura Publishers
London

This edition published 1980 by
Book Club Associates

By arrangement with Macdonald Futura Publishers

Copyright © Roy Nash 1980

First published in 1980 in Great Britain by
Macdonald · London and Sydney

Paperback edition first published 1981 by
Macdonald Futura Publishers
Paulton House
8 Shepherdess Walk
London N.1.

ISBN 0 354 04820 1

Design: Anne Davison

For
JOYCE

Filmset in Monophoto Apollo by
Servis Filmsetting Ltd., Manchester
Printed in Great Britain by
Fakenham Press Ltd, Fakenham, Norfolk

CONTENTS

ACKNOWLEDGEMENTS

The author and publishers wish to express their grateful thanks to the many people who offered generous advice and guidance on the preparation of this book and in particular the following: M. E. Bishop, MVO, Registrar, the Lord Chamberlain's Office; Bert Brampton, the Bramptons' Gallery, London (for assistance with picture research); Bruce Kemble (for assistance with research); the Librarian and staff, Guildhall Library, London; the Librarian and staff, the London Library; Michael Shea, Press Secretary, Buckingham Palace; and Mrs Michael Wall, CVO, Assistant Press Secretary, Buckingham Palace.

ILLUSTRATIONS

All the colour photographs appearing in this book are reproduced by gracious permission of Her Majesty the Queen: also the photograph of the state coach on page 23.

The author and publishers wish to acknowledge the following sources for the black-and-white illustrations:

pp. 8, 16, 22 (top), 27, 29, 34, 41, 46, 51 (top), 68: Guildhall Library, City of London

pp. 24, 31 (bottom), 47 (top), 50: Victoria and Albert Museum

pp. 11, 14 (top and bottom, by courtesy of the National Portrait Gallery, London), 18, 20 (top), 25 (top and middle), 30, 31 (top), 32, 36, 38, 44, 45, 47 (bottom), 49, 51 (bottom), 52, 54, 57, 59, 61, 64, 66, 67, 71, 74, 75, 76, 78, 80, 83, 84, 86, 87, 88, 89, 90, 93, 94, 96, 97, 99, 100, 102, 106, 107, 108, 113, 114, 116, 118, 124, 126, 127, 128, 129, 130, 133, 134, 136, 137, 138, 139, 141, 142, 144, 145, 147, 149, 153, 155, 157, 158: Popperfoto

p. 160: Camera Press

The illustrations on pp. 10, 19, 20 (bottom), 22 (bottom), 25 (bottom), 39, are from the author's own collection.

BUCKINGHAM HOUSE In St James's Park.

SIC SITI LÆTANTUR LARES

Buckingham House, 1754.

1

THE EARLIEST YEARS

JAMES I TO WILLIAM IV

BUCKINGHAM PALACE IS QUITE CERTAINLY the best-known residence of a head of state in the world today.

The Winter Palace of the former Czars in Leningrad is more impressively massive and, despite its somewhat deceptively bland façade, the White House in Washington, D.C., exudes a far stronger atmosphere of power. Yet, to millions of foreign visitors to London, the Palace is a 'must' on their sightseeing list – even although the vast majority come from modern republics in which royalty is an archaic concept. Somehow, for reasons too obscure or complex for definition, Buckingham Palace manifests a strange mixture of mystery and romance which has made it a remarkable piece of international public property.

Curiously enough, however, it was never originally intended as a public focal point. It first became a royal residence solely because a king so deeply loved his queen that he wanted to create a home that would be *private*, and in which the doors could be locked against the scandals and political turbulence of the outside world. It is even more curious that the king in question, George III, should have chosen Buckingham House, as it was then called, since scandal, intrigue and infidelity were firmly embedded in its very walls and in the site on which it stood.

The origins of the Palace's story hang on the diaphanous thread of a silk-worm. In the early 1600s enterprising English minds were fascinated by the possibility of amassing riches from the making of silk. King Henry IV of France (1553–1610) had whetted appetites by setting up a flourishing industry in his kingdom, and a technical manual, published in London in January 1607, noted that the first step towards limitless profit was to plant groves of mulberry trees in which the productive silk-worms could breed.

England's King, James I, studied the manual, consulted his advisers and promptly required landowners throughout the realm to purchase and plant ten thousand mulberry trees. To ensure that everyone clearly understood the meaning of the word 'require', he informed the Lords Lieutenant of the kingdom's shires that their vigilance in seeing that his will was done would be taken as 'an argument of extraordinary affection towards our Person'.

The mulberry plantations duly flourished; but, unhappily for the monarch and the Lords Lieutenant, they provided neither silk-worms nor the basis for extraordinary affection. James had somehow overlooked the essential fact that it was only *white* mulberry trees that nurtured the silk-worms. The more common variety, the black, which had been supplied to the landowners, produced nothing more profitable or original than berries. By chance a few white mulberry trees had been planted, and a handful of their silk-worms was enclosed in a casket presented to James. For as long as it survived he carried the little hoard with him wherever he went around his kingdom, almost as if in a gesture of rebuke to those who had failed to make his industrial dream come true.

On the King's personal orders and payment of £935, a Mr William Stallenge had planted one of the 'failed' mulberry groves on a four-acre site in London, close to

Two views of St James's Park, about 1680. The lines of trees mark the avenue that was to develop into the modern Mall leading to the main entrance of the Palace.

the royal palace of Westminster and eastwards of the villages of Chelsea and Knightsbridge. There the ground, fed by two streams, the Westbourne and the Tyburn, had a marshiness ideally suited to the nourishment of the trees.

Over the years, and as its growth matured, the plantation developed into an attractive garden and Londoners began to seek its benign and leafy shade on hot summer evenings. It was a time when open spaces in London were developing into popular pleasure gardens, where wine, food and entertainment were to be had and where the girls and young gallants of the town paraded up and down and paired off together.

Gradually the Mulberry Garden became not only a rendezvous for young lovers but a convenient outdoor brothel frequented by the professional ladies of the capital, each of whom had a territorial claim on a particular secluded arbour from which she scared away the enthusiastic amateur competition with shrill abuse.

The earliest of all the great English reporters, Samuel Pepys, recorded in his diary for 20 May 1668:

. . . to White Hall, and walked over the Park to the Mulberry Garden, where I never was before; and find it a very silly place, worse than Spring Garden [another pleasure garden], and but little company, and those a rascally, whoring, roguing sort of people, only a wilderness here, that is somewhat pretty, but rude. Did not stay to drink, but walked an hour, and so away to Charing Cross.

In 1633 George Goring, Earl of Norwich, had paid £400 to James's successor, Charles I, for the rights to the garden; and on its western side, to which he added twenty acres, had built himself a mansion that became known as Goring House. A contemporary print shows it to have been an elegantly gabled Jacobean building,

King Charles II (1630–85). His close friend and confidant, Henry Bennet, Earl of Arlington, built Arlington House on the site of the original Goring House, which was destroyed by fire.

Coronation of Charles II in Westminster Abbey, 23 April 1661. Somewhere in the vast onlooking throng was that great recorder of events, the diarist Samuel Pepys; but an over-stretched bladder obliged him to retreat from the Abbey 'a little while before the King had done all his ceremonies'.

with a dome rising above its roof and an iron balustrade fronting five first-storey windows. It was set on a small plateau beyond a rise in the ground, and rows of mulberry trees stood behind it and at its sides like well-girthed sentinels.

The life of Goring House, however, was a short one. During the night of 21 August 1674, it caught fire and was completely gutted. Henry Bennet, Earl of Arlington, who had by then purchased the property from Goring, was safely absent at the time, but the fire consumed the priceless collection of rare paintings, tapestries and furniture which he and his wife, two of the seventeenth century's great spenders, had devoted their lives to acquiring. The total loss amounted to £10,000.

Although the house had gone, there survived a particular legend – that in 1665 (the year of the Great Plague of London) Arlington had presented his wife with one pound of a mysterious substance, until then unknown in England, called 'tea'. He paid £3 for the gift. If the story is true, one of the first cups of the nation's most popular and sustaining beverage must have been brewed in Goring House.

Arlington, a tall, pompous, magisterial courtier who wore a black patch over a scar on his nose, had two main claims to fame: he was a self-appointed leader of fashion, with the peacock habit of dressing himself in exotic style, and he was also a close friend and political confidant of King Charles II. Having observed that one of the monarch's principal personal needs was for a regular supply of women, he set himself up as an unofficial court procurer.

Unhappily for Arlington, his attempts to establish a monopoly with his 'agency' for the provision of mistresses were challenged by an energetic rival in the same business – George Villiers, second Duke of Buckingham. The two men developed a pathological hatred for one another, and at times their rivalry descended into pure farce.

Buckingham, for example, made himself the helpful 'tutor' of Miss Frances Stewart, a vivacious but empty-headed thirteen-year-old girl on whom the King had begun to cast lascivious eyes and whom he was already earmarking as a future companion for his royal bedchamber. Infuriated by his opponent's smart move, Arlington hurried off to see the girl, delivered a homily on Buckingham's unsuitability as a guardian and vowed to 'assist you in conducting yourself in the situation to which it has pleased God and your virtue to raise yourself'. To his utter humiliation, little Miss Stewart responded by screaming with laughter. Buckingham had already been regaling her with hilarious imitations of Arlington's stuffy, windblown manner, and the personal live performance was too much for her. As it turned out, the two rivals had wasted their time and effort. King Charles's bed never was graced by Miss Stewart, who eventually married the alcoholic Duke of Richmond. The thwarted King was obliged to endure his nagging frustration until the happy day when news reached him that the former Miss Stewart's beauty had been so marred by smallpox that he would no longer wish to possess her even if he could.

Arlington, having failed to win renown as a procurer, sought solace in his true profession, the spending of money, and rebuilt the destroyed Goring House on a new and more extravagant scale. There were more domes, a broader and vastly more elaborate façade, great sweeping lawns and deer in the woods. Exotic plants throve in a magnificent greenhouse, and jasmine, set in profusion among stone terraces, filled the summer air with delectable perfume.

The interior of the mansion was as opulent as its exterior. The rare pictures and *objets d'art* destroyed in the fire were replaced by new and impressive acquisitions, a Raphael, two Vandykes and a Leonardo da Vinci bust among them. Window curtains were made of the finest Venetian brocade, and bed-hangings of rich green damask. The new mansion, at which the crowds came to stare in astonishment and envy, was named Arlington House, and in 1681 Arlington extended the estate by buying a plot of surrounding land from Sir Thomas Grosvenor for £3,500. He was still dreaming of spending and building and treasure-hunting when he died peacefully in his bed at Arlington House on 25 July 1685.

After his death the property passed to his daughter, Isabella, who had by then married the Duke of Grafton, but when she was widowed in 1690 she found the house too large for herself and her only son.

Part of a surveyor's report which has survived from the period describes Arlington House as 'a most neat Box, and sweetly sealed amongst gardens, besides the prospect of the Park and the adjoining fields'. The term 'Box' sounds oddly dismissive to modern ears, and, for all the stir it created in London, the place was no doubt modest by the standards of the largest country houses.

By a remarkable quirk of fate, Arlington House then passed into the possession of one who bore the name so bitterly hated by the late Lord Arlington – the name of Buckingham.

The new owner to whom the Duchess of Grafton sold the house was John Sheffield, Earl of Mulgrave and Duke of Buckingham, but neither a descendant nor a relative of Arlington's great rival. A master of several languages and an amateur poet, Sheffield had fought for England against the Dutch when he was a mere boy. By the time he was twenty, in 1669, he had established himself at the court of King Charles II and was bidding fair to outdo the merry monarch as a womaniser.

He was altogether a strange mixture of contradictions, for despite his gambling and inexhaustible roistering he was also the intellectual and political superior of most of the court's hangers-on. In 1679 he was appointed Lord Lieutenant of the county of York. But, a few years later, not only his career but his life itself was threatened when he turned a lustful eye on the Princess Anne, daughter of King Charles's brother, who was subsequently to succeed to the English throne as James II.

Whether it was a mere desire to conquer, or deeper political ambition, that attracted Sheffield to Anne is uncertain, but King Charles certainly thought he had detected some sort of dangerous conspiracy, and made up his mind to punish the importunate suitor. His way of doing so was not exactly true to the image of the jolly, loveable royal personage. He gave Sheffield command of an expedition to relieve the port of Tangiers, then besieged by the Moors, but arranged that he should be sent to sea in a ship with rotting timbers. Those 'advisers' who were in the plot with him assured Charles that the ship was bound to sink the moment she encountered heavy weather. The King appeared to regard that as a most satisfactory promise – despite the fact that among other innocent people who would also go to watery graves was the Earl of Plymouth, one of Charles's own illegitimate sons.

In the event, fate protected Sheffield. The expedition sailed to Tangiers in perfect weather, the ship and its company survived, the Moors retreated at the first sight of the English, and Sheffield returned home to be acclaimed a public

Queen Mary II (1662–94), the elder daughter of James II. After he was drummed out of the kingdom, she ruled jointly with her husband, William of Orange, who was also her cousin.

Queen Anne (1665–1714). By her decree John Sheffield was created Duke of Buckingham, and she gave him a parcel of land at the western end of St James's Park to add to his Buckingham House estate. It may be that she secretly admired him for having made advances to her in her days as Princess Anne.

James II of England and VII of Scotland (1633–1701). One of his ardent admirers was John Sheffield, Earl of Mulgrave and Duke of Buckingham, who acquired Arlington House and renamed it Buckingham House. When James was deposed, in 1688, the royal House of Stuart fell.

hero. Charles, the would-be murderer, added his own words of congratulation and, apparently resigning himself to the fact that higher powers were on Sheffield's side, resumed his friendship with his liegeman as though nothing had ever marred it.

Sheffield was, indeed, one of history's great survivors. After Charles's death he formed an equally close relationship with James II, and, when James was deposed and the House of Stuart fell, he kept his head above the choppy political waters throughout the reign of the joint sovereigns, William of Orange and Mary. He was fifty-four, when, in 1702, William died and was succeeded by Queen Anne, the former princess for whom Sheffield had nearly sacrificed his life.

Despite King Charles's murderous plot against him, there had never been any sign that Anne had objected to Sheffield's earlier advances, and her first actions on ascending the throne included having him sworn in as a member of the Privy Council and appointed as Lord Lieutenant of the North Riding of Yorkshire. By her decree he was created Duke of Normanby on 9 March 1703, and, only fourteen days later, Duke of Buckingham. The title happened to be 'available': the previous Duke, Arlington's old rival, had died without leaving a male heir.

Meanwhile, the new Buckingham, having already acquired Arlington House, had the mansion torn down; and, on the 'bigger and better' pattern so well established by previous owners, he built an even larger house to dominate the site of the former Mulberry Garden. Queen Anne added to the scope of his estate by presenting him with a piece of land that had formed part of the western end of St James's Park.

The new building was named Buckingham House, and a commentator of the time said that, although it was not the most beautiful house in London, its impressiveness was derived from its situation 'and the liberty it allows the spectator of seeing it from whatever point of view he pleases'.

The main structure had a bold, solid appearance, with two rows of tall windows set one above the other and a further line of nine smaller windows immediately below the chimney-tops. Radiating from the house, like huge arms set in an open embrace, were north and south wings consisting of walkways supported by Ionic pillars, leading to two tower-topped opposite-facing buildings that served as coach-houses and servants' quarters.

In the large forecourt of the house was set an octagonal pool, in the midst of which sprouted fountains supplied, by pump, from a lead storage tank holding fifty tons of water. The whole site was enclosed by an iron palisade, in whose centre, and in line with the main entrance of the house, stood a noble iron gateway giving access to the Mall. The gate was crowned by a superb representation of the Duke's coronet, his coat of arms, the Garter and St George.

A terrace of white stones, interspersed with dark-coloured marble, led up to the main entrance, and immediately inside the hallway the visitor was faced with the magnificent spectacle of three stone arches supported by Corinthian pillars. Beyond the arches stood the main staircase – forty-eight steps, each ten feet deep and each cut from a single piece of Portland stone.

The roof over the staircase was fifty-five feet above the entrance-hall floor, and its 1,400-square-foot area was adorned with paintings of gods and goddesses, with Juno and Venus as the central figures. One of the main ground-floor rooms, which Buckingham chose to call his 'parlour', was nearly forty feet wide by thirty-three feet long, and paved with white marble. Above that parlour, on the first floor,

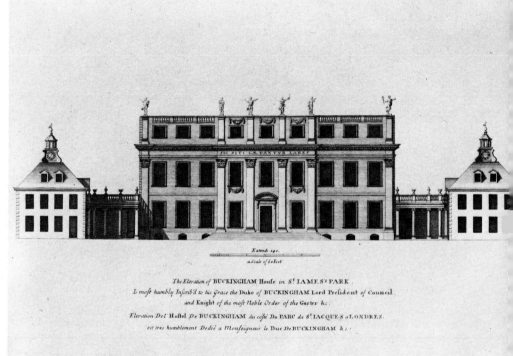

The Elevation of BUCKINGHAM Houfe in St IAMES's PARK
I moft humbly Infcrib'd to his Grace the Duke of BUCKINGHAM Lord Prefident of Council,
and Knight of the moft Noble Order of the Garter &c.

Elevation Del' Hoftel De BUCKINGHAM du cofté Du PARC de St IACQUES a LONDRES.
eft tres humblement Dedié a Monfeigneur le Duc De BUCKINGHAM &c.

A contemporary architectural drawing showing the elevation of the proposed Buckingham House. In the building's final form the two wings (housing servants, coaches and horses) extended outwards from the main building, instead of in line with it as depicted here. Translated, the inscription over the main building reads: 'The household gods delight in such a situation.'

stood the main saloon, with an enormous centrepiece painting on the ceiling depicting Apollo lying on a cloud beguiled by the arts of the nine muses. Everywhere there were fine paintings and statues, all perfectly lit by the great windows, and there was a library so meticulously organised that, according to Buckingham, 'by its mark a very Irish footman may fetch any book I want'.

Buckingham House certainly commanded one of the finest views in London. From his front windows the proud owner could see, beyond the sweep of the Mall and the adjoining avenues in St James's Park, Westminster Palace and the banqueting hall in Whitehall where Charles I had presented his neck to the executioner's axe. From the rear of the house he could gaze upon the Surrey hills and the market gardens of the tranquil little village of Kensington.

Altogether, true to the traditions of the site, the place was just a shade too ostentatious, and one London wag, summing up the derision that many people felt for the Duke, hung on the railings a placard which read: 'This is the House that Jack built.'

The building had been designed by a Captain William Winde, who discovered, to his rage, that Buckingham's philosophy was 'build now – pay later'. When delay in settlement of his architect's fees was bringing him close to bankruptcy, Winde took Buckingham up to a flat part of the roof – ostensibly to commend that magnificent city view – and threatened to jump off unless his client paid up forthwith.

'And what is to become of me?' cried the Duke, who was ever a man for getting his personal priorities right.

'Why, you shall accompany me!' the architect howled in reply.

Suddenly, as by a miracle, Buckingham recalled that this was, indeed, the very day he had set aside for paying the bill, and he hurried down from the roof at once to see to the arrangements.

After the death of his patroness, Queen Anne, and the accession of King George I in 1714, Buckingham finally retired from public life, and spent almost all his time at Buckingham House, quietly reading in his library. By the time he reached his sixties he had mellowed into a thoroughly domesticated, solid citizen. He spoke loftily of virtue and thought himself the adornment of his era.

He died at his home on 24 February 1721, aged seventy-two, and a friend remembered him as a 'good husband, a just and tender father, a constant, zealous friend and the most agreeable of companions'. Less charitably, but with greater accuracy, Dr Samuel Johnson, the great lexicographer and essayist, wrote: 'His character is not to be professed as worthy of imitation . . . . His sentiments with respect to women he picked up in the Court of Charles, and his principles concerning property were such as a gaming table supplies. He was sensual and covetous . . . .'

The widowed Duchess of Buckingham, who had been the Duke's third wife and shared her husband's taste for self-approbation, insisted on a lengthy lying-in-state of the corpse in the parlour of Buckingham House, and a funeral of royal proportions with the interment in Westminster Abbey. Bishop Atterbury, the Dean of Westminster, who officiated at the burial, was irritated by the Buckinghams' compelling need to overdo everything. The day before the funeral he wrote to his friend, the poet Alexander Pope: 'Tomorrow I go to the Deanery and I believe I shall stay there till I have said "dust to dust" and shut up that last scene of pompous vanity.'

As things turned out it was not quite the last scene, for the Duchess managed to persuade the ecclesiastical authorities to accede to the Duke's request that a splendid monument to his name (and for which he had willed the necessary money) should be erected in the Abbey's Henry VII Chapel. Bishop Atterbury did, however, jib at a line in the Latin epitaph to be inscribed on the monument, in which the Duke (who had helpfully composed the piece himself) was referred to as adoring Christ and trusting in God. In view of some much-gossiped-about aspects of Buckingham's private life, and his overweening conceit, Atterbury insisted on the line being omitted.

Once she had settled into her widowhood, the Duchess strove to turn herself and Buckingham House into the two leading social edifices of the age, out-royalling royalty whenever occasion offered itself. Indeed, she did her best to establish a kind of shadow court, with her own set of 'courtiers' who were required to stand in her presence and leave it by retreating backwards to the door.

She set tongues wagging not only by her eccentricities but by her blatantly militant adherence to the cause of the Jacobites, the sect which, since the dethronement of James II, had sought the restoration of the royal House of Stuart. Every 30 January, on the anniversary of the beheading of Charles I, she would sit, all in black, in a vast throne-like chair, also draped in black, and hold a lugubrious, day-long wake in the great salon of Buckingham House. Her courtiers, shrouded like herself in mourning, would cluster around, vying with each other to conjure up the most doleful mood of anguish.

Sir Robert Walpole, the Prime Minister, who was irked both by her silly Jacobite intrigues and by the manner in which she wafted about the London social scene dressed like a princess in red velvet and ermine, described her as 'more mad

George III (1738–1820), still young, handsome and regal, and soon after he had succeeded his grandfather, George II, in 1760. He gazes composedly upon a realm from which, in due course, his American colonies were to break away to independence.

Queen Charlotte (1744–1818), wife of George III. She loved her husband dearly and proved it by producing fifteen children – fourteen of them born at Buckingham House, later known as Queen's House. Some of the King's subjects thought Charlotte's attachment to domestic life and the rearing of children was (in the words of a contemporary verse-maker) 'vulgar and unamusing'.

with pride than any mercer's wife in Bedlam'.

Vanity lingered absurdly in the Duchess right up to her last conscious moments in 1742. As she lay dying in one of the lofty bedrooms of Buckingham House, she summoned her failing breath to issue orders for the splendour of her funeral. She was worried that a gorgeous canopy, which was hastily being prepared to cover her lying-in-state, might not be finished in time to receive her personal approval.

'Why don't they send it for me to see?' she croaked. 'Let them send it though all the tassels are not finished.' And she admonished her 'courtiers' to make certain at the end that she was genuinely dead, and not merely in a coma, before they sat down in her bedchamber. Within a short time of receiving that caution the anxious death-watchers were relieved to discover that they could safely be seated.

Edmund, the Buckinghams' son, had died in his early youth, and the Duke had therefore willed that Buckingham House should pass into the possession of one of his illegitimate sons, Sir Charles Herbert Sheffield. Unlike his colourful father, Charles Herbert lived a quiet life, largely away from the public gaze, and in 1761, some nineteen years after the Duchess's death, he sold the house and its land to the Crown, so that for the first time the mansion at the head of the Mall became a royal property.

In the intervening years two Georges, I and II, had worn the crown, and in October 1760 it had passed to George III, the first of the United Kingdom's Hanoverian monarchs to have been born within the boundaries of the realm. To George III, Buckingham House seemed ideal for his main purpose – to use it as a domestic hideaway in which he could concentrate on his beloved Queen Charlotte, younger sister of Adolphus Frederick IV, ruler of the tiny duchy of Mecklenburg-Strelitz on the Baltic coast of Germany.

George and Charlotte made a contrasting couple in public – he handsome and regal, she shortish and thin, with a rather flattened nose, but with a fine head of rich brown hair which helped to rescue her appearance from downright mediocrity. In private her vivacity and good nature amply compensated for her lack of feminine beauty, and the King, free of his ancestors' taste for promiscuity, loved her from wedding-day to deathbed.

George III had bought Buckingham House from Charles Herbert Sheffield for £21,000; but although it basically suited him domestically – and it was conveniently close to St James's Palace, the seat of the official royal court – he was not entirely satisfied with it as it stood. Very soon he began to alter some of its main features, and before long he grew obsessed with the need for alteration.

Some of his changes were for the better, but many were for the worse. For example, he had Buckingham's stately gateway removed, and the gap closed by railings, so that there was, oddly, no longer a main front entrance to the estate and visitors were obliged to make their way in through nondescript side-gates. He built four fine new libraries, but added a number of new adjoining buildings apparently without much concern for the order and balance of the main house itself.

One critic, noting the number of 'irregular additions' to each side of the mansion, said the general effect reminded him of a country parsonage 'to which every incumbent had added something, one a wash-house, another a stable, another a hen-roost, etc., till the whole is made a mere jumble of patchwork'.

The King furnished his own private apartments on the ground floor simply but

Buckingham House in 1775. For some eccentric reason George III had removed the stately centre gateway, erected by the Duke of Buckingham, and enclosed the whole forecourt with iron railings. Visitors, however notable, had to make their way into the mansion through small side-gates.

comfortably, but, in tune with his devotion to her, saw to it that the Queen's rooms were sumptuous. Her drawing-room and its neighbouring ante-room were upholstered in blazing crimson; but it may well have been that she found the colour too overwhelming, since she preferred taking her ease in the Green Closet — where, in course of time, the walls were hung with Gainsborough's portraits of the royal children.

To celebrate the completion of the main alterations, which had cost a total of £47,546, the King had arranged to hold a house-warming party at Buckingham House on 6 June 1763. Queen Charlotte had planned her own special gift to her husband, combining the house-warming with his birthday, which fell on 4 June, and contrived to get him away from the house for a few days while her plans were completed. When George returned, at ten in the evening of 6 June, Charlotte took him to a room on the rear of the first floor and threw open the shutters with an excited flourish. The King gazed down with delight upon the Queen's remarkable gift — a temple and bridge erected in the garden and illuminated by four thousand gas-lamps which also floodlit a large mural of George in the act of extending the blessings of peace to all the nations and peoples of the world. Beneath the royal feet cowered the miserable figures of Envy, Malice and Greed.

Apart from the rewards of love, which led to the birth of fourteen princes and princesses at Buckingham House in twenty years, Charlotte was not neglected by the state, and in 1775 the house was legally settled upon her by an Act of Parliament and became known as Queen's House.

It is, of course, for the tragedies of his life that George III is best remembered — his autocratic, unyielding political policies, which resulted in the loss of Britain's American colonies, and the frequent bouts of mental disturbance that finally bore him into the dark night of permanent insanity. Even before his health began to

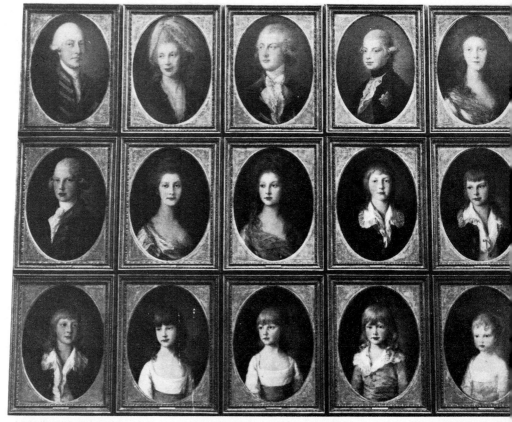

George III and Queen Charlotte and family: fifteen oval portraits painted in 1782 by Thomas Gainsborough. In the top row, third from the left, next to Queen Charlotte, is the Prince of Wales, the future George IV. To the right of him is the Duke of Clarence, the future William IV.

In the late eighteenth century the former Buckingham House was sometimes known as the Queen's Palace, more usually as Queen's House. Whatever its title, it had, as this engraving suggests, all the appearance of a country gentleman's country mansion.

decline, the earlier relaxed atmosphere of the house had gradually been replaced by an eccentric obsession with pernickety etiquette. No member of the household was allowed to pass a room occupied by a member of the Royal Family if the door stood open. There was a rigid rule that any servant seeking to enter any of the Queen's rooms should never knock but always rattle the doorhandle.

The general rule (a replica of that established in her day by the Duchess of Buckingham) was that no one ever sat in the presence of Their Majesties: and, through interviews lasting up to as much as two hours, even William Pitt the elder, the King's Minister, was obliged to stand. Pitt's agonising gout brought him no reprieve from the rule, although George was gracious enough, at the end of one exhausting meeting, to express the hope that Mr Pitt had not suffered unduly from being so long on his feet.

Every morning, promptly at nine, the King took breakfast with the Queen and the princesses, whose places down the table from their parents were arranged in strict order of seniority. The King ate his second meal of the day regularly at two in the afternoon, and the Queen and the princesses ate theirs at four. All the members of the family met together again at five for a glass of wine, and George then worked for an hour or two in his study until card-tables were set out for the royals and any guests. Card-playing was strictly for entertainment: gambling was barred.

The strangest moment of all came at around ten o'clock. Unfailingly, each evening at that hour, supper was laid out in the Queen's drawing-room; but, by a firmly established convention, no morsel of food ever passed any of the royal lips. At eleven, after having sat with eyes studiously averted from the laden table, the family retired to bed.

It was indeed a curiously routine-ridden, ineffably dull household, and only very occasionally was it disturbed by untoward events. One of these, which lasted long as a topic of household conversation, occurred in 1771 when Sarah Wilson, a servant of one of the ladies-in-waiting, broke open one of the Queen's private cabinets and stole a number of valuables, including jewellery. She was arrested, tried and sentenced to death, but Charlotte personally interceded for her, and her sentence was commuted to transportation for life to what was then still His Majesty's North American colony of Maryland. Upon her arrival in the colony Miss Wilson was purchased by a Mr Devall, of Bush Creek, Frederic County, but escaped and fled to Charlestown, South Carolina. There, according to legend, she assumed the title of Princess Susannah-Carolina-Matilda, passed herself off as a sister of Queen Charlotte and did very well for herself.

Charlotte's decision to become involved with the Wilson case cannot have been taken lightly. Like her husband, she shunned publicity. He enjoyed the quiet country life – he earned the title of Farmer George – and she was happiest when devoting herself to her children, her embroidery and music. Ironically enough, Charlotte's love of privacy made her unpopular with many of the King's subjects. Despite the widespread poverty of the time, they thought she should display greater majesty, and that Queen's House should be more of a state building and less exclusively a home. The idea of Charlotte fussily presiding over the nursery and sharing in her children's daily routine cares 'like a common mother' was too much for one 'poet', who was moved to proclaim:

> What vulgar, unamusing scene,
> For George's wife and Britain's queen!

The eastern (or main) front of Queen's House was like a magnet to which Londoners were irresistibly drawn. Outside the railings they met their friends and gossiped and hoped to be lucky enough to catch a glimpse of the royals.

Cattle graze in London's Green Park and, away beyond the trees, Queen's House (or Palace) basks in the sunshine of a tranquil 18th-century summer's afternoon.

Good-tempered and cheerful as she usually was, Charlotte was not above occasionally delivering a smart box on the ears to a servant who had displeased her, and George took quiet satisfaction from the spectacle of his teenage sons receiving corporal punishment. When one of them had erred in his tutor's eyes, the thrashing would be administered by two servants – one to hold the boy's arms and the other to wield the whip.

As compensation for such unhappy moments, George and Charlotte would turn to the consolation of music. While ministers of state met late into the evening to groan over their tiresome master's unceasing plots to dominate Parliament, the private apartments would be filled with the felicitous sound of the King, at the piano, accompanying Johann Christian Bach on the flute. Bach, son of the famous Johann Sebastian, often went to the house to give Charlotte music lessons. George Frederick Handel, too, was a frequent visitor.

Dr Johnson was generously allowed to browse among the marvellous collection of books in the Queen's House libraries, and after his first meeting with the King he declared: 'Sir, they may talk of the King as they will, but he is the finest gentleman I have ever seen.'

One of George III's most famous acquisitions, housed in the Royal Mews of Buckingham House (and used to convey Queen Elizabeth II to her crowning nearly two hundred years later), was the great state coach. This was designed by Sir William Chambers, the architect responsible for London's magnificent Somerset House, cost precisely £7,587 19s 9½d and was delivered to the King in November 1762. Joseph Wilton, one of the leading sculptors of the period, undertook the elaborate carving, which on the main body of the coach represents eight palm trees, branching at the top and supporting the roof. Two figures at the front are

The state coach, acquired by George III in 1762 and still in use today.

The fashionable and their families parade under the trees of St James's Park against the background of Queen's House. From a painting, in 1790, by Edward Dayes.

shown sounding eternal blasts on conch-shells to announce the sovereign's approach. Two figures at the rear carry, over their shoulders, the imperial fasces – bundles of rods and tridents. The centrepiece of the roof shows three cherubs, representing England, Scotland and Ireland, supporting the Royal Crown and holding in their hands the Sceptre, Sword of State and Ensign of Knighthood.

Giambattista Cipriani, the Royal Academician, painted the panels, including those on the doors that represent such features as Mars, Minerva and Mercury sustaining the Imperial Crown of Great Britain, and – in the words of the contemporary description – 'Industry and Ingenuity presenting a Cornucopia to the Genius of England'.

The coach is twenty-four feet long, eight feet three inches wide and twelve feet high, and weighs a total of four tons. But, for all its impressive air of regal authority, some of its early public appearances were not greeted with due deference. On its return to Buckingham House on 29 October 1795, after taking George III to the opening of Parliament, it was stoned by the mob, who were protesting against measures to relieve Catholics from civil restrictions, and every pane of glass in its windows was shattered.

Despite riots, despite political upheaval and even assassination attempts against him, George III continued to follow the rigidly dull pattern of domestic life at Queen's House until his mind deteriorated to such an extent that, in 1811, Parliament was obliged to introduce an Act creating his eldest son Regent for the remainder of the reign. George III's days at Queen's House then came to an end, but he lingered on in the seclusion of Windsor Castle – a sad, demented old man, blind in his right eye and with little vision in his left – until death released him on 29 January 1820.

Charlotte had already died, in November 1818, and one of the last tasks of her household had been to gather together her personal belongings. They searched around to find an empty box in which to pack her diamonds, but without success – until someone remembered having seen one in a small room which the late Queen had used as a store-room for junk. The box was found, thickly covered with dust. Inside, looking as though it had been carelessly discarded, was a collection of the King's royal regalia, including his sword, star, loop and garter. In such a forgotten tomb had some of the trappings of former power been buried.

The new monarch, who had spent nine years as Prince Regent, was George Augustus Frederick, now King George IV. When he was born, on 12 August 1762, his father had presented the bearer of the news with £500 to mark the royal pleasure at the arrival of an heir. But the gift was an expression of a joy which would not survive long with the King nor be shared by many others, once it was observed what kind of man his son had grown up to be. As far as Queen's House was concerned, George IV was to make important structural changes, and to leave its stones as a memorial to a profligacy and self-indulgence that, even in its previous chequered history, the site had not known.

At the age of twenty-one George, then Prince of Wales, had moved out of the family home and established himself at Carlton House, a sprawling, rat-infested mansion on the south side of Pall Mall, where Waterloo Place now stands. There he immersed himself fully in his favourite occupations: debauchery and the spending of money on a prodigious scale. Parliament had already granted him a stipend of £50,000 a year – an enormous fortune by the values of the time – but within three years the first of the many debts he was to accumulate throughout his life

George IV (1762–1830). the King in his younger days – a somewhat flattering portrait in which the high collar conceals the spreading flabbiness of his neck.

Mrs Mary Anne Fitzherbert (1756–1837), mistress of George IV. While Prince of Wales he married her secretly and in breach of the 1772 Royal Marriage Act, which still applies and decrees that no descendant of George II may marry without the consent of the sovereign.

The front of Carlton House, London, 1820. Here George IV lived while he was still Prince of Wales. He found it gloomy and rat-infested and planned to turn the rebuilt Queen's House into a palace that would make him the envy of the world's royal families. Waterloo Place, on the south side of Pall Mall, now stands on the original Carlton House site.

amounted to £160,000. Public money was called upon to pay that off, but nine years later he was once again in the red – this time to the tune of £630,000. He gambled wildly, lost heavily, handed out jewellery to his women friends like a berserk Santa Claus and developed a mania for building. The results included his famous Royal Pavilion in the Sussex seaside resort of Brighton.

In breach of the Royal Marriage Act,* which his father had pressured Parliament into passing in 1772, he secretly married his mistress, Mrs Fitzherbert, thus entering into an illegal alliance. But he also contracted an 'arranged' marriage with Caroline, Princess of Brunswick, whom he detested on sight and who was equally disenchanted with him. (The story is that, when he was introduced to the Princess at Queen's House and received her kiss of welcome, he staggered away and called in a loud voice for brandy. Whether his revulsion was due to Caroline's uninviting appearance or to the obvious indications of her notorious aversion to personal hygiene is not certain.)

Despite vast expenditure on Carlton House, George could not put the place into a shape that satisfied him, and in 1825 he proposed to Parliament that he should build himself a new palace to outshine the most glorious residence of any of the world's monarchs.

Parliament, already dazed by the drunken-sailor extravagances of its royal master, dug in its heels. Joseph Hume, the radical MP, summed up his sense of outrage with the terse comment: 'The Crown of England does not require such splendour. Foreign countries may indulge in frippery, but England ought to pride herself on her plainness and simplicity.' George, however, had no intention of allowing himself to be thwarted by a mere Parliament. What he could not achieve by direct and honest application he would secure by deception, and he found a willing accessory in the person of John Nash, the architect.

Nash had already helped to immortalise the King by laying out the London park that became known as Regent's Park and designing the broad highway, Regent Street, which ran directly from Carlton House to the park gates. He was among the very few whom George could claim as a genuine friend. Together, King and architect devised a plan that seemed foolproof. Queen's House, alias Buckingham House, would have to come down – that was indisputable, since neither man favoured the idea of adjusting to other builders' concepts of what was royally right. But (happy solution) why tell Parliament that a *new* palace was to be constructed? Let the operative words be 'repairs' and 'improvements'.

George was not without influence among some members of the House of Commons, and he was confident that the plan could be carried through successfully. And, as events showed, he was right. Parliament agreed that the estimated cost of the 'renovations' – £252,690 – should be found from the Crown's land revenues and the Department of Woods and Forests, and the work began. Nash set about dismantling the old building, but took as much care as he could to disguise the true nature of the operations. The new palace, as it slowly began to take shape, was confined to the area of its predecessor, and its elevation remained similar.

Very soon, however, a committee of the House of Commons was complaining in injured terms that the money allocated for the 'repairs' was rapidly running out

* This still applies today, and decrees: 'No descendant of George II shall be capable of contracting matrimony without the previous consent of the King, and signified under the Great Seal, declared in Council, and entered in the Privy Council books.'

The garden front of John Nash's building – sometimes called, as in the original caption to this engraving, 'the King's Palace at Pimlico'. The 'inverted egg-cup' dome is much in evidence.

Another view of the New Palace, with the dome just discernible above the main portico.

due to charges which (most inexplicably) 'had not been foreseen or ascertained at the time'. By then a revised estimate had put the cost of the work at £432,926. One of the reasons for this alarming increase in the budget was that the architect was plainly out of his depth and had made some incredible blunders. He was obliged to make the embarrassing confession that his design for the new wings of the building had gone awry, for 'I was not at first aware that the effect would have been so bad . . .'. The bill for correcting that one mistake came to £50,000.

A dome (later removed) that Nash had placed over the roof was execrated as 'a wretched inverted egg-cup', and the unfortunate architect was obliged to make an even more humiliating admission about that. He did not intend it to be visible from the front (or 'public') side of the palace, he said, and added lamely, 'nor was I aware that it would have been'. Not unreasonably, the impression got around that the 'repairs' envisaged by Nash on paper and those that actually emerged had little in common.

And by that time the soaring costs of the building – now variously known as Pimlico Palace and New Palace – were public knowledge, and George and his propensity for dipping his fingers in other people's pockets were lambasted in pamphlet and cartoon. The attitude of the man-in-the-street, the ultimate paymaster, was summed up in one lampooning verse, *The Palace That N--H Built*, which began:

> This is the man whom they Johnny Bull call,
> And who very reluctantly pays for it all,
> Who from his youth upwards he worked like a slave,
> But devil a shilling is able to save.

Johnny Bull notwithstanding, King George was not to be diverted from his purpose. In addition to the 'renovations', he had determined on a triumphal arch on noble Roman lines, which was to lead the way into the palace forecourt. It would be adorned with various emblems representing, among other things, the battle of Waterloo, Valour, Virtue and Victory. The arch was to be sixty feet high, and three gateways within it would be of mosaic gold. The Marble Arch did eventually arise in 1828, but later, in Queen Victoria's reign, it was uprooted and re-erected on its present site, on the north side of Hyde Park, where it now gives its familiar name to a station on the London Underground system.

When it had finally taken shape, the exterior of the new palace was castigated by one expert for exhibiting 'general feebleness and triviality', and royal glory was conspicuous by its absence. But, despite Nash's shaky, hit-or-miss efforts, some compensation was provided by features of the interior. Immediately inside the main entrance was a Grand Hall, fifty-five feet by thirty-six feet, and eighteen feet high. At the end, on the left, rose an imposing 'winged' staircase of white marble with a centre flight and two returning flights.

Above the staircase were the saloon, fifty feet long, and the throne chamber with a length of sixty feet and walls hung with rich crimson satin. The ceiling of the chamber was ornately carved, but the centrepiece, on which the eyes automatically focused, was a dais, three steps above floor level and carpeted in crimson velvet, on which the throne would stand. Over the dais was spread a canopy, also of crimson velvet and some eighteen feet high.

The King's bedroom was equally richly decorated, if not exactly cosy – like the saloon, it was fifty feet long. And even the smaller of two drawing-rooms boasted no fewer than eighteen Corinthian columns with lapis-lazuli plasterwork to simulate stone. There were music-rooms, picture galleries and libraries — all of them impressive. The suite of private apartments, wrote one commentator who had remained a faithful admirer of the architect, 'has an air of simple elegance, an unostentatious, luxurious comfort, enhanced in no small degree by the windows opening immediately upon the terrace . . .'

All in all, however, there is no doubt that Nash's New Palace was not a great and glorious work. Hapless Johnny Bull, for all he could see from the other side of the railings, had hardly been rewarded with a gallant spectacle. The more eloquent voice of the architectural critic, W. H. Leeds, spoke for him in one devastating, dismissive sentence: 'Uglier structures of the kind there may be many; yet scarcely any one that is more deficient in grandeur and nobleness of aspect.'

But, whatever critics might say, George was anxious that Nash should press on towards the completion of the place, however great the continuing costs. On 23 August 1829 the *Observer* newspaper wrote:

The New Palace: His Majesty has expressed his earnest desire for the speedy completion of his new Palace at Pimlico, in consequence of which additional hands have been put on the work and the number of persons now employed amounts to 1,000. At one time the enormous sum of £10,000 a week was expended on the work, but by order of the Duke of Wellington [the Prime Minister], the issue of money is now restricted to £30,000 a quarter . . . . We are credibly informed that Mr Nash has promised to have the new Palace ready for occupation by 12 August 1830.'

By November 1829, teams of construction workers were kept busy on the site each night until ten o'clock, working by candle-light. The rush and scurry, however, were all in vain, for George IV was destined never to occupy the Palace.

Plagued with gout, heavily dosed with laudanum against the pain of a bladder infection, he retired to Windsor Castle and spent most of his time in bed, looking sorry and worn-out, with a grubby flannel jacket covering his great bulk and a white nightcap perched on his head. On 26 June 1830, he suffered a stomach haemorrhage, grasped the hand of his physician, Sir Wathen Waller, and cried out with pathetic accuracy: 'My boy, this is death!'

Few mourned his passing. Indeed, the London *Times* — the great 'Thunderer' of its day — bitterly inquired: 'What eye has wept for him? What heart has heaved one throb of unmercenary sorrow?' If there were such eyes or hearts, the

A view of the Palace, in 1842, as seen across the lake in St James's Park — from a painting by Thomas Shotter Boys (1803–71).

*William IV (1765–1837).
The third son of George III,
he was born in Buckingham
Palace but could not abide
the place. When the Houses
of Parliament burned down,
in October 1834, he scurried
over to Westminster and
offered the parliamen-
tarians the Palace as their
new home. 'Mind,' he cried,
'I mean Buckingham Palace
as a permanent gift – mind
that!' To his fury the offer
was turned down.*

newspaper said, it had been unable to identify their owners. The editorial writer added: 'An inveterate voluptuary, especially if he be an artificial person, is of all known beings the most selfish. Selfishness is the true repellent of human sympathy. Selfishness feels no attachment, and invites none; it is the charnel house of the affections. Nothing more remains to be said about George IV but to pay – as pay we must – for his profusion; and to turn his bad conduct to some account by tying up the hands of those who come after him in what concerns the public money.'

The year after his royal client's death, John Nash retired to his house, East Cowes Castle in the Isle of Wight. He was old and exhausted – partly, no doubt, as a result of the problem of the Palace and his interrogations by the Commons committee – and he suffered from what he described as 'a rush of blood to the head'. The malady had been induced, he believed, by his 'standing on the pavement of St Paul's Cathedral' during a funeral. Four years after his retirement he died, aged eighty-two.

By then, relieved of two men who had hung financial millstones around its neck, Parliament took advantage of a much needed breather and suspended further work on the Palace. For a time, at least, it stood mute and unoccupied – a half-finished symbol of the folly of squandered money in an era of small liberties and large-scale poverty for most of the British people.

But in the summer of 1831 the government, with some reluctance, began to think once more about the royal building which, by general acceptance, was known at last as Buckingham Palace. Inevitably, the first and most pressing question was: 'How much will it cost to complete?' Preliminary reports were not encouraging. Much of the interior, it was disclosed, still awaited the attentions of the plasterers and painters.

With the approval of the new King, William IV (son of George III), the architect Edward Blore was appointed to prepare an estimate and to supervise any subsequently agreed work. Already the George IV–John Nash 'repairs' and 'improvements' had run up a bill of £644,000, and Blore, a careful, cost-conscious man, worked out that completion would require another £75,000.

Work was resumed, but this time there was to be a closer scrutiny of the doling-out of money. Blore was ordered to put in his bills quarterly and direct to the Treasury, where the ultimate accounting was done, and not to the Department of Woods and Forests. It says much for Blore's management that he both removed Nash's dome (the 'inverted egg-cup') and raised the top storey of the whole central block without exceeding his original estimate. By the late autumn of 1833, when it looked as though the work must be nearing its final stages, Parliament granted a further £55,000 to cover the cost of 'finishings, fixtures and furniture'.

Now, after all the expenditure lavished on the place, the nation seemed close to having a new royal palace ready and waiting. But what the Palace seemed unlikely to have was a royal resident. William IV detested the building and hoped that he would never be obliged to make it his home.

William, born in 1765 and the third of the fifteen children produced by George III and Queen Charlotte, had never expected to be King. In normal circumstances George IV would have been succeeded by his daughter, Princess Charlotte, or, in the event of her premature death, by his eldest brother, the Duke of Kent. But Charlotte had died in November 1817, at the age of twenty-one, and the Duke in January 1820.

The acquisition of the crown certainly delighted William, if only because his previous life had mostly been one of thwarted ambition in which he had been denied the status to which he felt himself entitled. He had spent the earliest years

The invitation card which was also the ticket of admission for guests to the Coronation, on 8 September 1831, of King William IV and Queen Adelaide.

Preliminary sketch by the architect Edward Blore for decorations in what, by 1831, had at last become known as Buckingham Palace. With the approval of William IV, Blore was appointed to supervise the completion of the Palace.

Mrs Dorothy Jordan (1762–1816), Drury Lane actress and, for twenty years, mistress of William IV. She bore William no fewer than ten illegitimate children but, in the end, he abruptly walked out on her and married Princess Adelaide of Saxe-Meiningen — mainly on the grounds that as an 'official' husband he would receive a higher state allowance. Ironically, none of his legitimate children born to Queen Adelaide survived and he therefore left no direct heir to the throne.

of his manhood at sea in the British Navy, experiencing a fair amount of action and acquitting himself well. Ashore, he devoted twenty years to the popular Drury Lane actress, Mrs Dorothy Jordan, with whom he lived openly as a devoted, if unofficial, 'husband' and by whom he had no fewer than ten illegitimate children.

True to Hanoverian form, he had been up to his ears in debt, and at the age of fifty-two he abruptly walked out on Mrs Jordan and married Princess Amelia Adelaide of Saxe-Meiningen, mainly on the grounds that as a married man he would receive a higher state allowance. But to everyone's surprise, including his own, the marriage turned out happily.

When he was presented with the news of George IV's death and his own accession, at six o'clock on the morning of 26 June 1830, he is alleged to have declared that he would be returning at once to the double bed he shared with Adelaide 'as I have long wished to sleep with a Queen'.

Alas for poor, undistinguished William, his reign was far from tranquil. A chill wind of unrest, sweeping across the English Channel from revolutionary France, blew through the realm. The central political topic was Parliamentary reform and an extension of the franchise. There were riots in the Midlands and in Bristol, but eventually, on 7 June 1832, the first Reform Bill was passed by an overwhelming majority and the foundation for modern democracy was laid.

Against the backdrop of a nation stumbling out of a secure, narrowly privileged past towards a broader-based but uncertain future, Buckingham Palace might well have been seen as a small piece of incidental stage scenery. But for King William it remained a pressing and irksome problem – until, in October 1834, a providential solution seemed to present itself. The Houses of Parliament burned down, and an inspired William hurried at once to the smoking ruins and there, on the spot, offered a group of Parliamentary 'mourners' the Palace as their new home. 'Mind,' he cried, 'I mean Buckingham Palace as a permanent gift – mind that!'

To the King's indignation, his government looked the gift horse in the mouth. Their misgivings about the unsuitability of the Palace were strengthened by Edward Blore, who reported, with a touch of acidity, that the royal proposal was 'attended with so many disadvantages and inconveniences that a worse selection could not be made'.

William withdrew into sulky solitude; however, by December of the following year he had an unexpected change of mind and astonished everyone by announcing that he wished to move into the Palace as soon as possible. But, now that he wanted the very thing he had previously rejected, he found that it was to be denied him. The work was still not finished. Part of the extra delay had been due to a last-minute decision to equip some areas of the building with the new-fangled gas lighting.

William had no choice but to continue to spend his days at Windsor, dogged by arthritis, asthma and an enlarged liver, cracking the occasional smutty joke and rustling his way through the morning papers with his favourite comment on the news: 'That's a damned lie!'

At last, after all the harrowing years and the endless outpouring of cash, Buckingham Palace was pronounced ready for occupation in May 1837. By then William had neither the health and strength nor the inclination to leave Windsor Castle; one month later, and just two months short of his seventy-second birthday, he died there.

The Long (picture) Gallery.

2

THE MIDDLE YEARS

QUEEN VICTORIA

PERHAPS THE MOST CRUCIAL DATE in the history of Buckingham Palace is 13 July 1837. For it was on that day that Queen Victoria formally moved in and became the first sovereign to make the reconstructed building an official royal residence.

It was not a notably happy day for her young Majesty – she was aged only eighteen – for she had been saddened at having to leave her previous home, Kensington Palace. But she was at least cheered by the evident pleasure in the great gardens shown by her devoted spaniel, Dash. Her loyal (and equally devoted) subjects were delighted, too – just to have her on the throne. They had had more than enough of old George III's offspring, and only by the Grace of God were they being spared yet another of his debt-ridden heirs.

William IV had most certainly been a monarch fashioned for fatherhood, as his ten illegitimate children had proved, but no child had survived from his marriage to Queen Adelaide. Destiny had therefore beckoned, as next in line of succession, the Princess Victoria, born on 24 May 1819, daughter of Edward, Duke of Kent – George III's fourth and youngest son – and his Duchess, Victoria of Saxe-Coburg.

It was in a curious way that the young Princess was said to have discovered that destiny for herself. On 11 March 1830, when Victoria was not quite eleven years old, her governess, Baroness Louise Lehzen, slipped into the child's history book a piece of paper outlining the royal genealogical table. According to the Baroness – who sometimes took the line that 'colour' in a story was more attractive than fact – Victoria studied the paper for a moment and then declared: 'I see I am nearer the throne than I thought.' Dewy-eyed, she placed 'her little hand' in the Baroness's and added: 'I will be good.' Lehzen, squeezing the last drop out of her account of the great occasion, alleged that she then told the Princess: 'Your Aunt Adelaide is still young and may have children and, of course, they would ascend the throne after their father, William IV, and not you, Princess.' To which Victoria solemnly replied: 'And if it was so I should never feel disappointed, for I know by the love Aunt Adelaide bears me, how fond she is of children.'

In the event, it was at five in the morning of 20 June 1837, that the Archbishop of Canterbury, Dr William Howley, and the Lord Chamberlain, Lord Conyngham, arrived at Kensington Palace to inform Victoria of her succession. It took several minutes of hammering on doors and ringing of bells before a half-asleep porter admitted them and sent for an equally drowsy Baroness Lehzen, who peevishly announced that the Princess was in a 'sweet sleep' and was not to be disturbed. But for once the garrulous Baroness was stunned into silence by what the Lord Chamberlain said next: 'We are come to the QUEEN on business of state, and even her sleep must give way to that!'

By the end of the year Parliament had granted the new Queen an annuity of £385,000, out of which £131,260 was for her household salaries, £172,500 for

Queen Victoria's Coronation procession leaves the Palace, on the morning of 28 June 1838, through the Marble Arch. Later the Arch was dismantled and re-erected on the north side of Hyde Park where it still stands and gives its name to the Marble Arch Underground station.

household expenses and £60,000 for her Privy Purse – her personal 'salary'. Unlike her predecessors, Victoria was prudent about money, and just over a year after she had moved into Buckingham Palace she had paid off all the debts accumulated by her late father.

At the time of her move Pimlico, the area adjoining the Palace, was what one Victorian writer, Sarah A. Tooley, called a 'most desolate suburb' of 'dirty roads and squalid alleys'. But Victoria's presence brought about a swift transformation. Hovels vanished, shops smartened themselves up, local business boomed and the Palace itself developed into a centre of attraction for both the fashionable and the 'lower' classes.

Sarah Tooley, looking back on those earlier days from the latter part of the reign, recalled that from 'eight in the morning until eight at night a crowd waited outside the gates on the chance of seeing the Queen drive out for an airing; and if only a royal servant walked across the courtyard everybody was in a state of excited expectation . . . .

'The sight of [Victoria] in the large, round bonnet of the time, with a wreath of daisies or roses inside, framing her fair, girlish face, was indeed sunshine to the crowds who waited daily at Hyde Park Corner to see her drive into the park. Most eyes grew moist at sight of her; she looked so like a child beside her big, elderly aunts and uncles . . . .

'One gentleman of position was reduced to weeding the Round Pond in Kensington Gardens in the hope of obtaining a sight of her, and when the Queen left for Buckingham Palace he had his phaeton [carriage] in readiness and drove in front of her carriage all the way to town. He continued to make himself so obtrusive that the authorities were obliged to take him in hand.'

Despite the fact that today's popular image is of Victoria as a little old widow in black, being constantly unamused and giving her name to a repressive age, it was the young Queen who brought Buckingham Palace to life. She loved singing and dancing and what she called 'mirth'. Imprisoned within that little girl – she was only a fraction over five feet tall – was a passionate woman awaiting her hour of fulfilment.

She set up a court orchestra, arranged a regular weekly dance on Monday evenings at the Palace, and held whole series of formal receptions and smaller, more private gatherings. She delighted in card games of all types – played for 'mirth' rather than money – and would show visitors over the Palace, from state apartments to kitchens, rather like a young housekeeper proudly over-awed at having found herself a post in such a vast, imposing establishment.

She took the greatest delight in trying out the new throne that had been specially built for her and installed in the throne room. Its gilded framework was carved with leaves and scrolls, branches of oak and acanthus foliage. The elaborate carvings on the back – which was five feet ten inches high – represented the royal emblems of the rose, shamrock and thistle, and the upholstery was crimson velvet and gold. Altogether, with its canopy, this elegant object cost £1,187 to make. Victoria skittishly pronounced it 'the most comfortable throne I ever sat upon'.

On the pretext of presenting loyal addresses, hordes of stiffly respectable dignitaries from universities, local authorities and societies for the promotion of various good works trooped into the Palace to gape at their remarkable girl Queen. Palace factotums sweated away at the onerous task of ensuring that precedence and etiquette were properly observed. They came near to crisis when confronted

An after-dinner gathering in the Yellow Drawing Room of the Palace (probably 1847). Queen Victoria sits on the sofa, with a protective arm around the little Princess Royal, and Prince Albert leans over mother and daughter.

by a deputation of Quakers who courteously but adamantly refused to remove their hats, since their doctrine required that they should never voluntarily uncover their heads in the presence of either sovereign or lesser mortal. A quick-thinking official solved the problem brilliantly: as the Quakers mounted the grand staircase in pairs, two Yeomen of the Guard, one standing to the left and the other to the right, lifted off each man's hat as he passed so that the letter of the pious ruling remained inviolate. Afterwards someone asked the deputation's leader, Joseph Sturge, if his principles had allowed him to kiss the Queen's hand, to which he replied enthusiastically: 'Oh yes, and found that act of homage no hardship, I assure thee. It was a fair, soft, delicate little hand.'

Understandably, Victoria herself was at first puzzled by some of the rigid rules which sovereigns, like Quakers, were expected to follow. When called upon to preside over a Chapter of the Order of the Garter, she summoned her premier Duke, the Duke of Norfolk, and inquired, blushingly, 'My Lord Duke, where am I to wear the garter?' Norfolk, never a man at a loss when it came to the niceties of ceremonial, answered with poker-faced dignity, 'Ma'am, it may be worn as an armlet, which would be in accordance with the custom adopted by Her Majesty Queen Anne.'

In matters of government and the handling of state formalities Victoria had two principal advisers, who went often to the Palace to give her instruction – Lord Melbourne, her Prime Minister, and Lord Palmerston, her Foreign Secretary. Many times Melbourne had to summon all his patience to sit quietly while the Queen insisted on reading every line of every government paper before adding her signature. Once, when he apologised for the day's heavy load of paperwork, she commented, 'My Lord, the attention required from me is only a change of occupation. I have not hitherto led a life of leisure, for I have not long left my lessons.' To the Palace Palmerston took specially drawn maps to enable the Queen more clearly to understand the latest developments in foreign affairs, and during one audience he devoted three hours to a painstaking outline of the history of Greece.

Victoria's early interest in foreign affairs had at the time no direct connection with Britain's imperial role. The empire on which the sun would never set was not to begin its great expansion for another two decades, but Britain was already recognised as a formidable and rapidly growing world power. For that reason the government was keen that Victoria's Coronation, in the summer of 1838, should be stage-managed as a major public relations exercise. It would help to unite the great mass of people in the kingdom, and also suitably impress all those others who were covered by the single, appropriately disparaging word 'foreigners'.

At eight on the morning of the great day –28 June – huge crowds flocked to Buckingham Palace. In addition to Londoners it was estimated that some half a million people from the provinces had poured into the capital. A few lucky ones had secured places on wooden stands erected opposite the Palace, for which they each paid 2s 6d (12½p). Others packed into St James's Park and Green Park and filled Constitution Hill.

The coaches of foreign ambassadors formed into imposing line in Birdcage Walk, the most admired belonging to Marshal Soult, Duke of Dalmatia, Ambassador Extraordinary of France. It was painted a rich cobalt, relieved with gold. Its raised cornice was of chased silver and at each of the four corners was a large ducal coronet. As only twenty-three years had passed since the Duke of Wellington had trounced Napoleon at Waterloo, Marshal Soult no doubt felt it right to remind the British that France was alive and well and as stylish as ever. (Later that day the crowds, brimming with goodwill, sentiment and ale, cheered

In the Palace Throne Room the girl-queen, Victoria, receives a loyal address from an Oxford University deputation. Dignitaries from learned institutions and a host of other public bodies descended on the Palace immediately after the accession — ostensibly to pay their respects but actually to gaze with wonder upon the petite eighteen-year-old who had become their sovereign.

vigorously when the sixty-nine-year-old Iron Duke warmly and publicly shook the Marshal's hand.)

At a quarter past ten the state coach, drawn by eight cream-coloured horses, trundled slowly out of the Palace forecourt, attended by Yeomen of the Guard walking alongside each wheel and footmen walking beside each of the two doors. Riding on either side, each accompanied by two grooms, were the Gold Stick, Viscount Combermere, and the Captain of the Yeomen of the Guard, the Earl of Ilchester. Through the coach windows the beguiled masses glimpsed the diminutive figure of the sovereign – 'gay as a lark and looking like a girl on her birthday', as one eye-witness reported.

At five o'clock the crowned Queen returned to the Palace. Even after the lengthy, exhausting Coronation ceremony at Westminster Abbey she did not, according to the *Times* reporter, 'evince any particular symptoms of fatigue'. How he knew that is not clear, since the day's public relations programme did not extend to inviting a mere scribbler into the Palace. But a member of the royal entourage, who *was* inside, later recalled that Victoria's first words on entering the Palace and hearing her spaniel bark were, 'There's Dash! I must go and give him his bath.' Before she did so, however, she rushed off to her bedroom to soak her left hand in a basin of iced water to help remove the ruby Coronation ring which, although it was the right size for her little finger, had been agonisingly forced on to her fourth finger by the Archbishop of Canterbury.

That night there was a family dinner party at the Palace, and afterwards Victoria went out on to the balcony to watch London's fireworks celebration. The Coronation had cost £200,000 – £150,000 more than had been spent for William IV – but the general view was that it had been worth every farthing. Even the poorest of the poor had been looked after, and the authorities of the St Martin-in-the-Fields workhouse proudly disclosed that every inmate had that day received 'six ounces of roast beef (free from bone), half a pound of potatoes, three-quarters of a pound of plum pudding and one pint of porter'.

Long after the Queen had retired to bed, those of London's fifty thousand prostitutes whose 'beat' covered the West End – an eight-minute hansom-cab drive from the Palace – enjoyed a bonanza, at an average fee per client of anything from a few shillings to a guinea. In the early hours of the following morning the lesser ranks of the free-and-easy sisterhood were still busy 'working' the fringes of St James's Park, around the Mall and just across from the darkened Palace windows.

In sexual matters the girl-Queen herself was an innocent, and in so far as the subject was ever mentioned she shared the attitude of all 'respectable' women of the time that sex was alarming – something one might secretly consider to have been God's only and inexplicable aberration. And it was the prevailing, dark-minded fear of sexual passion that was, for a time, to send a chill draught of scandal through the interminable corridors of Buckingham Palace.

By January 1839 Victoria began to hear disturbing but persistent whispers of tittle-tattle about Lady Flora Hastings, an unmarried lady-in-waiting to the Queen's mother, the Duchess of Kent. Lady Flora looked drawn and pale and was clearly unwell, and, as Victoria and the gossip-sniffing bloodhound Baroness Lehzen noticed, her figure was suddenly expanding. Leaping to the 'obvious' conclusion, the Queen wrote in her diary: 'We have no doubt that she is – to use plain words – *with child*!!'

(Above) Grand Hall: reached through the main entrance, this is for many distinguished visitors their first sight of the Palace interior. Each pair of columns was cut from a single block of veined Carrara marble.

(Below) Throne Room: the 'real' royal throne is at Westminster – all others in the Palace (like those shown here) are, strictly speaking, 'throne-chairs'. The four Louis XVI-style wood-carvings (two on each side of the thrones) demonstrate the intermingling of musical instruments, birds, foliage, fruit and arrow quivers.

(Above) Blue Drawing Room: until 1854 this was the Palace ballroom. A main feature is the magnificent ceiling with its series of inset, inverted domes. The astronomical clock on the marble mantelpiece shows the passing of hours, days, weeks and months and the lunar changes.

(Below) The Ball Room: added to the south wing of the Palace in 1854 and set out here with white and gold chairs ready for an investiture. This is the largest of all the state apartments. The canopy over the thrones is formed from the awning beneath which George V and Queen Mary were seated at the Delhi Durbar in 1911.

Grand Staircase: the top of the double flight of stairs which leads up to the marble-framed doorway giving access to the main state apartments. The portrait, to the left of the doorway, is of Queen Adelaide, wife of William IV, whose own portrait (of which only part of the frame can be seen here) hangs to the right.

(Above) White Drawing Room: often used by members of the royal family as a centre for assembling before a banquet or other state function. The sculptured frieze depicts children at play, and its twelve panels were designed by the artist William Pitts in 1831.

(Below) State Dining Room: the great dining-table top is of Spanish mahogany and can be extended to seat up to sixty guests. Above the mantelpiece is Sir Thomas Lawrence's portrait of the creator of the modern Palace, George IV. Flanking the King are portraits of his father, George III, and his mother, Queen Charlotte.

The new Queen Victoria returns in her coach to the Palace from the House of Lords. In the background loyal subjects wave their hats in enthusiastic greeting; those in the foreground seem rather disloyally engrossed in their own private fashion parade.

Victoria at once confided to her great guide and mentor, Lord Melbourne, that an 'awkward business' was brewing at the Palace. Melbourne, who customarily took the view that all troubles disappeared if ignored, advised the Queen to do nothing, and added hopefully, 'If you remain quite quiet, you'll get through it well.' As it turned out, that advice belonged in the category of famous last words.

Victoria, who disliked Lady Flora anyway, couldn't keep quiet, and the scandal gathered daily momentum. The unfortunate victim, who had already voluntarily consulted the Duchess of Kent's doctor, Sir James Clark, about her health, was now persecuted by Sir James, who stoked himself into a temper and demanded that she 'confess' to what was unmistakably an illegitimate pregnancy. It was not long before details of the 'awkward business' leaked out of the Palace into the newspapers. One editorial writer, who not so many months before had been reflecting the popular adoration of the Queen, expressed the withering opinion that Lady Flora was the 'victim of a depraved court'.

Eventually Lady Flora took a course that was deeply distasteful to her. She agreed to submit to what, in effect, amounted to a public medical examination, to be conducted by Sir James Clark and a second doctor, Sir Charles Clarke. On 17 February the two men issued a certificate, under the 'dateline' Buckingham Palace, announcing that there were no grounds for suspicion that Lady Flora was, or had been, pregnant. Indeed, although he did not say so publicly, the bumbling James Clark had known all along that the girl was *virgo intacta*. (He originally said she might well have conceived but still retained evidence of virginity.)

In her drawing-room at the Palace the ill-advised Queen tried – late in the day – to make amends. She received Lady Flora and embraced her. In her own account of that embarrassing moment she wrote – probably more in hope than anticipation: '[Lady Flora] expressed herself exceedingly grateful to me and said that for Mama's sake she would suppress every wounded feeling, and would forget it etc.' That significant and dismissive 'etc' was undoubtedly Victoria's way, in line with Melbourne's doctrine, of leaving trouble to skip away on its own two feet. Unfortunately for her, trouble was this time not so fleet of foot.

The Opposition Tory party, which had been trying for years to oust the Whig government led by Lord Melbourne, saw that the affair offered a plum ripe for the picking. In her inexperience Victoria had made the mistake of behaving as though Melbourne (and therefore his party) was her personal, permanent ally, and the Tories her enemies.

In July poor Lady Flora died of enlargement of the liver – the true, agonising cause of the ludicrous scandal – and so incensed with the Palace had popular opinion become that the Queen was publicly accused of having hastened her death. Both Lady Flora's family and the Tory party demanded a public apology from the Queen, but Victoria was warned that such an admission of error could not constitutionally be made by the sovereign. These events were to have the most extraordinary consequences for Victoria, Melbourne and the nation. Even in Melbourne's own Whig party there were many who felt that the Queen should not be dependent upon one political faction or its leader, and it soon became clear to the Prime Minister that he was without majority support in both Parliament and Cabinet. He therefore resigned. Victoria shut herself up in her room at the Palace and wept in sorrow and anger.

Within a few days Buckingham Palace was once again the setting for trouble, this time in what became known as 'the Bedchamber Crisis'. The new Tory Prime Minister, Sir Robert Peel, proposed that, in accordance with custom, the government should choose the senior court officials, so that Tory-nominated ladies would replace Victoria's Whig ladies-in-waiting.

It was a milestone in Victorian history, for it afforded the first direct glimpse of the imperious woman into whom the girl-Queen would shortly blossom. Affronted by so calculated and immediate an example of Tory impertinence, Victoria vehemently rejected Peel's proposal. Still angry, she scribbled off a note to her lost protector, Melbourne: 'They wanted to deprive me of my ladies, and I suppose they would deprive me next of my dressers and my housemaids; they wished to treat me like a girl, but I will show them that I am Queen of England.'

In further defiance of protocol she called on Melbourne, her 'unofficial' Prime Minister, to draft a letter for her confirming her rejection of the proposal of her 'official' Prime Minister. Obediently he did so: 'The Queen, having considered the proposal made to her yesterday by Sir Robert Peel to remove the Ladies of her Bedchamber, cannot consent to adopt a course which she conceives to be contrary to usage, and which is repugnant to her feelings.'

Peel, who could have avoided the upset by showing more patience and tact, replied by declining to form a government, and overnight Melbourne resumed office. Charles Greville, the great diarist of the period, summed up this incredible round of political musical chairs with the comment: 'It is a high trial to our institutions when the wishes of a Princess of nineteen can overturn a great Ministerial combination, and when the most momentous matters of Government and legislation are influenced by her pleasure about her Ladies of the Bedchamber. This is making the private gratification of the Queen paramount to the highest public considerations.'

Melbourne himself was, on reflection, disturbed by the longer-term dangers inherent in the Bedchamber affair, and subsequently he and Victoria agreed that the Queen's Mistress of the Robes should be a political appointment, and that all the rest of the Ladies of the Household should be selected from both Whig and Tory families. On that issue, at least, peace was once more restored to Buckingham Palace; and, a few years later, a more mature, experienced Victoria admitted: 'It was entirely my own foolishness. I took no advice on the matter.'

The Flora Hastings tragedy and the Bedchamber farce served in their own ways to confirm the Palace, in many people's minds, as a continuing symbol of the royal court's corruption and disdain for public opinion. Memories of a long line of sub-standard royals died hard. What was needed was some important event which would change what, in late twentieth-century jargon, might be called the 'images' of Crown and Palace.

The heralding of such an event came on 23 November 1839. Victoria summoned her Privy Council to the Palace and announced portentously: 'It is my intention to ally myself in marriage with the Prince Albert of Saxe-Coburg and Gotha. Deeply impressed with the solemnity of the engagement which I am about to contract I have not come to this decision without mature consideration, nor without feeling a strong assurance that, with the blessing of Almighty God, it will at once secure me domestic felicity and serve the interests of my country.'

Those words enabled Victoria to unite her people round her. Nothing succeeds with the British like a royal marriage; indeed, there have been occasions in more recent times when politicians have welcomed one as the best means of distracting minds from economic crisis or plain administrative incompetence.

Edward Blore immediately put three hundred men to work at the Palace, making a number of minor alterations and redecorating the private apartments. Everything was ready by 8 February 1840, when the Queen's husband-to-be arrived at Dover and was acclaimed, all the way to London, by crowds who were relieved to see that the Prince was an upright, handsome man who appeared to fit the fairytale concept of a royal spouse. As soon as he reached the Palace Albert was plunged into his first formal ceremony – his naturalisation as a British citizen.

Victoria had first met Albert, her cousin, in May 1836, when he had visited Kensington Palace with his father, the Duke of Coburg, and his brother, Ernest. He was three months Victoria's junior, and both their families had decided from the beginning that one day they should be matched. Fortunately for the young people themselves, this arranged marriage would prove to be deeply happy.

At Westminster, across the park from the Palace, all had not been so rapturous in the weeks before Albert's arrival. To Victoria's humiliation, Parliament had wrangled noisily over the Prince's 'salary', and an original proposal of £50,000 a year was voted down to £30,000. Joseph Hume, the Radical MP, who had not forgotten the spendthrift Hanoverian royals, warned the government that it 'must know the danger of setting a young man down in London with so much money in his pockets'.

Parliament also declined to meet the Queen's wish that the Bill to naturalise Albert should include a clause giving him rank in the realm next to herself. In practice she was to ignore that omission whenever she and Albert travelled

Domestic bliss at the Palace – circa 1842. Queen Victoria with the Princess Royal, nestling against her right shoulder, and the Prince of Wales (the future Edward VII), cradled in her left arm. Victoria bore her husband, Albert, four sons and five daughters, but hated and feared childbirth.

through Britain and the dominions. To her annoyance, however, certain foreign sovereigns chose to follow the letter of the British law, and when, duty-bound, the royal couple submitted to being their guests the Prince found himself received as a second-rater. As best she could, Victoria consoled herself with a treasured letter Albert had written to her at Buckingham Palace after the Parliamentary skirmishes, in which he declared: 'While I possess your love they cannot make me unhappy.'

The royal wedding, on 10 February in the Royal Chapel of St James's Palace, was a suitably grand occasion. From early morning, and despite heavy rain, people thronged around Buckingham Palace, where in the forecourt the band of the Regiment of the Blues played. From the gates to the garden entrance of St James's Palace the route was lined with Horse Guards. Soon after dawn Victoria sent a note to Albert in his bedroom a couple of corridors beyond hers: 'Dearest: How are you today, and have you slept well? I have rested very well and feel very comfortable today. What weather! I believe, however, the rain will cease. Send one word when you, my most dearly beloved bridegroom, will be ready. Thy ever faithful, Victoria.'

As Albert descended the Palace's Grand Staircase, even the most blasé courtiers were fascinated by the sight of this fine young man, superb in his perfectly fitted uniform of a British field-marshal, with the ribbon of the Garter adorning his masculine breast. The trumpets sounded, the colours were lowered in salute and the onlookers cheered wildly as his carriage rolled out of the main gates. When the Queen left, loyal Lord Melbourne, crushed into the open doorway beyond the Grand Staircase with a bevy of assorted royal relatives and statesmen, cried, 'God bless you, Ma'am,' and shed a sentimental tear.

Appropriately, Victoria was 'radiant, if pale' in her bridal gown of Honiton lace over white satin. The lace had been made by two hundred women in the village of Beer, next to Honiton, in Devon, and, as the indefatigable chronicler, Sarah Tooley, observed, they may have been poor but their joy at being commanded to produce the lace 'was unbounded and they could not sufficiently express their gratitude'. Once the lace had been completed the pattern was destroyed so that no opportunistic couturière could cash in by selling copies of the royal wedding gear to the shopkeeping classes.

At the Queen's personal request the word 'obey' was included in the marriage vows, for, as Victoria had previously informed the Archbishop of Canterbury, she wished to 'be married as a woman, not as Queen'. One observer, eyes unwaveringly fixed on Victoria, reported that she gave Albert a little quizzical smile when he repeated the words 'With all my worldly goods I thee endow.'

The reporter from the *Morning Post*, himself wedded to accuracy, noted that the Queen wept precisely two tears; the Duke of Sussex, who gave the bride away, was greatly affected; and a loud sobbing, issuing from the chapel gallery, was traced to Lord FitzWilliam. The Queen's mother was grave and dignified.

On the royal couple's return to the Palace the clouds had fled and the sun was shining. The most memorable feature of the wedding breakfast that followed was a giant cake, three yards in circumference, fourteen inches deep and weighing three hundred pounds. It was topped by a miniature piece of sculpture, depicting Britannia blessing the newly-weds and Cupid writing the date in an open book.

After the meal Victoria and Albert drove off for a three-day honeymoon at Windsor Castle, where the Prince was given grounds for concern about future

The fast-growing royal family: Victoria and Albert, in 1846, with the first five of their nine children. Left to right: Alfred, Duke of Edinburgh; the Prince of Wales (later Edward VII); Princess Alice; Princess Helena; and Princess Victoria, the Princess Royal, who was destined to be the mother of Wilhelm II, the notorious German Kaiser of the First World War.

royal privacy by the discovery that a communicating door from the bridal suite led directly into the bedroom of the always hovering Baroness Lehzen.

In November the couple's first child, Princess Victoria Adelaide Mary Louise (the Princess Royal), was born at Buckingham Palace, followed a year later by the Prince of Wales, who would subsequently become King Edward VII. That was the year, too, of the curious case of an errand-boy named Jones, who three times somehow slipped into the Palace and nosed around, gaping at all its wonders. Before he was finally caught he succeeded in sneaking into the private apartments, hid under a sofa and eavesdropped on a conversation between the Queen and Albert. What he heard was, regrettably, not disclosed.

Life at the Palace took on a new air of animation and colour. The Queen launched a series of magnificent fancy-dress balls, and there were musical evenings at which she and Albert, an accomplished musician, joined in singing Rossini and Haydn quartets. The composer Mendelssohn was a frequent visitor, and especially delighted the Queen by performing 'Rule Britannia' on the piano with his left hand while simultaneously playing the Austrian national anthem with his right.

More royal infants arrived in swift succession, and altogether Victoria and Albert produced nine children – five girls and four boys. But there was a dark side to their parenthood. Victoria was a transmitter of the then little-understood hereditary condition of haemophilia, or the 'bleeding disease', in which the blood refuses to clot, so that even an ordinary casual wound caused by a fall or a mishandled knife can lead in some cases to death. The condition, although passed

Little Victoria, the Princess Royal, sits for her portrait in the Palace while Ladies-in-Waiting keep her amused and the Queen and Prince Albert observe the work in progress.

on by the mother, manifests itself only in males. Three of Victoria's daughters, the Princess Royal and the Princesses Alice and Beatrice, were haemophilia carriers, and through their marriages the condition spread to other European families. One of history's future and most famous victims was Alexis, the only son of the ill-fated Czar Nicholas II of Russia and his wife, Alexandra, one of Victoria's grandchildren. (In 1957 an effective antidote to the disease was developed by the Lister Institute for Preventive Medicine.)

The growing size of her family and the wearing-off of the novelty of dances, masques and musical evenings found the Queen tetchily concerned with the inadequacies of Buckingham Palace. On 10 February 1845 she wrote a sharp note to Sir Robert Peel, now back as her Prime Minister:

Though the Queen knows that Sir Robert Peel has already turned his attention to the urgent necessity of doing something to Buckingham Palace, the Queen thinks it right to recommend this subject herself to his serious consideration. Sir Robert is acquainted with the state of the Palace and the total want of accommodation for our little family, which is fast growing up. Any building must necessarily take some years before it can be safely inhabited. If it were to be begun this autumn it could hardly be occupied before the spring of 1848, when the Prince of Wales would be nearly seven and the Princess Royal nearly eight years old, and they cannot possibly be kept in the nursery any longer. A provision for this purpose ought, therefore, to be made this year. Independent of this, most parts of the Palace are in a sad state, and will ere long require a further outlay to render them *decent* for the occupation of the Royal Family or any visitors the Queen may have to receive. A room, capable of containing a larger number of those persons whom the Queen has to invite in the course of the season to balls, concerts, etc., than any of the present apartments can at once hold, is much wanted. Equally so, improved offices and servants' rooms, the want of which puts the departments of the household to great expense yearly. It will be for Sir Robert to consider whether it would not be best to remedy all these deficiencies at once, and to make use of his opportunity to render the exterior of the Palace such as no longer to be a *disgrace* to the country, which it certainly now is. The Queen thinks the country would be better pleased to have the question of the Sovereign's residence in London so finally disposed of, than to have it so repeatedly brought before it.

Peel replied that he thought it would be diplomatic, before announcing any new expenditure on the Palace, to see how the public reacted to the government's proposal to continue applying income tax as one of its means – one much detested – of raising revenue. So the Palace file went temporarily back on to the Treasury shelves, and in due course the country accepted the continuance of the tax, at 7d (about $3\frac{1}{2}$p) in the pound, on all annual incomes of £150 and over. Since an agricultural worker earned no more than between £20 and £26 a year, and a skilled woollen cloth weaver £44 at the most, the matter was of purely academic interest to the mass of ordinary working people, whose permanent lot was grinding poverty.

In May 1846 the government, despite its preoccupation with a series of crises – including the Irish potato famine, which was to lead to more than a million deaths from starvation and drive 800,000 Irish emigrants to seek salvation in North America – appointed a commission to look into improvements at the Palace. Edward Blore was once again chosen as supervising architect.

Blore reported in August, by which time Robert Peel had been replaced by Lord John Russell as Prime Minister, and disclosed that the royal children were housed in attics in the Palace's north wing that had originally been intended for servants.

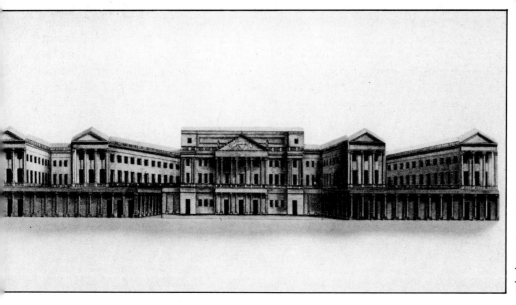

The fame of Victoria's Palace, like that of the Queen herself, spread far and wide. This is a German representation of the east front (about 1845) in the form of building blocks for children to assemble.

Part of the basement of the same wing was used as store-rooms and workshops, and the royals complained that their private apartments were constantly permeated by the cloying odour of oil and glue. Blore concluded that there was not 'the slightest means of extension or improvement within the existing building'.

By early the following year the sum of £150,000 was voted for a new wing on the east side of the Palace courtyard, the removal of the Marble Arch, the re-planning of the south wing and the building of a new kitchen and ballroom. Part of the money was to be raised by the sale of George IV's Pavilion at Brighton, which, as it happened, Victoria abhorred. (In 1850 Brighton Town Council bought the building with a Bank of England loan of £60,000, and it has remained a tourist attraction ever since. Much of its furniture and many of its carpets, clocks and other ornaments were distributed between Buckingham Palace, Windsor Castle and Kensington Palace.)

Blore's new east wing was not considered a success – 'dull' and 'little more than an ordinary piece of street architecture' were two typical comments; but his need to pack in as many rooms as possible meant that the façade was hampered by long rows of identical, unappealing windows. He also used stone from Caen, in Normandy, which proved too delicate for London's polluted atmosphere, quickly disintegrated and had to be protected by continual painting.

After a policy change Blore was replaced by James Pennethorne, an architect who was Nash's nephew and had been trained in Nash's office. He built a high block at the south-west corner of the Palace. One of his most notable contributions, however, was to remove Nash's octagonal apartment in the south wing and to replace it with the State Supper Room. This was an impressive addition to the Palace – sixty-five feet long, fifty-eight feet wide and forty-five feet high. It could be used for a variety of functions; its outstanding features were its six tall doorways fitted with mirror-panelled doors, its five bowl-shaped crystal chandeliers and its two magnificent marble mantelpieces, on one of which were carved miniature busts of George IV and William IV.

Queen Victoria in 1855. From a watercolour painting by Franz Xavier Winterhalter (1806–73), the German artist.

Pennethorne also built the largest of the state apartments, the 123-foot-long Ball Room, decorated in Italian style and with a great organ whose gilded pipes were set against a crimson background. Wall paintings represented the twelve hours of the day, and the huge room was illuminated at night by six elaborate lustre chandeliers. (Later, in Edward VII's reign, the Ball Room was to be further enhanced by two splendid thrones placed beneath a gold-embroidered canopy of crimson velvet.)

Certainly the new additions meant greater comfort for the royal family and eased the problems of official entertaining. But neither Victoria nor Albert ever greatly cared for Buckingham Palace, and although they spent much of their time at Windsor they were happiest at Balmoral, in Scotland, and at their new Osborne House, on the Isle of Wight, which Albert had designed in co-operation with the builder Thomas Cubitt. Among Osborne's ornaments were marble carvings of the royal children's infant legs and of one of the Queen's hands. The house itself cost around £200,000 and was paid for by the Queen entirely out of her personal income.

At the Palace, as at Windsor, the daily routine seldom varied. Victoria and Albert rose at 6.30 in summer and 7.30 in winter and, after morning service with members of the household, breakfasted on coffee, bread and butter, and eggs or cold meat. If the day was fine the royal pair would then take a stroll around the gardens, but by ten o'clock Victoria would be at her study desk, conscientiously working her way through the mounds of state papers which arrived every day in government despatch-boxes.

In the late morning or early afternoon she received those visitors who had been 'commanded' to attend upon her, and who might include anyone of note from a general to a foreign dignitary or an artist or musician. She and Albert lunched at two, and, as her plump little figure testified, Victoria habitually over-ate. If there were no official engagements the royals spent the afternoon relaxing, sometimes working at etchings on copper or taking a drive through Hyde Park.

Dinner was at eight, with the food served by scarlet-clad servants and a military band playing in an ante-room. Guests who were not being addressed by the Queen were permitted to talk to their neighbours at table – but only in whispers. On one occasion a duchess found that a fellow-guest with whom she wished to take wine was a total abstainer, and jokingly appealed to Victoria to 'command' the man to partake of the claret. Graciously the Queen replied; 'There is no compulsion at *my* table.' Often a musical evening, with Victoria and Albert as active participants, would follow dinner, and the Queen once insisted on taking the place of a professional musician at the piano and personally accompanying the famous visiting soprano, Jenny Lind, widely publicised as the 'Swedish Nightingale'.

Much though she enjoyed good food, the Queen insisted that her children, when small, should not be spoiled by over-indulgence. So, while the best fare flowed across the parental dinner table, up to the nursery went what one servant gossiped about as 'quite poor living – only a bit of roast meat and perhaps a plain pudding'. Occasionally, though, the royal offspring would show their discontent. When, by some mischance, an iced pudding was set before the young Princess Beatrice, Victoria declared, 'Baby must not have any of that; that is not good for Baby.' To which the infant replied, 'But Baby likes it, my dear.'

Victoria was a pleasant, courteous and considerate hostess, always using the first names of her ladies-in-waiting, receiving them with a kiss and inquiring after

Royals are expected never to let it be seen that they are bored. Here, in the Palace Throne Room, Victoria braces herself for yet another loyal address — this time, in 1853, from the Convocation of the Clergy.

their relatives. When she held formal receptions, seated on her throne in the Throne Room, she ordered that all women guests should make their curtsies at the foot of the dias steps and need only take a couple of paces backwards – so as to avoid the difficulties arising from the long trains to their gowns.

A good test of a woman's personality is the regard in which she is held by other women, and Victoria passed that test with full marks. After lunching with her, the Baroness Bunsen, English-born wife of a Prussian diplomat, wrote to her son that 'she is the only piece of *female royalty* I ever saw who was also a creature such as God Almighty has created. Her smile is a *real smile*, her grace is *natural*, although it has received a high polish from cultivation – there is nothing artificial about her.'

A gracious sovereign, an idyllic marriage – serenity appeared the order of the royal domestic day. Yet there was another side to the two sensitive and extraordinary royals. From time to time the sound of bitter quarrelling was heard echoing through the corridors of the Palace's private apartments. Victoria feared and detested child-bearing and suffered from acute bouts of post-natal depression. Some chance remark by Albert, a suspected critical tone in his voice, would send her into petulant rages and she would follow him from room to room, upbraiding him shrilly. When attempts to talk her out of her tantrums failed, Albert would have the servants hurrying back and forth taking admonitory notes from him to the bedroom where she had gone to sulk.

This was a curious trait in Victoria, which had its darker aspect. It is clear that she found the actual process of childbirth 'degrading' as well as frightening. And despite her devotion to Albert – which never fundamentally wavered, the silly

Scots Guards parade in front of Victoria (on the Palace balcony) in 1854 just before their departure for the Crimean War. Many were never to return home. Britain lost 19,600 fighting men – but 15,700 of them died not at the hands of the Russian enemy but from cholera and other diseases.

(Inset) Her Majesty's Escort, the 16th Lancers, see Victoria safely home to the Palace.

A word or two of encouragement for the young never came amiss. Respectfully bowing the knee, boys of the Bluecoat School show their drawings to Victoria at the Palace in 1873.

Victoria and her ninth and youngest child, Princess Beatrice (1857–1944), pose for the camera around 1880. The clasped hands and the tightly held umbrella are not mere affectations but aids to steadiness – an absolute necessity at a time when early, 'slow' photographic plates required several minutes of exposure.

Four generations of royalty: distinctly unamused Victoria with the future Edward VIII in a sailor-suit and two other future Kings in the background – George V on the left and Edward VII on the right.

quarrels notwithstanding — she felt herself to be his intellectual inferior. The irksome restrictions of the final stages of pregnancy and her sense of dependence on others at the delivery may well have underlined that feeling of inferiority. They were also reminders of the deep resentment, shared by many Victorian wives, of men as the 'users' of women and the instruments of pain.

Writing from the Palace to the Princess Royal, after she had become a mother for the first time, Victoria said of women: 'We poor creatures are born for Men's pleasure and amusement.' (The Princess had a difficult time during labour and, in the course of the birth, permanent dislocation was caused to the left arm of the infant who was to grow up to be Kaiser Wilhelm II of Germany.)

Victoria had, in an instinctive sense, a livelier understanding of people than Albert had. She felt genuine concern for the sufferings of her soldiers in that shambles, the Crimean War, in which Britain and France were pitched against the Russians. She made her own protest to the government about the lack of care for them, and saw something of the ravages of war when she met badly wounded Grenadier Guards in the Marble Hall of the Palace. And it was her own awareness of the meaning of battlefield heroism that led to the institution, in June 1856, of the Victoria Cross, which even today continues to be Britain's highest military decoration. (All the medals were originally struck from the bronze of Russian cannon captured at Sebastopol in the Crimea, until 1942, when that supply of metal finally gave out.)

After meeting Charles Dickens at Buckingham Palace, Victoria found herself sharing his hope that one day rigid class divisions would disappear from British society. She certainly had occasion to appreciate something of the squalor and disease-ridden conditions in which so many of her subjects lived. During a summer drought she and Albert set out for a boat trip on the Thames, but were forced to turn swiftly back because of the overpowering stench of the capital's rotting sewage uncovered by the low water-level.

Indeed, it was the bad sanitation at Windsor Castle which brought Victoria the greatest disaster of her life. From the contamination of the drains Albert contracted typhoid, which his weakened constitution was incapable of resisting, and he died at Windsor on the evening of 14 December 1861.

Without Albert, Victoria sank into a long period of apathy and withdrew from the public gaze. Writing of herself in the third person, she said: 'To express the Queen's desolation and other misery is almost impossible; every feeling seems swallowed up in that of unbounded grief.'

Her original dislike of the Palace was heightened by memories of happy times there with Albert, and she could not bear to linger in rooms where they had been together. She seldom returned except, later, for a special occasion such as the celebration of the Diamond Jubilee of her reign on 22 June 1897. (The actual day, to the sixtieth year, was 20 June, but that happened to be a Sunday and was reserved for a private thanksgiving.)

When she descended the great staircase of the Palace on that Jubilee morning on her way to St Paul's Cathedral, she was seen to have taken on the image that has now become her stereotype — that of the little, old, forbidding widow in black.

She died at Osborne House on 22 January 1901, rousing herself in the final moments to lift up her arms and utter the single word 'Bertie'. On the point of her departure she had recognised, at her bedside, her eldest son, the Prince of Wales, who now became King Edward VII.

KING EDWARD HEARTILY BIDS YOU WELCOME TO HIS CORONATION DINNER, ON JULY 5TH. 1902.

A royal invitation.

3

THE MIDDLE YEARS

EDWARD VII

AT THE TIME OF VICTORIA'S DEATH Buckingham Palace was something of a mausoleum, dedicated to the memory of the late Queen's beloved Albert and seldom occupied. The Prince Consort's rooms had been left exactly as they were when he died in December 1861. Even his medicine glass still stood on his bedside table.

The first task of the new King, Edward VII, the former Prince of Wales, was to brighten up the place and rid it of its atmosphere of morbid gloom. The private apartments were stripped clean and renovated, new bathrooms were built, the plumbing modernised and electric lighting installed. In the main entrance hall – Edward spoke of it as the 'sepulchre' – the dingy ravages of age and London smogs were removed from the imitation-marble decorations. After years of neglect and stuffiness the Palace began to breathe freely again.

Edward personally supervised much of the refurbishing, often wandering into rooms and issuing instructions to startled workmen perched at the tops of ladders or scaffolding. (He confessed to a friend that he was not very knowledgeable about art – 'But I do know something about *arrangement*.')

Despite the renovations Edward could not bring himself to think of the Palace as a home in the true domestic sense. It symbolised too many of his past frustrations – his uneasy boyhood, when over-zealous parents had laboured to hammer him into the mould of heir apparent, the unavailing struggle to meet his mother's hungry need to possess a replica of the incomparable Albert, and the long, restless years when he lingered in the wings of the royal stage, an actor without a significant role to play.

Prince Albert had been the principal driving force behind the Prince of Wales's education and, following the Consort's directions to the letter, his tutor, Frederick Waymouth Gibbs, kept the boy at his lessons in the Palace seven hours a day, six days a week. Understandably, Edward developed symptoms of acute exhaustion accompanied by fits of uncontrollable rage. His father ignored these obvious appeals for rescue and his mother was merely puzzled by her son's inexplicable behaviour.

The pressure-cooker system of education to which the Prince was subjected became public knowledge, and the editor of the magazine *Punch* was subsequently moved to publish a poem of eight stanzas, the first of which ran:

> Thou dear little Wales – sure the saddest of tales
> Is the tale of the studies with which they are cramming thee;
> In thy tuckers and bibs, handed over to Gibbs,
> Who for eight years with solid instruction was ramming thee.

In Edward's youth the longer-term effects of that tyrannical upbringing manifested themselves as boorishness and a near-hysterical suspicion of almost everyone with whom he came into contact. Yet one of the many creditable facets of Edward's character was that he was able, when he came to manhood, to throw off the legacy of the shadowy Palace years and emerge as a charming and courteous personality.

The genuine love-match that brought him, on 10 March 1863, to marriage with the Danish Princess, Alexandra Caroline Marie Charlotte Louise Julie, helped to soften his nature. Even when the first bloom of their relationship had worn off and Edward resumed the womanising which he could never resist, Alexandra remained a loyal and extraordinarily tolerant wife.

Many of King Edward's subjects, gazing with awe at his enormous bulk, often chose to see him as the epitome of the phrase 'Laugh and grow fat'. But, as the Palace cooks quickly discovered, laughter was not the basic cause. He was a gargantuan eater. At the Palace, as at other royal houses and when staying with friends, the King ate four meals a day – breakfast, lunch, tea and dinner; and, until his final years, his usual breakfast consisted of four dishes: poached eggs, bacon, haddock and chicken. Dinner rarely involved fewer than twelve courses, all of them rich. The Palace chefs were instructed that the King's favourite food was grouse, partridge and pheasant stuffed with snipe and woodcock. A royal 'special' was snipe, stuffed with *foie gras* and highly seasoned mincemeat, shaped into small cutlets, grilled and then served with slices of truffle and madeira sauce. 'It's terrible, he eats anything and everything,' Queen Alexandra confided to a friend. 'I've never seen anything like it.'

Some of his Palace guests felt constrained to fast on the day after dining with him, and he was infuriated when he learned that leaders of London's smart set had nicknamed him 'Tum-Tum'. One of Edward's friends, excluded for some time

Song for Coronation Day

JUNE 26, 1902.

H.M. KING EDWARD VII.

H.M. QUEEN ALEXANDRA.

I.

Up, ye British boys, be gay!
Deck yourselves in bright array,
This is Coronation Day—
    Hark, the glad bells ring!
Garlands stretch from door to door,
Through the streets the people pour,
While the joyful cannons roar,
        Long life to the King!

II.

Long life to King Edward! Shout!
Hang the Royal Standard out,
Wave your Union Jacks about,
    Laugh, and dance, and sing!
For you live on British ground,
Where the truest freedom's found,
Let your loyalty abound—
        Honour to the King!

III.

Honour to the King! Rejoice!
Hark, the Empire's mighty voice!
Grateful hearts with offerings choice,
    Loyal tributes bring;
From where'er the sun doth shine,
Southern palm to northern pine,
Thoughts to Homeland now incline,
        For they crown the King!

IV.

Yes, they crown the King! Arise!
Note the glad news as it flies,
Hist'ry's made before your eyes—
    'Tis a famous thing!
Shout then with exultant tone,
Make the duty each your own,
"Goodwill to the King and Throne!"
        Three cheers for the King!

V.

Three cheers, too, for England's Queen,
Model woman she hath been—
Kindly deed and smile serene,
    Pure as is the Spring!
Hers the Lily and the Rose,
For unconscious sweetness grows,
When the heart with love o'erflows—
        Fortune's blest the King!

VI.

Fortune's blest the King! Bravo!
Ring the bells, the trumpets blow,
In procession gaily go,
    Step, and dance, and sing!
Mark the day with festive game,
Close it with the bonfire's flame,
All for noble Edward's name—
        God protect the King!

PLUMSTEAD,
MAY 14TH, 1902.

G. O. HOWELL.

A souvenir of Edward VII's Coronation, complete with specially composed song, presented to the boys of Vicarage Road School in Plumstead, south-east London, by the Mayor of Woolwich. Printed well ahead of the crowning, the souvenir bears the originally planned date of 26 June 1902. But Edward's illness and operation caused the postponement of the Coronation to 9 August.

from the Palace and the royal company in general, was Sir Frederick Johnstone, whom the King chided one evening at Sandringham, 'Freddy, Freddy, you're very drunk'. Jabbing a finger into the King's middle, the baronet replied, 'And you, Tum-Tum, you're very fat!' Instantly, Edward turned on his heel and barked at an equerry, 'This gentleman will be leaving in the morning – *before* breakfast. Please see to it.'

Unusually for a trencherman, the King was a moderate drinker and, in a significant way, he changed the after-dinner habits of wealthy men. His meals ended, Continental-style, with coffee, which was also a signal that no more wine would be served. In that way he ended the long-accepted ritual in which the gentlemen dismissed the ladies and then swilled port until they fell into a drunken stupor.

Earlier, as Prince of Wales, he had also achieved a revolution in formal dinner dress. He hinted that his male guests should discard their traditional swallow-tail coats in the evening in favour of something new that had taken his fancy: a dark blue jacket, black trousers and black bow-tie. Men therefore dined at the Palace in the uniform that developed into the modern dinner-jacket. However, in other ways he was pernickety about the wearing of the 'right' clothes for the right occasion. Once, when Lord Rosebery, the Liberal statesman and racehorse owner, arrived for a formal ceremony at the Palace wearing trousers instead of the regulation knee-breeches, Edward crushingly inquired, 'Have you come in the suit of the American Ambassador?'

Edward loved pomp and ceremony, and the first court, which he and Alexandra held on Friday 14 March 1902, was one of the most glittering affairs ever seen at Buckingham Palace. Sir Lionel Cust, Surveyor and Keeper of the King's Pictures and a Gentleman-Usher, left the best eye-witness account of the memorable occasion:

The whole ceremony takes place in the Ball-Room, where a dais is raised at one end with a canopy of rich curtains, in front of which are placed two thrones on which the King and the Queen-Consort take their seats. The general assembly of ladies and gentlemen in attendance occupies the further part of the Ball-Room with the Great Supper-Room and the East Gallery adjoining. Members of the Diplomatic Corps and other guests with the privilege of the Entrée are directed through the State Drawing-Rooms to the special places reserved for them. The royal procession assembles in the White Drawing-Room and the Royal Closet, and at the given hour starts in a slow progress through the Drawing-Rooms to the Ball-Room, at the door of which a signal is given and the band in the gallery strikes up the National Anthem, as their Majesties reach their thrones. The King and Queen now stand, while the Marshal of the Ceremonies presents the lady who on behalf of the Government is entrusted with the duty of introducing the ladies of the Diplomatic Corps. Then the Secretary of State for Foreign Affairs, who has been standing by the King, steps back, and the lady retires to her appointed seat, and after a pause the general procession begins, headed by those ladies who have the privilege of the Entrée. In order to expedite the passing of [name] cards, three Gentlemen-Ushers are stationed at the door of the Ball-Room, who take the cards from the ladies and pass them on to the three minor officers of State, the last of whom hands the card to the Lord Chamberlain, by which time the lady whose name is on the card is usually ready to pass the presence. [The general guests] approach the Ball-Room by the East Gallery, and those who arrive early enough are given seats in the further half of the Ball-Room, special seats being reserved for the ladies who enjoy the Entrée. Meanwhile, the ladies and gentlemen of the Diplomatic Corps are shown into an annexe beyond the actual Ball-Room in which they wait under their special

Seated on adjoining thrones in Westminster Abbey, 9 August 1902, Edward VII and Queen Alexandra are crowned – he by Dr Frederick Temple, Archbishop of Canterbury, and she by Dr W. D. Maclagan, Archbishop of York.

shepherds from the Foreign Office. When the seats in the Ball-Room are all occupied, the ladies are then diverted into the great Supper-Room, where they sit and wait their summons . . . . After the Diplomatic Corps has started and vacated the Annexe, the ladies of the Entrée are invited to start and enter this Annexe, joining up behind the Diplomatic Corps. The general company are then invited to leave their seats and form a single-file procession through the Annexe to the door opening back into the Ball-Room. There each lady is met by two pages, who take her train for her, and spread it skilfully, while she has, or should have, her card ready to hand to the Gentleman-Usher, who is standing nearest the door. Sometimes a lady forgets to hand her card, or is so much engrossed by the sight of the King and Queen that she can think of nothing else, and a little tact is required in extracting the card from her reluctant grasp. Here she is started along the carpet which leads to the presence, and soon the two curtseys are made, and she is safe, her duty done.*

Some of the royal courts were less sedate than that first one. After the presentations the King and Queen would process around the room, stopping here and there to talk to selected guests. But there were times when the behaviour of the 'ladies' was not entirely ladylike. Having come prepared to outdo each other in their particular choice of the regulation court dress – ostrich-feathers, a veil and a long, flowing train – they would nudge, push and scramble to show themselves to the royals; or, at any rate, to the King. Sir Lionel and his fellow Gentlemen-Ushers were obliged to shove them, politely, away from the central carpet which formed Their Majesties' parade-ground.

For Edward, the courts were useful opportunities for surveying the females on display. For Alexandra, who suffered from slight lameness and increasing

*King Edward VII and his Court, John Murray, 1930

deafness, they were occasions of duty, to be endured. They were so, too, for Sir Walter Parratt, who as holder of the ancient post of Master of the Queen's Musick directed the musicians in the Ball Room gallery. Sir Walter favoured the classical composers, whereas the King preferred what one of his acquaintances called 'tumti-tiddly' music. Later, after a comment in which, referring to the American composer of marches, he had declared that 'if the King prefers Sousa's band he had better have it', his 'assistance' at the royal courts was dispensed with. He and his musicians were replaced by a military band.

It was in June 1902 that the Palace played host to one of the greatest assemblies of foreign royalty ever seen in Britain. They arrived by boat-train on the 21st for the Coronation, which had been set for the 26th, and even the usually imperturbable Palace officials flinched at the sight of the mountains of baggage and the armies of retainers. It looked as though the world had suddenly disgorged crown princes from all its multitudinous comic-opera star productions – from Russia, Italy, Denmark, Rumania, Portugal, Saxony, Greece, Sweden, Norway, Siam, Montenegro, Monaco, Korea, Ethiopia, Zanzibar, Egypt, and so on and endlessly on. A few years later many of the princes from Europe were to be blown away by the gales of war. Indeed, the representative of Austria-Hungary was the Archduke Franz Ferdinand, whose assassination in the Bosnian capital of Sarajevo in June 1914 was to be the spark that ignited the First World War.

On the evening of their arrival the royal hordes sat down with Edward and Alexandra to a magnificent banquet at the Palace, but next day the King, who had been unwell for some time, collapsed in extreme agony. Acute appendicitis was diagnosed, and on 24 June, in a specially prepared room in Buckingham Palace, Edward underwent surgery. Despite the great hazards presented at that time by an appendectomy – the odds on death were even – the operation was successful and free of complications. The doctors decided, however, that a 'reasonable' period of recuperation would be necessary, and the London *Times* explained: 'In view of this it is hoped that the British public, and the people of the Empire, will not feel too disappointed or downhearted and will content themselves with a day's holiday (on 26 June); even if the occasion for it has been spoiled.'

The Coronation was re-arranged for 9 August. By then the busy princes and potentates had remembered previous engagements and departed; but, although the average British citizen managed to endure their absence with his usual stoicism, Palace kitchen staff were left to cope with the problem of a vast stock of uneaten food. It was not so much the caviare and the 2,500 quail that worried them, as a royal chef, Gabriel Tschumi, later recalled. There were 'huge amounts of cooked chicken, partridge, sturgeon and cutlets, not to mention all the fruit and cream desserts which would not keep. A little could be put aside for the staff but the rest, it was decided, would have to be given to charitable organisations.

'We were in touch with a good many of these charities, who had literally hundreds of hungry and homeless families on their books, and the Buckingham Palace staff often passed on to them broken or spoilt food. In this case they would be receiving something a little different – six or seven courses from the Coronation banquet of a King, and from all the many charities it was hard to choose one which could be relied upon to handle the disposition of the food fairly and discreetly. Finally we stored the food in hampers for the Sisters of the Poor. . . . On 26 June, the date the banquet was to have been held, it was the poor of Whitechapel and not the foreign kings, princes and diplomats who had the *Consommé de faison aux*

Coronation, 1902. The great state coach, with Edward VII and Queen Alexandra, passing through Whitehall on the return procession from the Abbey to the Palace.

quenelles, *Côtelettes de bécassins à la Souveroff* and many of the other dishes created by the royal chef.'

As a pleasure-loving man himself, the King sympathised with the disappointment felt by so many of his subjects at the postponement of the Coronation, despite the hopes expressed by *The Times*. But nothing astonished the convalescing monarch so much as reports of the reaction of people in the small town of Watford in Hertfordshire, seventeen miles north of Buckingham Palace.

Infuriated by the thoughtlessness of the King's appendix at interfering with their eagerly awaited local celebrations, a mob of some five hundred drunken townspeople went on the rampage on the night of 26 June. They set light to the town's massive bonfire, which festivity organisers were trying to keep intact until the revised Coronation date, smashed windows, burned down the butcher's shop owned by the president of the organising committee and looted other shops. A local magistrate read the 1714 Riot Act, but it was three o'clock in the morning before the police were able to disperse the mob and take command of the badly dented High Street and Market Place. Thirty ringleaders, including eight women, were subsequently sent to prison for terms ranging from one year's hard labour (for arson) to two weeks (for stealing a pair of stockings from a haberdasher's).

After the Coronation the King was curious to know what had happened to the town on the actual day of celebrations, and was shown a newspaper report which recorded: 'The day passed peacefully and amid scenes of great and decorous joy. Watford had learned its lesson and of brutality there was no more.'

To Edward, as to his friends, such behaviour merely confirmed the fact that the 'lower orders' of the kingdom were a race apart, worthy of a hand-wave and a bow on public ceremonial occasions but of no political significance. Yet, in general, the 'lower orders' of Buckingham Palace found the King a good master. Undoubtedly, he could often be bad-tempered, and according to Queen Alexandra he had 'a bellow you could hear all over the corridors'. But he could also be extremely courteous to those who worked for him, and he would invariably raise his hat when he met any of his servants off-duty.

Partly perhaps as a reaction against the austerity of his own upbringing, he had a deep and genuine love for children – his friends' as well as his own. 'You can call me Kingy,' he told one small boy at a party at the Palace; and, even when immaculately clad in full evening dress, he would amuse young visitors by letting slices of buttered toast 'race' down his trouser-legs, the buttered side inwards.

Racing, with horses rather than buttered toast, made as strong an appeal to the King as did women, and it sometimes seemed as though the enthusiasm of the crowds who waited at the Palace to catch a glimpse of him owed as much to his success as a racehorse owner as to any of his regal attributes. However, the 'sport of kings' was not merely a pastime for Edward VII; it was a highly lucrative occupation. From winnings and stud fees he had, by the end of his reign, earned himself a total of £415,880. But all his racing life he was generous to those who contributed towards his successes. When, in the year before his accession, his horse *Ambush II* won the Grand National and £1,975, he at once gave £500 to the jockey, £250 to the head stable-lad and £50 to the boy groom.

Although they never replaced his affection for his horses, he was also proud of his motor-cars – all in a claret-coloured livery – housed in the Palace stables. He delighted in being driven fast, and boasted that his chauffeur had exceeded sixty miles an hour when taking him from the Palace to Brighton. Most royal trips were less enjoyable for the chauffeur, however, who was obliged to endure a stream of abuse from the King in the back seat if he failed to overtake any other vehicle.

To the very end the King remained almost pathologically superstitious. The Palace valets, for example, were forbidden to turn the mattress of his bed on Fridays, and he suffered one of his worst moments when he discovered that there were to be thirteen at table for a dinner-party. He finally consented to sit down to the meal only after being informed that one of the women present was pregnant and that therefore the party could properly be said to number fourteen 'persons'.

Nothing could moderate his voracious appetite for food, and at his last formal dinner at the Palace, on 5 March 1910, he romped through no fewer than nine dishes, including salmon steak, grilled chicken, saddle of mutton and several snipe stuffed with *foie gras*.

Two months later a bulletin issued from the Palace by his doctors disclosed that the King was suffering from bronchitis and that there was 'some anxiety' about his condition. In the early afternoon of 6 May he collapsed in his bedroom, where he had just finished the lightest lunch of his whole adult life, and his nurses propped him up in an armchair before sending for the Queen.

He was wracked by a swift series of heart attacks, but he insisted on remaining in the chair. During his occasional periods of consciousness he received a succession of visitors who came ostensibly to wish him well but actually to pay their last respects. It was in his last hours that Queen Alexandra made a remarkable and compassionate gesture by inviting Mrs Alice Keppel, one of Edward's longer-reigning mistresses, to say farewell to the departing monarch. Quite without malice or jealousy, she told Mrs Keppel, 'I am sure he would want to see you.'

Soon after five in the afternoon the King's eldest son, George, Prince of Wales, breathed into his semi-comatose father's ear the news that his horse *Witch of the Air* had won the Spring Two-Year-Old Plate at Kempton Park by half a length. Edward whispered, 'I am very glad.'

Death finally came at 11.45 that night; soon afterwards his son, who had now become George V, wrote in his diary: 'I have lost my best friend and the best of fathers. I am heartbroken and overwhelmed with grief.'

The coffin of the dead King lay in state, first in the Throne Room of Buckingham Palace and subsequently in Westminster Hall. Nine European crowned heads and a vast concourse of other royals were among the mourners who on Friday 20 May followed the body in procession from the Palace to Paddington Station and thence by special trains to Windsor Castle for the funeral service.

Edward VII had reigned for only nine of his sixty-nine years, and after his boyhood had spent comparatively little time at Buckingham Palace. Unhappily, when he had gone the Palace became the setting for an immense ceremony-by-fire. In accordance with Edward's will, all his private papers and personal letters were burned. Before him, Queen Victoria had ordered her private diary to be consigned to the flames, and after him George V destroyed a large number of documents concerning George IV. It rather looked as though the Palace was taking on a secondary function as crematorium for priceless records whose destruction has robbed historians of many important and enlightening details of the lives of past sovereigns.

George V and Queen Mary.

4

THE MIDDLE YEARS

GEORGE V

SOVEREIGNS MAY INHABIT PALACES BUT only public sentiment can turn those palaces into shrines. And, in the first years of the twentieth century, Buckingham Palace was still without the final public seal of acclaim mingled with reverence. It badly needed two things: a popular monarch, cast in the deeply ingrained 'respectability' of the age, and an 'occasion' that would project it clearly into the foreground of national consciousness.

The Palace soon achieved both objectives: the first with the accession of King George V, and the second with the 1914 declaration of war against Germany.

If tolerance is indeed a special British characteristic, it had been clearly demonstrated by the people's patient acceptance of their royals up to 1910. They had put up with the profligate Hanoverians, shuffled uneasily between adoration for, and exasperation with, Victoria, and been bewildered by occasional misty glimpses of Edward VII as lecher and gaming-table companion of the parasitical idle rich. All in all, it had not been a pretty picture. The nation had learned the hard way that kings and queens are chosen by unpredictable fate, and that, even in sober, conservative Britain, there was no guarantee that a new run of second-class monarchs might not eventually lead to a republic.

Palace eye-view of the return of the procession after the Coronation of George V and Mary. The great state coach, bearing the King and Queen, is about to enter the main gates. Crowds line the Mall away down to the distant Admiralty Arch.

But George V's head came made to measure for a crown, and by happy chance (for those who preferred royals to republics, at least) he and his remarkable wife, Mary of Teck, were destined to lay the foundations for the modern popular concept of the British royal family as solidly permanent and dependable (despite one or two setbacks under Edward VIII).

It was towards the Palace that a crowd of some six thousand people poured down the Mall on the evening of 3 August 1914, as the last frail strands of peace between Great Britain and Kaiser Wilhelm's Germany finally began to snap. They pressed around the Palace railings singing the National Anthem, the 'Marseillaise' (in honour of their French allies) and 'Rule Britannia'. The King and Queen appeared on the central balcony for five minutes to acknowledge the cheers.

The next night the crowds were even larger, and the passing moments of the crisis were signalled by the lighting-up of first one window and then another until the whole of the front of the Palace was one blaze of illumination. The King recorded the decisive events in his diary: 'Tuesday, 4 August: I held a Council at 10.45 (p.m.) to declare war with Germany. It is a terrible catastrophe, but it is not our fault. An enormous crowd collected outside the Palace; we went on the balcony both before and after dinner. When they heard that war had been declared, the excitement increased and May [Queen Mary] and I with David [Prince of Wales, later to be Edward VIII] went on to the balcony; the cheering was terrific.' The cheering and singing outside the Palace lasted, without a break, for four hours.

In those vast crowds there were few who understood precisely the tortuous reasons that had led Germany and Austria to embark on war with Czarist Russia and France and to Britain's commitment to go to the aid of the French. But the enthusiasm for war was overwhelming, and in that hysterical night the Palace was promoted to its position as the centre around which, from then on, people would gather in times of great national rejoicing or grief.

Ironically, only three years beforehand the same crowds had cheered the Kaiser when he had visited the Palace for the unveiling of the memorial to his grandmother, Queen Victoria, set on its great stone island outside the gates at the top of the Mall. He had looked on appreciatively as King George had pulled the cord releasing the white canvas shroud under which the great memorial had been hidden.

By the time of the declaration of war the Palace had been converted, by one more piece of renovation, into the form in which it is seen today. The instigating force had been an anonymous letter (signed 'Anglus' but almost certainly inspired in high places) which had appeared in *The Times*. It read:

Kaiser Wilhelm II (left) rides with George V in Berlin in 1913. King George was attending the wedding of the Kaiser's only daughter to the son of the Duke of Cumberland. One year later Kaiser and King and their two peoples embarked upon the horrors of the First World War.

1st June, 1910.

Sir: Whatever form the national tribute to the memory of our late King [Edward VII] may take, may I suggest that some part of the funds raised should go to the decoration, as a personal tribute, of the eastern front of Buckingham Palace which was King Edward's home during the whole of his reign. As it stands now, it is mean and ugly, but it is a well-proportioned building and, if it were treated architecturally, might be made a worthy termination of the Mall, which will some day be one of the finest avenues in the world, and which is especially associated with the reigns of our last two sovereigns.

In due course approval was given to a design for improving the front of the

In Berlin in 1913 George V (right) poses with his cousin, the Romanov Czar Nicholas II of Russia. In July 1918 Nicholas and his whole family were to be murdered by the Bolsheviks.

Robed and coroneted peers and peeresses queue for transport outside Westminster Abbey after George V's Coronation.

Palace submitted by Sir Aston Webb, the architect responsible for a number of other London buildings, including the Imperial College of Science and Technology in South Kensington. The subtlety of Webb's plan – the cost of whose execution was estimated at an acceptable figure of £60,000 – was that it left the interior of the building and its levels and windows undisturbed. Webb's major alteration was to replace the crumbling Caen stone façade with Portland stone and to erect a series of pilasters and rounded columns supporting a bold cornice running from wing to wing. Along the top a balustrade hid roof and chimneys. The total result was a new, clean outline to the eastern front.

Eight hundred workmen, operating in day- and night-shifts, completed the whole job in the three months from August to October 1913. Exact timetables for each weekly phase were meticulously worked out, and every one of the Portland stone blocks – altogether totalling 5,757 tons – was given an identifying mark so that its place in the scheme could be instantly pinpointed. The scaffolding was some of the most elaborate of its time, consisting of five thousand poles and nearly twelve thousand boards. Six large derricks, five electric hoists and two electric passenger lifts were employed.

When the work was finished, all the workmen were given a celebratory dinner by the King at London's Holborn Restaurant. For speed and impeccable organisation their work has rarely been equalled in Britain since. The contractors' ability to have every piece of building material on the site the moment it was needed came close to genius.

With its new forecourt gates, the Victoria Memorial, and a widened Mall with the handsome Admiralty Arch (built in 1910) at its eastern end, Buckingham Palace was ready for royal and public business, twentieth-century style. The new

The unveiling of the Victoria Memorial, in front of the Palace, in 1911. Somewhere, under one of the plumed helmets visible at the base of the Memorial, is Kaiser Wilhelm of Germany. On that day Londoners cheered him through their streets; three years later, on the outbreak of the First World War, 'Kaiser' became a hated term in Britain.

The wartime Palace – an artist's impression drawn for a 1915 calendar. The royal standard, flying from the centre flagpole, indicates that George V is in residence.

dignity of the Palace was admirably suited to the quiet dignity of the new King, who would, in contrast to his father, spend a very large part of his reign in residence.

There were to be many occasions in George V's reign when national attention would be focused on the Palace, and one of the most memorable came on 17 July 1917, when the King issued a dramatic proclamation. Its most decisive paragraph ran:

We, out of Our Royal Will and Authority, do hereby declare and announce that as from the date of this Our Royal Proclamation Our House and Family shall be styled and known as the House and Family of Windsor, and that all the descendants in the male line of Our said Grandmother Queen Victoria who are subjects of these Realms, other than female descendants who may marry or may have married, shall bear the said name of Windsor . . . .

The decision to change the name of the House was not arrived at by the King voluntarily; it was forced upon him by mass public hysteria. All things supposedly pro-German, from dachshunds to certain, naturalised British subjects, became anathema to millions of otherwise sensible people. Prince Louis of Battenberg, father of the late Lord Mountbatten of Burma, was obliged to resign from his post of First Sea Lord, which he had held with distinction (and to the benefit of the Royal Navy and the prosecution of the war at sea), simply because of his German name. If Battenberg was held to be an 'unacceptable' name, Saxe-Coburg and Gotha, the Royal family's designation, was even more alarmingly alien, reeking most suspiciously of pillaging, raping Huns. Angered and bewildered though he was, King George had no choice but to submit to the hue and cry. A long list of possible new names was considered and rejected before Lord Stamfordham, the King's private secretary, made the brilliant discovery that for a time Edward III had been known as Edward of Windsor.

A more felicitous, English-sounding title could not have been devised, and Lord Rosebery wrote to Stamfordham at the Palace: 'Do you realise you have christened a dynasty? There are few people in the world who have done this; none I think. It is really something to be historically proud of. I admire and envy you.' Honour – and the wartime British people, who did not share Shakespeare's attitude of 'What's in a name?' – were satisfied.

On that, as on so many other matters, the outlook of the man at the Palace was level-headed and rational. George V was no intellectual, and neither was he clever in the quick-witted business sense. But he was one of that curious breed who are often assumed to be dull because of an outward personality that does less than justice to their inner private selves. Behind the starchy appearance lay a man of considerable qualities. Brought up to regard even the most moderately radical views with concern, he nevertheless took it upon himself to urge his wartime government to ensure that prisoners-of-war and conscientious objectors were fairly treated. And even in smaller ways he could sometimes show politicians that example was more impressive than precept.

At an early stage of the war David Lloyd George – then Minister of Munitions but later to be Prime Minister – was convinced that the drinking habits of the workers were holding up the flow of guns and shells. He dithered between the possibilities of putting a complete ban on the public sale of beer and of nationalising the liquor industry and controlling supplies.

While the Minister vacillated, however, the King announced that he would set an example 'by giving up all alcoholic liquor himself and issuing orders against its consumption in the Royal Household, so that no difference shall be made, as far as His Majesty is concerned, between the treatment of rich and poor in this question'. Significantly, the King adhered rigidly to his pledge, but Lloyd George failed to follow his lead — as did everyone else in high places except Lord Kitchener, Secretary of State for War, who was killed in 1916.

In peacetime George V's life-style at the Palace was firmly based on rigid routine — a factor which helped to contribute to his stolid image. The King would rise early and be bathed and dressed by eight o'clock. Before breakfast, if the day was fine, he would take a canter on horseback through Hyde Park's Rotten Row. If the weather was poor he would make a start on dealing with the morning's correspondence.

At nine-fifteen precisely he and the Queen sat down to a simple breakfast of China tea, toast, marmalade, and fish or eggs. During the morning he received the principal members of the household in his study, talking to them from behind a desk on which all the documents and files were arranged in apple-pie order. At around eleven the morning's newspapers were brought to him, with news stories and articles of special note marked in blue pencil by royal officials. He would tolerate no time-saving news clippings; every newspaper had to be unmutilated.

Every morning, too, the King telephoned his sister, Princess Victoria, one of the few people apart from his wife who was allowed to speak openly and bluntly to him. It was the regular procedure for the Palace operator to put the daily call through to the Princess without waiting for the King to ask for it. One morning Princess Victoria snatched up her 'phone the moment it rang and shouted boisterously, 'Hello, you old fool!' Blandly, the Palace operator replied, 'Beg pardon, Your Royal Highness, but His Majesty is not yet on the line.'

Like breakfast, the royal lunch, at one-thirty, was simple: fish, meat, a sweet, fruit and one cup of coffee. In the afternoon the King worked again in his study until three, when he took a couple of hours off to play rackets or stroll around the lake in the Palace gardens.

In the warmer months of the year he often completed his afternoon's work in the garden summerhouse or in a tent on one of the lawns. George V had the typical Englishman's obsession about the weather, and even in times of national crisis would almost invariably begin every private diary entry with a comment on the day. A stickler for punctuality, he was also constantly checking on the time, and insisted that every clock in the Palace should always be accurate — and since there were more than three hundred clocks, including one dating back to 1695, the clock-winder had a full-time job.

At eight-thirty the royal pair dined — in their private Chinese dining-room — and, except when they had guests, the meal was as modest as lunch. Afterwards George, who was moderate in all things, smoked one cigarette. Queen Mary, too, enjoyed an occasional cigarette, an early royal gesture of women's liberation which would have been severely frowned upon had it been publicly known.

Until bedtime, at eleven sharp, the King either studied his famous and valuable stamp collection or read. He had no great taste for literature but he kept a list of all the books he read and it contained some unexpected titles — among them D. H. Lawrence's notorious *Lady Chatterley's Lover*, which, twenty-four years after George V's death, was the subject of an unsuccessful indictment for obscenity.

So domestic life at the Palace was serene and unexciting, and the oddly matched couple – the rather arty, intellectual wife and the strait-laced husband – built themselves an affectionate and happy relationship. George, although not greatly adept at verbal endearments, nevertheless summed up his feelings in a touching and revealing note written, a few months after their wedding, to his 'May': 'When I asked you to marry me I was very fond of you but not very much in love with you. . . . I know now that I do *love* you, darling girl, with all my heart and am simply *devoted* to you. . . . I adore you sweet May.'

Father and son – and future Kings. George V-to-be with the ten-year-old Edward VIII-to-be outside the Palace in 1904.

Those feelings were genuinely reciprocated, and George and Mary were deeply hurt by the extraordinary assertion made in a magazine, the *Liberator*, at the beginning of the reign that the King was, in fact, a bigamist. The article's author, a young anti-royalist named Edward Mylius, declared that three years before taking Mary as his wife – in July 1893 – he had entered into a secret but legal marriage in Malta with Elizabeth Culme-Seymour, elder daughter of a British admiral. A son, Mylius alleged, had been born of the marriage, which was never dissolved and which therefore made the King's 'second' marriage, to Mary, an example of what the magazine headlined as 'Sanctified Bigamy'.

In February 1911 Mylius was arraigned on a charge of criminal libel, and one of the trial's highlights was his remarkable contention that the King should be summoned from the Palace to appear in court. 'I demand his presence', he said, 'on the grounds, first, that every accused person has the right to be confronted with his accuser in court. Second, that no action for libel is usually taken without the prosecutor being in court where the jury can see him.' Lord Alverstone, the Lord Chief Justice, retorted: 'You are perfectly well aware that the King cannot be summoned here.'

Evidence proved that Miss Culme-Seymour – who, by the time of the trial, was a Mrs Napier – had never been in Malta at the alleged time, and had met the King only once, briefly, at a Buckingham Palace garden party. Mylius was jailed for twelve months.

The piquant fact was that Mary's only serious rival for the King's affection was his mother, Queen Alexandra, for whom he had coined the special title 'Motherdear'. But Mary was astutely capable of safeguarding her domestic empire. When his newly married wife was visiting relatives, George – then still Prince of Wales – wrote to her to say that 'Motherdear' had been to lunch at their York Cottage, in the grounds of Sandringham, 'and afterwards moved the furniture in the drawing-room, which certainly gives us ever so much more room'. Mary's polite reply was a model example of how to contain a busybody mother-in-law: 'I am so glad "Motherdear" tried to arrange our drawing-room; she has so much taste.'

On 22 January 1924 Ramsay MacDonald, leader of the Labour Party, entered the Palace doors and kissed hands with the King on his appointment as head of the first socialist government in Britain's history. That night George V wrote in his diary: 'Today 23 years ago dear Grandmama died. I wonder what she would have thought of a Labour Government?' She would probably have expected the Palace to fall about her ears, and would no doubt have found it unbelievable that her grandson could bring himself to add: 'I had an hour's talk with him [MacDonald] and he impressed me very much; he wishes to do the right thing.'

The historic encounter threw a remarkably illuminating light on both MacDonald and the monarch. In his sensible, correctly constitutional manner,

George assured his new Prime Minister of his fullest assistance and in return asked only that they should always be completely frank with each other on matters of state. He could not, however, resist disclosing a hint of foreboding by referring to what he described as an 'unfortunate incident' at a recent left-wing meeting at the Royal Albert Hall at which the 'Marseillaise' and 'The Red Flag' had been sung.

MacDonald's reply was eminently reassuring. He hoped the King would sympathise with the problems he had in dealing with his party's 'extremists' and said that if he had tried to ban 'The Red Flag' he, as chairman of the meeting, would have had a riot on his hands. As it was, he had successfully used his influence to prevent a repeat performance – in the Commons – the previous day (21 January) when the Conservative government had been defeated by seventy-two votes. And, for good measure, he added that he hoped to break his party followers of the 'Red Flag' habit.

A few days later the King received MacDonald again, together with three of his new ministers, one of whom, J. R. Clynes, described the meeting in his *Memoirs*:

King George sent for Mr MacDonald. Arthur Henderson, J. H. Thomas and myself accompanied our leader to Buckingham Palace, to that fateful interview of which we had dreamed, when a British Sovereign should entrust the affairs of the Empire to the hands of the people's own representatives.

As we stood waiting for His Majesty, amid the gold and crimson of the Palace, I could not help marvelling at the strange turn of Fortune's wheel which had brought MacDonald, the starveling clerk, Thomas, the engine-driver, Henderson, the foundry labourer, and Clynes, the mill-hand, to this pinnacle beside the man whose forebears had been Kings for so many splendid generations. We were making history.

We were, perhaps, somewhat embarrassed, but the little, quiet man whom we addressed as 'Your Majesty' swiftly put us at our ease. He was himself rather anxious; his was a great responsibility, and I have no doubt that he had read the wild statements of some of our extremists, and I think he wondered to what he was committing his people. . . .

I had expected to find him unbending; instead, he was kindness and sympathy itself. Before he gave us leave to go, he made an appeal that I have never forgotten: 'The immediate future of my people, and their whole happiness, is in your hands, gentlemen. They depend upon your prudence and sagacity.'

To Motherdear, the King wrote: 'I have been making the acquaintance of all the Ministers in turn & I must say they all seem to be very intelligent & they take things very seriously. They have different ideas to ours as they are all socialists, but they ought to be given a chance & ought to be treated fairly.'

And, with typical consideration and courtesy, he instructed his private secretary to send MacDonald a memorandum on the traditional procedures between monarch and ministers so that, as men unaccustomed to governing, they might be spared the embarrassment of errors of protocol. He also waived the ruling that knee-breeches should be worn on formal Palace occasions, and Lord Stamfordham obligingly passed the word to 'the people's own representatives' that, 'from £30 complete', a modified form of levee dress could be hired from the famous firm of Moss Bros. (He pointed out that the hire price included 'a cock-hat and sword'.)

However, the swing of the political pendulum ensured that the total hire bill for the Labour ministers was negligible, for within six months they had been ousted from office and the Conservatives were back in power.

Unemployment, industrial unrest, and the fear of what he himself called 'class

From the Royal Collection: Van Dyck's portrait of King Charles I with M. de St Antoine, which hangs in the East Gallery of the Palace. The great Flemish-born artist (1599–1641) was for nearly seven years Charles's Court painter and was knighted by the King in 1632.

(Above) An Evening Landscape, *by Albert Cuyp (1620–91), artist son of a Dutch landscape and portrait painter. Cuyp's work was curiously neglected in his homeland after his death and was 'rediscovered' by English art-collectors in the 18th century.*

(Below) The Shipbuilder and his Wife, *by Rembrandt (1606–69), greatest painter of the Dutch school. He is believed to have visited England in 1661 when the Mulberry Garden – the site of the Palace – was becoming one of London's best-known attractions.*

Samuel Cooper's unfinished miniature of Frances Stewart (1647–1702), whom Charles II at one time saw as a possible future companion for his bedchamber. In 1667 she became the third wife of the Duke of Richmond, but he died five years later.

(Above) A Gobelins tapestry (dated 1780 and acquired by George IV) illustrating the story of Jason and the Golden Fleece. When Jason fell in love with Creusa and abandoned his wife, Medea, she in revenge killed Creusa, burnt Corinth (in flames in the background), murdered her two children by Jason (their bodies are draped over the front of her chariot), and drove her team of dragons to Athens. The yapping King Charles spaniel seems strikingly out of place.

(Below) Part of the Picture Gallery which occupies the whole of the centre area of the first floor on the west side of the Palace. Some of the canvases on display are 'rotated' between this gallery and the Queen's Gallery where they can be seen by the public.

warfare' were constant anxieties for the King, and, together with a great many other people, he thought the worst had happened with the declaration of the General Strike in the spring of 1926.

The strike was due to start at midnight on Monday 3 May, and on the morning of that day George V was at Windsor. He returned at once to Buckingham Palace – confirmation, if it were needed, that the Palace was the rightful standard-bearing centre of the monarchy in a time of crisis.

Once the strike had begun, hourly reports of its progress were delivered to the King in his study. But as he pored over each message and as the hysterical posturings of some politicians became daily more evident, George exactly understood his delicate role in the whole unhappy affair. When it was suggested to him that he should call a conference at the Palace to discuss the setting up of a so-called 'committee of reconciliation' he replied firmly that he would not even consider any personal intervention in the dispute. His proper task was to ensure that the Crown remained above and beyond the political battle.

Only when the strike had ended, on the evening of 12 May, did the nation hear directly from the King. In a special message from Buckingham Palace addressed to 'My People', he declared:

At such a moment it is supremely important to bring together all my people to confront the difficult situation which still remains. This task requires the co-operation of all able and well-disposed men in the country. Even with such help it will be difficult, but it will not be impossible. Let us forget whatever elements of bitterness the events of the past few days may have created, only remembering how steady and how orderly the country has remained, though severely tested, and forthwith address ourselves to the task of bringing into being a peace which will be lasting because, forgetting the past, it looks only to the future with the hopefulness of a united people.

That message and the King's conduct of affairs at the Palace during the strike helped to underline George V's right to the accolade bestowed on him in later years by the historian, Lady Longford, as 'the first great constitutional monarch'. He had most certainly benefited from the lessons in constitutional history given to him by one of his boyhood tutors, Dr J. R. Tanner, the Cambridge historian, and he kept always in mind the precept of the economist, Walter Bagehot, that the British monarch's principal task is to 'advise, to encourage and to warn'.

It was a delicate role for him in a realm where national crises are as familiar as soggy weather, and sometimes seem as persistent. Ministers were constantly trooping to the Palace to tell him of the country's latest package of troubles – as in the summer of 1931, when the effects of the world's great economic depression sent shivers of alarm throughout Britain.

On 24 August he held a crucial meeting in the Indian Room at the Palace to discuss with ministers the formation of a National Government composed of all three major political groupings, Conservative, Liberal and Labour, with Ramsay MacDonald as Prime Minister. This coalition was intended as a temporary measure, designed specifically to steer the nation through the crisis, but it lasted in various forms until the defeat of Germany in the Second World War, although MacDonald resigned in 1935. The King was convinced that without the establishment of an all-party government, undertaken at the Palace that August day, there would have been 'a national disaster in a few hours'. But the majority of the Labour Party branded MacDonald as a renegade who had 'sold out' to the

George V faces a BBC microphone. He was the first British sovereign to speak directly to his people at home and overseas by means of radio and regularly broadcast a Christmas message – a tradition that has been maintained by Elizabeth II.

Conservatives, and some of its leaders thought they detected a sinister monarchical hand behind the new administration.

One of those leaders, Sir Stafford Cripps – destined to emerge as a distinguished statesman in the 1945 Labour Government – told a political meeting that if Labour were ever returned to power 'there is no doubt that we shall have to overcome opposition from Buckingham Palace and other places as well'. Chastened by the public outcry that followed press reports of his speech, Cripps quickly tried to make it clear that he was referring not to the monarch personally but to what he vaguely described as 'court circles'. On hearing of that retraction, George V demanded: 'What does he mean by saying that Buckingham Palace is not me? Who else is there, I should like to know? Does he mean the footman?'

Despite that light-hearted quip, the King probably had, in supporting the formation of the National Government, come close for the only time to exceeding his royal authority. But if that really was so – and political historians still argue the matter – the most likely reason is that he had failed to understand that MacDonald was acting without his party's mandate.

A letter he wrote from the Palace to the Archbishop of Canterbury contained a sentence which showed that the King's personal convictions were as honest and straightforward as they were politically unsophisticated: 'Thank God I am an optimist and I believe in the common sense of the people of this country, if only the situation is properly explained to them.' The people themselves would have endorsed that. There was a strong popular and romantic belief – not all that inaccurate – that the Palace's royal resident was the kind of man whose companionship one could readily have enjoyed in the local pub. The King may not have been witty but he had a bantering sense of humour, of the jolly saloon-bar variety, and he loved children and domestic pets. Many hearts were touched by the rumour that during one of his serious illnesses, from which it seemed he might not recover, his Cairn terrier Snip lay whimpering hour after hour outside his Palace sick-room.

And there were times when Palace visitors, navigating their way through the maze of corridors, were startled to be greeted with the shrill, squawking demand, 'Well, what abaht it?' They were apologetically informed that it came from the royal parrot, Charlotte, acquired by the King in Port Said during his Royal Navy service as a young man. But no Palace official was able to say who had taught the bird its only spoken line or what, indeed, the curious question meant. One old lady, who assumed that Charlotte's presence indicated George V's personal devotion to all birds, sent the Palace a couple of doves in a wooden cage with the advice that if the King's health troubled him again 'these birds should be placed in His Majesty's bedroom and their breathing will purify the air'. On royal instructions the doves were allowed to go free and purify the air of the Palace gardens.

The King's love of children was especially marked in his deep affection towards his first granddaughter, Elizabeth (now Elizabeth II), his 'sweet little Lilibet', in whose company he was always totally relaxed. On one occasion the Archbishop of Canterbury, Gordon Cosmo Lang, entered the private apartments at Buckingham Palace to find the King-Emperor on his hands and knees playing the role of horse while Elizabeth, as the groom, led him around the room by his beard.

In an era when there existed a remarkable popular antagonism towards any kind of music that might have been called 'classical', the King was happy to

6 May 1935, the first day of celebrations for the Silver Jubilee of the reign of George V and Queen Mary. Flanked here by her grandparents, the young Princess Elizabeth waves to the crowds from the Palace balcony. To her right the top of little Princess Margaret's head is just visible.

*Family group at the Palace
– Silver Jubilee, 1935. Left
to right: Duke of York (later
George VI); the Princess
Royal; George V; Lord
Harewood; Princess Mar-
garet (who can just about see
over the balcony); the Hon.
Gerald Lascelles; Princess
Elizabeth; Queen Mary; the
Duke of Gloucester (in the
background); the Duchess of
Kent (Princess Marina); the
Duke of Kent; Lord Lascel-
les (in background); and the
Duchess of York (now Eliz-
abeth, the Queen Mother).*

*People waited in the streets
of London throughout the
night of 5 May 1935 so as to
be in the best position for
seeing the following day's
royal procession to St
Paul's Cathedral for the
Silver Jubilee Thanksgiving
service.*

acknowledge himself – in private, at least – to be a convinced 'lowbrow'. (For a long time the word 'highbrow' confused him; never having seen it written down, he thought it was 'eyebrow' and could not imagine what its connotation could be.) After private dinner-parties he often entertained his guests with gramophone records, mostly of cloying sentimental ballads. Satirists would have gloried in the fact that the King's favourite composition was the national anthem. 'That good old thing', he called it, and grew quite misty-eyed when he heard it played by a military band in the Palace forecourt.

Among other traits he shared with his people was an instinctive distrust of all 'foreigners'. There were times when he had to make a special effort to stifle his bluff personal opinions on the subject – as, for instance, when political considerations obliged him to receive King Fuad of Egypt as a three-day guest at the Palace. He was astonished to see that the visitor's retinue included a food-taster and a chemist to test all the royal food before meals, and he was revolted by the discovery that Fuad's preferred dish was horse-flesh steaks.

Few visitors to the Palace roused such deep prejudices in the King as Mahatma Gandhi, the 'rebellious' leader of the Indian Congress Party. George V saw him, as did popular opinion of the time, as a thorn in the Empire's flesh, spreading the virus of independence in the great sub-continent. And the King was both resentful and embarrassed at the prospect of meeting a man who, wherever he travelled, insisted on wearing a simple Indian peasant's loin cloth and revealing his bare and bony knees.

Yet at the Palace meeting in 1931 it was 'the little man with no proper clothes on', as George V called him, who scored a famous diplomatic victory. After being rather petulantly warned by the King against encouraging terrorism in 'my Empire', Gandhi, the advocate of non-violent protest, replied in his gentle, fluting English: 'I must not be drawn into a political argument in Your Majesty's Palace, after receiving Your Majesty's hospitality.' The King was nonplussed. He had not expected a 'rebel', inflated to Satanic proportions by British propaganda, to have such charming manners. (The Mahatma's good impression did nothing, of course, to change the immediate political attitude of the King and his government, and not long after the Palace visit Gandhi was back, as he had been so many times before, in a British jail in India. George V did not live to see the 'impossible' realised – the creation of India and Pakistan as sovereign independent republics within the British Commonwealth.)

No record exists of the manner in which the King may have spoken of the Mahatma in private, but he was certainly never at a loss for ripe language when he thought the occasion demanded it – although not in the presence of Queen Mary. Towards the end of his days, when it was suggested that he might consider a health-restoring visit to the south coast resort of Bognor, where he had recuperated after a previous illness, he replied succinctly, 'Bugger Bognor!' And he refused medicine from one of his doctors with the cry, 'I'm not taking any more of your bloody muck!'

Occasional outbursts of anger towards Palace staff usually left him with a feeling of nagging guilt, and he would try whenever possible to make amends with a friendly word before the day was over. On some problems, too, he could be much more understanding than most of his subjects might have been in similar circumstances. Told that a manager of one of his estates intended to take a harsh line with an unmarried daughter who had become pregnant, he declared, 'He must

In their open-top coach George V and Queen Mary pass Temple Bar (the western entrance to the City of London) on their way to the St Paul's Jubilee service.

show mercy to her. Tell him he must treat the girl gently.'

Progressively minded on some of the wider political developments of his age, he was nevertheless extremely wary of change in small matters. All his life he wore his trousers pressed at the sides, instead of at the back and front, and when a collar-stud he had used for fifty years began to fall apart he had it repaired with gold filling rather than throw it away.

In 1932 he made royal history by becoming the first British sovereign to speak directly to his people at home and overseas by radio (which he and everyone else still called 'the wireless'). His short Christmas message, which was to be established as an annual event, was prepared at the Palace although the actual broadcast was made from Sandringham. The voice, over headphones and primitive loudspeakers, sounded dry and remote – the King was understandably nervous – but the huge listening audience loved it, and many people wept openly when it pronounced the sentence: 'Your loyalty, your confidence in me, has been my abundant reward.'

Three years later his people had a special opportunity for further demonstrations of that loyalty when kingdom and Empire celebrated the Silver Jubilee of the reign. Hundreds of thousands of visitors flooded into London and many camped out in the capital's parks for the week of festivities. On the morning of Monday 6 May, 1935, the opening day, the whole area around the Palace was one vast throng of people.

'At night, too,' the author and journalist Sir Philip Gibbs recalled, 'flood-lighting etched London's chief buildings in a new silver tint and Buckingham Palace, thrown up against the night by the lights, drew thousands upon thousands up the Mall, along Buckingham Palace Road, down Constitution Hill and Birdcage Walk and through the parks to form a mass of surging humanity before it, such as these old stones had never before witnessed. Graciously the King and Queen appeared night after night in that Silver Week, and sometimes several times a night, upon the balcony, in response to the never-ending chant of "We want George".'

The King also broadcast a radio message to his people that night, but what worried him most was a ten-minute speech he was due to make in Westminster Hall and which was to be preserved for posterity on a gramophone record. He feared that his voice would break – as it did, and as it can still be heard today – when he came to the point at which he would pay tribute to his wife. As he was dictating the passage to a secretary he paused and then said, 'Put that paragraph at the very end. I can't trust myself to speak of the Queen when I think of all I owe her.'

Seven months later, throughout the days and nights of 19 and 20 January 1936, crowds again gathered outside the Palace; but this time they stood in complete silence, staring sadly at the darkened windows. At Sandringham, where he had gone to spend Christmas and the New Year, the King lay dying. The whole kingdom had been warned of the approaching end by one of the most famous radio bulletins in history. It had been scribbled on a piece of card by the King's principal doctor, Lord Dawson of Penn. The simple words were memorable: 'The King's life is moving peacefully to its close.' By eleven o'clock on the night of the 20th the crowd around the Palace had been increased by late-comers from theatres and restaurants. Soon after midnight an awesome whispering, like a great final sigh, spread from those nearest the Palace railings, who could read the notice posted there, to people on the outer fringes of the crowd. The King had died at 11.55.

Edward VIII and Cosmo Lang (right).

5

THE MIDDLE YEARS

EDWARD VIII

THE NEW KING, EDWARD VIII, THE FORMER Prince of Wales, disliked Buckingham Palace. He objected to what he thought was its musty, damp smell and complained that, among other things, the lighting in the state reception rooms was too harsh and made women guests 'look ghastly'. During his short reign he spent as little time as possible in the place, finding real comfort and relaxation only at Fort Belvedere, his eighteenth-century pseudo-castle near Windsor Great Park.

For a time the widowed Queen, Mary, stayed on at the Palace while the new King, although he set up an office in a small Chinese-style room on the ground floor facing on to the great courtyard, continued to live at York House, St James's Palace, the London residence in which he had established himself while still Prince of Wales.

Most of the King's subjects had a very clear picture in their minds of the new man at the Palace. He had arrived in the Chinese room more handsomely packaged by the exhaustive public-relations efforts of newspapers and popular magazines than any previous incoming sovereign.

He was (so the picture showed) the world's most attractive and eligible bachelor, forceful, dynamic, progressive without being revolutionary, caring and compassionate about ordinary people: a King who would continue in the great constitutional role created by his father, but with a younger, more modern touch. But there were other facets of the King's life which were as yet of no public interest – that, for example, he was irresistibly drawn towards married women, had dismissed one of them after a sixteen-year love affair and was determined to make another his wife.

Dr Cosmo Lang, Archbishop of Canterbury, one of the first of the notable visitors to the Chinese room immediately after the accession, clearly had such matters on his mind, but according to Edward's subsequent account the interview was conducted largely in double-speak. While the King sat glumly listening, the Archbishop discoursed on those of his meetings with George V at which Edward had been the subject of discussion. Although he apparently declined to be specific, he made mysterious references to the late King's disapproval of Edward's conduct; but he added the footnote that he, the Archbishop, had 'tried in your interest to present it in the most favourable light'. It was no wonder that, as Edward noted, after Lang had departed the atmosphere in the Chinese room was 'heavy with portent'.

One moment of gravity at the Palace in those first days was counterbalanced by a moment of farce. Neville Chamberlain, the Chancellor of the Exchequer, came to talk about deciding the new King's income – it was finally fixed at £410,000 a year; and a sorrowing Cabinet minister, J. H. (Jimmy) Thomas, came to hand over his seals of office. Thomas, a former railway-engine driver and trade-union leader, drummed out of the Labour Party for remaining as a member of the National Government, had been forced to resign his ministerial post and House of Commons seat for leaking Budget secrets to some of his wealthy friends. 'It's a bloody conspiracy!' the earthy Thomas cried; and, recalling his long and oddly matched friendship with George V, added tearfully, 'Thank God your old Dad is not alive to see this!'

Anthony Eden, the Foreign Secretary, returned from the Chinese room to 10 Downing Street to inform the Prime Minister that the King had rejected the government's advice on a matter of diplomatic policy. He had bluntly refused to grant an audience at the Palace to the Ethiopian Emperor, Haile Selassie, who had been driven out of his kingdom by the invading forces of Benito Mussolini, the Italian Fascist dictator. To Eden's plea that the reception of the Emperor would be a popular move, Edward had replied acidly, 'Popular with whom?' (Later the King effected a compromise by instructing his brother, the Duke of Gloucester, to call on Haile Selassie at his London hotel. When he came to write his memoirs, Edward explained that he had been worried that his government was 'coercing' Mussolini and would drive him into closer alliance with the German dictator, Adolf Hitler. But this has a touch of post-war hindsight; at the time the King had strong sympathies for the two western dictatorships.)

King George V had been meticulously attentive to the daily task of reading through the state documents sent to the Palace from Whitehall in red despatch-boxes – 'doing my boxes', he had called it; but Edward found the desk-work of the Chinese room irksome. He started off with a brave enough will, but, not being a man much taken with the written word in any form, he began to skip first one paper and then another until most were being returned to the Cabinet Office unread. Once he realised that the King was neglecting his duty, Stanley Baldwin, the Prime Minister, restricted the flow of papers to those that required the royal signature. And Edward, only too happy to see his burden lightened, made no comment about his right to see all state documents.

Bored as he was by such routine, Edward would sometimes spend inordinate energy on quite trivial matters. One of the most bizarre examples was an almost farcical wrangle in which he involved himself with officials from the Royal Mint – the government department responsible for manufacturing the coins of the realm. Sir Robert Johnson, Deputy Master of the Mint, brought to the Palace a group of artists from whom he had commissioned designs for the new Edward VIII coins. After one brief glance at the examples the King exploded with anger. The artists had portrayed the right-hand side of the King's head, and Edward demanded that the coins should show the left side – his 'better' one.

Sir Robert was embarrassed, but insisted that the Mint must be allowed to follow its tradition that each new sovereign's head should be shown facing in the opposite direction from the head of his, or her, predecessor. George V had faced to the left, Edward must be seen facing to the right.

'Now I see,' said the King derisively. 'It's just as if the sovereigns of England were following a perpetual tennis game from the side-lines!' And he ordered Sir Robert to take his artists away and not bring them back until they had submitted to the royal command.

Sir Robert, however, was not a man to be deflected from duty to tradition by an 'unreasonable' order – even one direct from the lips of the monarch himself. He pondered deeply and arrived at a neat solution. A few days later he returned to the Palace with a sheaf of new designs in which the left-hand side of the King's head

A bored Edward VIII endures the interminable presentation of debutantes at his one and only Palace garden party. Soon after this photograph was taken a heavy downpour of rain left the 'lucky' young women with soaked and ruined dresses but gave the King a welcome excuse to curtail the proceedings and flee indoors.

Edward VIII rides to Hyde Park, July 1936, to present Colours to the Guards. It was on his return from the ceremony that there occurred what at first was thought to have been an attempt on his life.

Constitution Hill, 16 July 1936. In the centre of the picture just to the right of the St John Ambulance first-aid truck, a policeman can be seen strong-arming a man believed at the time to have tried to assassinate Edward VIII. The mounted King continued on his way to the Palace, unharmed, at the head of six battalions of Guards. The would-be 'assassin', as it turned out, had thrown a revolver at the feet of the King's horse in order to publicise an imagined personal grievance against the Home Secretary.

was duly depicted, but reverse-printed so that it faced to the right. Edward gaped in disbelief at such an outrageous display of insubordination, and without argument banished Sir Robert from the Palace until he had done as he was told. In the end the curious little battle turned out to have been pointless, for Edward was no longer King by the time the first batch of coins had been minted.

The annoyance of the 'battle of the coins' was at least offset by the quiet enjoyment which the King gained from the fiasco of his one and only Palace garden party. He had anticipated it with dread but, on the day, a sudden downpour of rain gave him the excuse to hurry indoors and rescued him from the tedium of receiving an endless line of curtseying debutantes from among the six hundred guests. A photograph taken shortly before the deluge shows him sitting sunk in boredom in a gilt-framed chair, impatiently fidgeting with his fingers.

His public-relations image was given a boost, however, on 16 July, 1936, when he escaped what appeared to be an attempt on his life. He was returning on horseback to Buckingham Palace at the head of the six battalions of Guards to whom he had presented new colours in Hyde Park. As the procession moved along Constitution Hill a revolver, loaded in four chambers, was thrown into the roadway and fell within a few feet of the King's horse.

Edward gave no sign of alarm, and the procession continued on its way uninterrupted. The next day's newspapers paid special tribute to the calmness of the King, and the Archbishop of Canterbury – leaping at this opportunity to view the King's conduct in the most favourable light – was among the many people from all walks of life who showered the Palace with messages of congratulation. (The owner of the gun, which had been knocked from his hand by an alert special constable, turned out to be an Irish journalist named McMahon who believed that his plan to launch a journal called the *Human Gazette* was being frustrated by Sir John Simon, the Home Secretary. In some tortuous way he had convinced himself that a dramatic demonstration in the presence of the King would bring him helpful publicity for his cause. In the event it brought him a year in jail.)

The general public, while relieved to learn that no harm had come to the King, were still completely ignorant of the steady progress of events that were to bring King Edward VIII's reign to a swift and sensational conclusion. But to people with inside information – from the government, members of Parliament and the Archbishop to Fleet Street editors and London's society cliques – the King's love affair with the American-born Mrs Wallis Warfield Simpson was well-known and continually discussed. To one prominent MP, dismayed by a press picture of the King actually walking out of the Palace on a rainy day under his own umbrella, it seemed quite natural that he should ask Mrs Simpson, a fellow-guest at a dinner-party, to pass on his disapproval to Edward. (Sniffily the politician declared, 'The monarchy must remain aloof and above the commonplace. We can't have the King doing this kind of thing. He has the Daimler.')

The King himself saw no harm in that kind of newspaper publicity, but he was very acutely concerned about the possible coverage of Mrs Simpson's forthcoming petition for divorce from her stockbroker husband, Ernest, due to be heard in the eastern county town of Ipswich, seventy-two miles from London. At his invitation, Lord Beaverbrook, the owner of the London *Express* group of newspapers and the most powerful of the Fleet Street proprietors, went to the Palace to hear the King's plea that he should use his influence to hush up the divorce proceedings.

A moment of off-duty re-laxation before the abdi-cation storm broke. Edward VIII and Mrs Simpson watch the floor-show in a London night-club.

Beaverbrook promised to do his best, and his best could not have been bettered. By a sudden inspiration he and his fellow-proprietors realised that the freedom of the press, to which they were all devoted, included the freedom not to publish. This 'gentleman's agreement', as it was called, could not, of course, be extended to the foreign, and especially the American, press, which was already avidly reporting on the 'King-and-Wally' romance. But Palace officials whose task it was to keep an eye on foreign publications were relieved to find that certain pages of *Time* magazine were being regularly removed before distribution to British buyers. No one, either in the government departments of Whitehall or in the Palace, could say who was responsible for the vandalism of such a reputable publication.

On 27 October King Edward held a Privy Council at the Palace, and soon after lunch the telephone rang in the Chinese room and brought him the news for which he had been eagerly waiting. That same morning Mrs Simpson had been awarded a decree *nisi*, meaning that, unless (*nisi*) circumstances changed within the then statutory intervening period of six months, her marriage would be irrevocably dissolved. Although not a notably witty man, the King might have noticed a piquant touch about the evidence on which Wallis Simpson's petition relied. Mr Simpson's ultimate undoing, it seemed, was a cup of very English morning tea brought to him in bed at a small hotel in Bray, a Thames-side village (which happened to be only four miles from the royal residence of Windsor Castle). Unfortunately for him – or so it appeared – hotel chambermaids and others were able to confirm that the lady in the double bed next to the tea-sipping Mr Simpson was most positively not the real Mrs Simpson. She was in fact the delightfully named Miss Buttercup Kennedy, whose presence was the essential factor in Ernest Simpson's chivalrous gesture to free his wife from what was already a shattered marriage.

Immediately after the Ipswich court hearing Mrs Simpson returned to London, and that night the King dined with her at her four-storey house, 16 Cumberland Terrace, Regent's Park. It was a happy evening, a celebration of what the King hoped was a positive step along the road towards their marriage; and the surroundings of Cumberland Terrace were a good deal more congenial to Edward than those of the Belgian Suite at the Palace, which he had by now taken over as his private apartments.

The Belgian Suite, named in honour of Queen Victoria's uncle, Leopold I of the Belgians, is in the north-west corner of the Palace, with an entrance from the garden. It consists of five rooms, with the Regency Room, decorated in 1922 under Queen Mary's direction and furnished in Regency style, as the main living-room. Elegant though he found it, with its grey walls and emerald-green carpets and curtains, it was not the King's idea of cosy homeliness. On the walls the features of George III and Queen Charlotte and family stared fixedly from eleven portraits painted on copper, each two feet high. The passing hours of Edward's brief reign were marked off by an exquisite mahogany mantelpiece clock of the French Empire with elaborately chased ormolu mounts.

It was during his final days at the Palace that Edward escaped from the museum atmosphere of the Belgian Suite to the exploit that was to bring him a curious kind of personal fame, long to be remembered despite the overriding notoriety of his eventual abdication. He paid a visit to south Wales – then officially listed as a 'depressed area', with widespread unemployment and crushing poverty – and

On his famous tour of South Wales, in November 1936, Edward VIII greets ex-servicemen in Pontypool. He is shaking hands with Mr J. H. Williams, who won the Victoria Cross during the First World War.

caught the nation's imagination with his reported declaration: 'Something must be done.'

For all its constant repetition there is evidence for doubting that the King made such a comment. It was more probably – as two of them privately claimed in later years – the product of a group of experienced Fleet Street industrial reporters, tagging along on the King's tour and anxious to put a few words into Edward's mouth to 'personalise' the visit. It was certainly a journalist's ideal 'quote'. It illuminated the King as a caring person, and, most important, it was hardly the kind of comment that Palace officials could subsequently deny. In his memoirs, Edward himself recalls the occasion in strangely circumspect language: 'I was *quoted as having said*, in the midst of some dismal scene of ruined industry, that "something must be done" to repair the ravages of the dreadful inertia that had gripped the region. The statement was the minimum humanitarian response that *I could have made* to what I had seen.' (Emphasis added.)

That statement about the unemployed – if it was made – was in marked contrast to the personal action of the King in cancelling an unwritten rule that no Buckingham Palace servant should be fired (except for the most extreme offence) without being found another job.

From his tour the King came back to the Palace to find that nothing could now prevent his relationship with Mrs Simpson from causing a constitutional crisis. He had already told the Prime Minister that he would marry Mrs Simpson in the face of the government's opposition even if it meant abdication. And, soon after his return from Wales, he again summoned Stanley Baldwin to the Palace and demanded to know for certain if Parliament would refuse to consent to a morganatic marriage Act, under which Mrs Simpson would be his wife but not his queen and under which no child of the marriage would have any right to succeed to the Throne.

Astutely Baldwin laid a trap for the King by asking, almost casually, if His Majesty wished him to 'examine the question formally'. Edward readily agreed that he did, thereby missing the Prime Minister's point that 'formally' meant consultation not only with the Cabinet but with the British dominions. The catch there was that Edward would inevitably be made to appear as though he were going over the heads of his own imperial ministers in the search for allies. No dominion government would risk the responsibility of appearing to split the Empire over the King's intention to marry a twice divorced woman of whom the British state and church disapproved. Predictably, the dominions supported the British government, as did the two opposition parties in the House of Commons, Labour and Liberal.

At the beginning of December the British press at last broke silence on the affair, and once more the Prime Minister was called to the Palace. While he stood nervously fluttering his right hand back and forth past his ear, snapping thumb and forefinger – a habit that grated on the King's nerves – Edward brandished the script of a radio speech that he wished to broadcast to the nation.

When Baldwin protested that such a proposal was 'quite unconstitutional', the King shattered the quiet of the Chinese room by bellowing, 'You want me to go, don't you?' In as soothing a tone as he could muster the astonished Prime Minister replied: 'What I want, sir, is what you told me you wanted: to go with dignity, not dividing the country and making things as smooth as possible for your successor.'

On 3 December Edward left Buckingham Palace for the last time and, until the

The exiles. The Duke of Windsor (lately Edward VIII) with Mrs Wallis Simpson in France shortly before their marriage, on 3 June 1937, at the Château de Candé, Tours.

Will he, won't he, abdicate? Londoners gather outside the Palace in the concluding days of the Edward-Mrs Simpson crisis. But the culminating drama was being staged at Edward's country retreat, Fort Belvedere, where he made the irrevocable decision to put love before crown and kingdom.

final scenes of the drama were played out, shut himself away in Fort Belvedere.

But even though they knew the King was no longer there, people gathered in front of the Palace, staring bemusedly at its grey stones. A few carried posters with slogans supporting the King – one of them pleaded 'God save our King – from Baldwin' – but there were no fervent demonstrations. No one rioted in the streets, the economy did not collapse, the Empire did not fall: in short, none of the dire predictions exchanged by customers in a thousand and one pubs came true.

At ten o'clock on the morning of 10 December, at Fort Belvedere, Edward VIII began to inscribe his name on the abdication document. By five minutes past ten his three brothers had added their signatures as witnesses and, before the hands of the clock in the deserted Belgian Suite moved forward another second, Britain had a new King, George VI.

At least one member of the Palace staff recalled a prophecy said to have been made by a gypsy at Windsor Fair on the day, 23 June 1894, when the prince who was to become Edward VIII arrived in the world at nearby Royal Lodge: 'Today a prince has been born and when the hour comes he will approach the Throne of England. He will be king in name only, but never the crowned king. Remember that – this, the king who never wears the crown!'

Outside the Palace the stolid expressions on the faces of the crowds relaxed. The old building seemed suddenly once again as substantial as the traditional British belief that everything always turns out all right in the end. In this one short reign the bachelor monarch had been no more than an occasional and reluctant tenant. But in public estimation nothing so well becomes royals as a royal *family*, and there was widespread satisfaction that the new incumbents would be just that. After all, in his farewell broadcast, the departing King had said of his successor – quoting words specially composed for him by Winston Churchill: 'He has one matchless blessing, enjoyed by so many of you, and not bestowed on me, a happy home with his wife and children.'

Scurrying to endorse the same line came the newspapers, which had so recently tried, in their own questionable way, to protect the former King. In a 'guidance' note, Geoffrey Dawson, editor of *The Times*, told his journalists: 'Try to spread the loyalty of our readers a little more widely over the royal family.' They tried, and succeeded memorably; as did the rest of Fleet Street.

The royal family.

6

THE LATER YEARS

GEORGE VI

TO THE NEW KING, GEORGE VI, Buckingham Palace was in every way forbidding – a gloomy new home that, together with the Crown, he had been obliged to inherit suddenly and unwillingly. Its vast, sprawling and impersonal bulk lay like a barrier of solid stone across his life, a depressing reminder that he was no longer the relatively private person he had hoped to remain.

Many of his boyhood memories of the place were unhappy ones. He had spent many hours alone there with his parents while his brothers and sisters were away, often being subjected to nagging criticism by his father. One of George V's deficiencies had been an unimaginative attitude towards his children. Fond of them though he certainly was, he put the maximum of emphasis on discipline and the keeping of a proper distance between offspring and parents, and the minimum on demonstrations of affection. He was a father to be respected but also to be feared. And her own primly austere view of life, plus her belief in support for her husband as head of the family, made it impossible for Queen Mary to offer much in the way of motherly and compensatory warmth. For someone as naturally sensitive as George VI, such deep-rooted childhood impressions were bound to contribute to an antipathy towards the Palace.

There were some at the Palace, indeed, who privately wondered if he would prove capable of kingship. They brooded over reports of his outbursts to his cousin, Lord Mountbatten, on the eve of his accession: 'Dickie, this is absolutely terrible! I've never even seen a state paper. I'm only a naval officer; it's the only thing I know about!'

At forty-one he was still as shy as a young boy, and his health had never been robust. An illness had interrupted his service in the Royal Navy during the First World War and left him with a sense of angry frustration – not only because he had been at his happiest as a member of a ship's company but also because he had been forced, against his will, out of active service. Moreover, he suffered from a persistent stammer.

Perhaps he was indeed too fragile for his role at the Palace? A weak man, even? The censorious tongues clattered, but courtiers and others who posed such questions could not more grossly have misjudged their man. A knowledge of the history of the king's stammer would alone have revealed some significant clues to the tenacity and dogged perseverance that they were to encounter in their new master.

George VI was not born with his affliction – it developed when he was between the ages of seven and eight, and it has generally been attributed to his having been compelled to abandon his natural left-handedness and to write with his right hand. In private conversation his speech appeared to be almost unimpaired, but public speaking was an agony for him. Ironically, the word 'king' had always presented a particular difficulty, and in referring to his late father and his recently departed brother he habitually used the more easily articulated 'His Majesty'.

From early manhood he had waged a valiant struggle against his handicap, and in gaining the will to sustain that effort he owed an enormous debt to his wife, Elizabeth, the former Lady Bowes-Lyon – now the Queen Mother. It was she who, in their days as Duke and Duchess of York, persuaded him not to accept the failure of a succession of specialists to help him, but to try a new therapist.

This was an Australian, Lionel Logue, who had originally embarked on a career as an engineer but became fascinated by speech therapy and developed a highly successful practice in London. He based his theory on correct breathing and encouragement to his patients to have confidence in themselves. For two and a half months the Duke went almost daily to Logue's consulting-rooms and conscientiously followed the prescribed exercises. Often the Duchess accompanied him so that she might more fully understand the treatment and help her husband at home and in his preparation for public speeches.

Close observers noted that, whenever possible, the Duchess contrived to stand close to the Duke during his public-speaking engagements, and that when he struggled with an intractable word she would surreptitiously reach out to touch his hand until the moment of crisis passed. The improvement in the Duke's speech, under Logue's guidance, was swift, but the exercises and efforts of concentration were – and would remain – all-important. As the Duke explained in a letter to his father: 'I am sure I am going to get quite all right in time, but twenty-four years of talking the wrong way cannot be cured in a month.'

By the time he became King, 'Bertie' (as he was known to his family) had gained considerable mastery over his impediment. But it was a savage irony that, in the very moment of bracing himself to shoulder the unwelcome and daunting burdens of the monarchy, he should have suffered a setback as the result of a foolish

King George VI (1895–1952) is crowned in the Abbey. To the left of the throne-chair, Queen Elizabeth is seated, looking on, and, beyond and above her, the King's mother, Queen Mary, watches.

broadcast by the Archbishop of Canterbury – that very same Dr Cosmo Lang whom Edward VIII had seen as one of his implacable enemies. Speaking of the new King, then very little known to most of his people, Lang told the nation: 'In manner and speech he is more quiet and reserved than his brother. And here I may add a parenthesis which may not be unhelpful. When his people listen to him they will note an occasional and momentary hesitation in his speech. But he has brought it into full control and, to those who hear, it need cause no sort of embarrassment, for it causes none to him who speaks.'

Logue was furious, George dismayed. Both rightly feared that, each time the King spoke publicly in future, he and his listeners would be in a state of tension, uncomfortably anticipating the 'momentary hesitation'. It meant that at the very outset of his reign the King had to summon up extra and often exhausting effort to regain the ground stripped from under him by the Archbishop's ill-advised and patronising intervention. This unhappy incident contributed to the King's decision not to make a radio broadcast at Christmas 1936 – thus creating a break in the regular series of royal messages instituted by his father. (BBC engineers helped to make later broadcasting easier for George by recording each of his talks in short 'takes' and then re-recording the parts into one continuous whole.)

George VI and Queen Elizabeth, with their two daughters, Elizabeth and Margaret Rose, formally moved into Buckingham Palace on 17 February 1937. The gloom with which the King and Queen had viewed the prospect of life at the Palace was confirmed by immediate experience. Time and neglect were beginning to take their toll of the building. George complained that it was like an 'icebox', and indeed the heating and electricity systems were badly in need of modernisation. Mice scuttled busily behind the wainscoting, there were rats in cellars and kitchens, and one of the hardest-worked members of the staff was the full-time 'vermin man' engaged in an endless battle to keep the rodents under control.

In their previous home, 145 Piccadilly, overlooking Green Park, they had been cosy and private, devoting their lives mainly to their small family, rarely dining out and giving only occasional dinner-parties. When they did entertain, the guests were often industrialists or trade-union leaders; as a result of his interest in industry and its problems, George had been affectionately nicknamed by his brothers as 'the Foreman'.

By contrast with their Piccadilly house, the echoing, cavernous Palace seemed more like a prison. The two young daughters – Elizabeth was rising eleven, Margaret six – modelled their own distaste for the place on their parents' reactions, although they enjoyed the spaciousness and 'adventure' possibilities of the gardens. Margaret was especially miserable at first, wandering the corridors disconsolately on her own. For a time she attached herself to the Palace clock-winder, 'shadowing' him as he tramped from room to room attending to the innumerable clocks. When she tired of that, her favourite indoor game – until her mother put a stop to it – was to lurk in dark corners and leap out shouting 'Boo!' at startled dignitaries or Palace servants. In her innocent way she seemed acutely conscious of the fact that the move into the Palace had confirmed the mysterious and unwelcome change in the family's life. She was particularly bewildered by the instruction that she could no longer use the family name of York, and complained, 'But I've only just learned how to spell it – Y-O-R-K!'

Palace life at least seemed to give Princess Elizabeth more authority over Margaret. Staff were amused to hear her frequent admonition: 'You really *must*

The mother who neither wanted nor expected to be Queen. The Duchess of York (later to be Queen Elizabeth) with her first-born, Princess Elizabeth, who was one month old at the time of this portrait, May 1926.

stop being so silly, Margaret!' Both the 'Little Princesses' – the joint title had been conferred on them by the press – were learning that their roles in life were destined to be very different. Some day Elizabeth would be Queen. 'And I', said Margaret, sensing already her outsider's place in the scheme of royal affairs, 'am nothing!'

At the time that the new arrivals took up residence in the Palace, the 'Little Princesses' were much better known to the public than their parents were. The seal of public approval had been put upon them in November 1934 when they had appeared on the Palace balcony after the wedding of George, Duke of Kent, to Princess Marina of Greece. The *Daily Telegraph* had declared that one of the day's memorable moments was when George V had 'lifted up on the parapet his granddaughter, Princess Margaret Rose – a fairylike figure in a short, spreading white frock who waved her hand to greet the roaring throng below'. Earlier, Princess Elizabeth had delighted the wedding-guests with her graceful perform-ance as Marina's chief bridesmaid.

The press was finding it rather more difficult to 'project' the new King and Queen, and the *Illustrated London News* testified to the uncertainty by finding itself limited to the word 'charm' to describe the Queen. 'H.M. Queen Elizabeth: Her charm in childhood and girlhood days' its headline ran above one page of pictures and, two pages further on in the same issue: 'H.M. Queen Elizabeth: The charm of the first lady in the land'.

It was left to an American, Janet Flanner, London correspondent of the *New Yorker* magazine, to produce the most apt summary of the widespread view of the King: 'No one knows how the future will stylise him – whether as a distinct character or as a piece of national property, whether he will fit the picture or make his own portrait. In either case, he will unquestionably be very popular – and very soon. When he is seen in the ordinary way here, wearing a derby, what the common people invariably say, in a kind of thoughtful concurrence, is '''E's got a nice face''.'

The former King, too, had had 'a nice face', but there was still something the government wanted done to ensure that, metaphorically, it was turned to the wall. One of the first official duties of the new King was to create for his departed brother the title of Duke of Windsor; but with the proviso that he alone, and not his Duchess, would be permitted the use of the style 'Royal Highness'. It was a final reprimand to the man who had caused such a constitutional hubbub, and carried the implication that he had been put out of the realm on the toe of Stanley Baldwin's boot. The snub rankled with the Duke and Duchess from the day in June 1937, when they were married in France, for the rest of their lives.

Financially, the Duke of Windsor was well provided for. Details of the arrangements, privately undertaken by the new King, have never been officially confirmed, but are thought to have included £60,000 a year and around £1,000,000 for the transfer of Sandringham and Balmoral, of which Edward VIII had enjoyed the rights of lifetime tenancy. Whatever the precise figures, it was undoubtedly one of modern history's most notable golden handshakes.

So the file on a failed sovereign was closed at last; but once again, as in all times of national stress, what was really needed to set minds looking ahead was a festive royal 'occasion'. In British popularity charts royal weddings rate highly and royal births come a close second – but nothing beats a Coronation. Edward VIII's Coronation, for which he had not stayed, had originally been set for 12 May 1937,

On Coronation Day itself, the top of a 'No Entry' sign in Piccadilly Circus serves as a well-placed perch for two adventurous sightseers.

and the government and Palace authorities decided that there were many valid reasons, both practical and psychological, for sticking to that date. Many of the plans were already well advanced; the people had expected a King to be crowned that day, and crowned a King would be – and, even better than had been anticipated, a Queen as well.

The sudden concentration of energies helped to take the royal family's mind off the discomforts of the Palace. There was so much to do: for the Princesses, lessons in the significance of the hallowed occasion from their governess Miss Crawford (the legendary 'Crawfie') and Queen Mary, and the making of their first long dresses; frequent visits to the Palace by Norman Hartnell, the thirty-three-year-old top dress designer of the day, to advise the Queen on her gowns for the crowning ceremony and the Coronation Ball. (When Hartnell's name had first been mentioned, Queen Elizabeth had protested: 'Oh, I'm not smart enough to be dressed by him!')

One of the busiest parts of the Palace was the Royal Mews, where George III's state coach was brought out and sparkle-polished. A grey gelding named Silver Fox was selected to lead the eight horses drawing the coach and to be ridden by the head postillion in his £120 regalia. Like the coach, the state harnesses were brightly burnished – each weighing 128 pounds, and with the metal parts gold-plated. The white legs of some of the seventy Cleveland bays taking part in the procession were brushed with lamp-black to tone in with the black legs of their companion horses.

On Coronation Day morning the testing of loudspeakers on Constitution Hill woke the King and Queen at three o'clock, and to that noise was soon added the clump of marching feet as troops moved towards their stations on the processional

In Hyde Park, on the night of 11 May 1937, crowds bed down on the grass to snatch a few hours' sleep before the next day's Coronation procession passes.

The great state coach, twenty-four feet long, was delivered to George III in November 1762 and cost just a few pence short of £7,588. Here, in May 1937, and now priceless in value, it leaves the Palace and is about to turn into the Mall, carrying George VI and Elizabeth to Westminster Abbey.

route to Westminster Abbey. The royal couple decided that further sleep was impossible, but the King was too strung-up to face breakfast, and had, he said afterwards, 'a sinking feeling inside'. The hours of waiting until it was time to leave the Palace were nerve-wracking'

In an ordinary school exercise-book, in red pencil, Princess Elizabeth later wrote down her own account of that morning: 'At five o'clock I was woken by the band of the Royal Marines striking up just outside my window. I leapt out of bed and so did Bobo [Margaret MacDonald, her nurserymaid].

'We put on dressing gowns and shoes and Bobo made me put on an eiderdown as it was so cold and we crouched in the window looking on to a cold, misty morning. There were already some people in the stands and all the time people were coming to them in a stream with occasional pauses in between. Every now and then we were hopping out of bed looking at the bands and the soldiers. At six o'clock Bobo got up and instead of getting up at my usual time I jumped out of bed at half-past seven.'

Just before half past ten, the King, pale and tense, and the Queen, relaxed and smiling, took their seats in the state coach, and the long procession moved out of the Palace forecourt on its half-hour walking-pace journey to the Abbey. At eleven, almost precisely to the minute, the royal couple entered the Abbey's west door, to be greeted by the Westminster choir intoning the anthem 'I was glad when they said unto me'. They had scarcely advanced a dozen paces up the nave when a Presbyterian chaplain fainted away in front of them and was held, sagging sideways, by his immediate neighbours in the solidly packed congregation. King George's face betrayed a momentary alarm and he half-paused, but Elizabeth moved forward unhesitatingly. In that briefly flickering incident there was much to be seen of the sustaining influence this Queen was to have on her King.

In the splendour of the ceremony the remnants of those haunting memories of recent months were banished. For the first time in history the Coronation proceedings were broadcast by radio, and countless millions in Britain and overseas found themselves hypnotised by the extraordinary medieval ritual.

Two minor hitches added to the tension endured by King George: one occurred while he was seated in the Coronation Chair, and the other as he was leaving it. The first was caused by some tidy-minded official who had removed a thin strand of red cotton purposely inserted under one of the jewels of the Crown of England, St Edward's Crown, to mark the front edge. For a few seconds the Archbishop of Canterbury and the Dean of Westminster were obliged to juggle with the seven-pound crown in a desperate attempt to decide which was the back and which the front, and neither of them was afterwards quite sure whether it finally rested correctly on the royal head or not.

The second hitch occurred when a rotund bishop, following the King too closely, planted an outsize boot on the hem of the King's robe, bringing His Majesty to an abrupt, choking halt. The boot leapt away, as if activated by a powerful electrical charge, when a ripely worded royal rebuke was hissed into the wearer's ears.

At 3.20 p.m. the crowned King and Queen came out of the Abbey to find London shrouded in heavy cloud and soaking in a downpour. But neither the rain nor the travelling difficulties caused by a bus strike had deterred the multitudes who cheered the royal procession back to the Palace.

Sound-measuring equipment set up in Whitehall showed that Queen Mary received the greatest ovation – eighty-five decibels of cheering, compared with eighty-three for the King and Queen. But then, there was a rather special warm feeling for the Dowager Queen that day. As an elderly woman squeezed into the front rank of the crowds at Marble Arch put it, 'If you're a mother you can't help wanting her to know we understand what she's had to put up with, poor dear!'

Back at the Palace the appearance of the royal family on the balcony was received ecstatically. The crowds sang the national anthem and 'Land of Hope and Glory'. The King looked drawn and tired, but the Queen was still smiling. On the day they moved into the Palace she had said: 'We must take what is coming to us, and make the best of it.' Now, looking down from the balcony, they could both draw great satisfaction from an initial victory gained: the people were un-questionably on the family's side.

That evening, with Lionel Logue sitting next to him to give encouragement, the King delivered a live Coronation broadcast. Despite the travail of the long day, he acquitted himself well, without undue hesitation, and pledged his duty to his subjects with the words: 'If, in the coming years, I can show my gratitude in service to you, that is the way above all others that I would choose . . . for the highest of distinctions is the service of others, and to the Ministry of Kingship I have in your hearing dedicated myself, with the Queen at my side, in words of the deepest solemnity. We will, God helping us, faithfully discharge our trust.'

The Coronation, with its radio coverage and subsequent film, proved to have been one of the biggest international prestige events of modern times. Naturally enough, in view of the recent abdication, not only the Empire but the world beyond it had been watching the King and Queen with especial interest. Some of

The real reward for a rank-and-file guest at a Palace garden party is to be close enough to the sovereign to hear what is being said to the Top People. At this, the first garden party of his reign, George VI exchanges a few words with the senior French representative.

the results were evident in the spring of 1939, when George and Elizabeth were fêted, as visiting royalty had never been before, on a tour of Canada and the United States. On their return, abroad the liner *Empress of Britain*, they were met by the two princesses – by now known to the royal household as 'PI' (Elizabeth) and 'P2' (Margaret) – and children and parents drove together from London's Waterloo station to the Palace in an open carriage. Harold Nicolson, member of Parliament and biographer of George V, cheered wildly, along with the rest of the crowds in Parliament Square beneath Big Ben, and afterwards recorded in his diary that 'The King wore a happy schoolboy grin. The Queen was superb . . . . She is, in truth, one of the most amazing queens since Cleopatra.'

This time the public welcome had about it a particular depth of feeling that several observers found greater even than at the Coronation, and the reasons were not difficult to analyse. There was anxiety and a sense of impending doom among the British people, and a strong need, even if it was not precisely defined, to draw closer to the symbol of their nationhood.

War was chillingly imminent. A year previously, Nazi Germany's Chancellor, Adolf Hitler, had been awarded large slices of Czechoslovakia in the notorious pact entered into in Munich to which Britain's Prime Minister, Neville Chamberlain (successor to Baldwin), was one of the signatories. But in March 1939, and in violation of the agreement, Hitler had seized the rest of Czechoslovakia and was now making threatening gestures at Poland. Any attack on Poland would make war unavoidable. Britain, therefore, was looking afresh to old friends and allies, and the reception given to the royal couple in north America aroused hopes that, if the worst should happen, they might not have to look in vain.

During most of that hot, cloudless summer of 1939 the King remained at the

A moment of peace in a world at war – on Princess Elizabeth's fourteenth birthday at Royal Lodge, Windsor, in 1940. Princess Margaret holds the family's lion-dog, Choo-choo.

Palace, occupied almost daily in meeting his ministers and members of the Privy Council as final negotiations with Germany over the threatened invasion of Poland dragged on. But when, on 22 August, a stunned world heard the incredible announcement that the two great rival dictators, Hitler and the Soviet Union's Josef Stalin, had formed an alliance, government and King knew for certain that peace was almost spent.

Under the King's direction the Palace staff had already put into operation the air-raid precautions advised by the government, and on George VI's study desk lay a well-thumbed copy of *The Protection of Your Home Against Air Raids*, a thirty-six-page official booklet distributed by the government to every household in the land.

Three of the country's thirty-eight million civilian gas-masks had been sent to the King: one for the Queen and one each for the Princesses. His Majesty, who as sovereign was also Supreme Commander of the Armed Forces, had his own rather more elaborate 'service respirator'.

From sunset to dawn, again as in every other home, Buckingham Palace was blacked out; the servants played their part in what was to become the nightly national ritual, known simply as 'doing the black-out' – drawing heavy curtains over some windows and putting up wooden frames covered by light-tight material over others.

Schoolchildren from London and other large population centres had already been evacuated to what the authorities hoped would be safer areas, and as it happened the two princesses were staying at Balmoral. The Queen telephoned them, telling them to stay put for the moment, and the King sent a telegram to

'Crawfie', on holiday, instructing her to join his daughters at their Scottish home.

Before he had breakfasted on 1 September, the King received a note from 10 Downing Street informing him that German troops had crossed the Polish frontier at 4.45 that morning and were already bombing Poland's capital city, Warsaw. He was told that the Cabinet was urgently considering its next move, and after a snack of coffee and toast he went to his study to begin work on the text of a radio message he would deliver once a formal declaration of war had been announced.

By the evening, when the first draft of the message was almost ready, no further news of the expected declaration had reached the Palace. The truth was that the Prime Minister, deeply shocked by Hitler's 'dishonourable' conduct, still could not make up his mind to take the irrevocable step that would lead to a new European war. Throughout 1 September and until after midnight on the 2nd he continued to hesitate, hoping against hope that Hitler could be persuaded to pull back. In the end, under growing pressure from his Cabinet colleagues, he reluctantly gave orders for an ultimatum to be delivered to the Nazi leaders in Berlin. The deadline for a reply was set at 11 a.m. on Sunday 3 September.

That Sunday morning the King and Queen sat down by their radio in their private sitting-room, waiting for the announcement by the Prime Minister which was due at 11.15. They listened impatiently, with all their subjects throughout the kingdom, to selections from Gilbert and Sullivan and to a talk on 'making the most of tinned foods'. Soon after the scores of Palace chiming clocks had sounded in their medley of voices, the King took a telephone call telling him that the war had officially begun. When he broke the news to Queen Elizabeth, she could see that he seemed suddenly relieved – the end of the waiting and uncertainty was like an intolerable burden lifted.

After the chirpy voice had finished discoursing on the attributes of tinned foods, the dry, weary tones of the seventy-year-old Prime Minister began to issue from the Palace radio's loudspeaker.

'I am speaking to you from the Cabinet Room at number 10 Downing Street,' it muttered. 'This morning, the British Ambassador in Berlin handed the German government a final note, stating that unless the British government heard from them by eleven o'clock that they were prepared, at once, to withdraw their troops from Poland, a state of war would exist between us.'

The Prime Minister paused for a moment, as though the effort to come to the decisive point of his announcement was almost too much. Then he added: 'I have to tell you now that no such undertaking has been received and that consequently this country is at war with Germany.'

Later that afternoon a hollow-eyed Neville Chamberlain called at the Palace. The King listened sympathetically as his Prime Minister spoke, like a man betrayed, of his efforts to save the peace. He defended the Munich agreement and protested that, whatever his critics might say, it had prevented a war in 1938. The King did his best to reassure him, for – mistakenly as it had turned out – he had also shared Chamberlain's belief, after Munich, that Europe had secured 'peace in our time'.

At six the same evening, dressed in his admiral's uniform, His Majesty sat at a table in his study, facing a pair of BBC microphones, and spoke to his peoples at home and throughout the Empire. 'I ask them to stand calm and firm and united in this time of trial,' he said' 'The task will be hard. There may be dark days ahead and war can no longer be confined to the battlefield. But we can only do the right

Winston Churchill joins Elizabeth and George VI in the gardens of the Palace on the way to inspect the damage from the September 1940 air-raid.

as we see the right and, reverently, commit our cause to God.'

Even in times of national crisis royals can, if they go about it discreetly, continue to enjoy enormous privileges. But, so far as their special position allowed, George VI and Queen Elizabeth actually wanted to share the austerities and dangers which were about to descend on Britain's home front. Some of the courtiers close to them at the time thought Their Majesties grasped at the notion of duty almost obsessively – as though anxious to take the opportunity of proving to themselves that their unsought jobs were not merely status symbols.

With brisk enthusiasm they set about organising their wartime lives. Many of the rooms at the Palace were put under dust-sheets and closed 'for the duration', and all the public measures necessary for sustaining a country that relied on imports were accepted fully by the family and the royal household. In common with everyone else they had their own ration-books for food and clothing, and the variations in amounts of foodstuffs that were to apply over the war years also operated at the Palace. The meat ration, for example, started at 1s 10d a week – roughly equivalent to 9p – for everyone above the age of six, and at one time fell to 1s 1d, or around $5\frac{1}{2}$p.

When tinned foods disappeared from the shops they disappeared from the private royal tables as well. The national effort by housewives to make do and mend – the sewing-machine renovation of old clothes to save on precious material needed for uniforms and parachutes – was supported by the Queen and the Ladies of the Household. Following government advice that people should take baths in no more than five inches of water – 'Your personal share in the Battle for Fuel' – the King had a five-inch 'Plimsoll line' painted on the inside of all Palace baths. A drastic cut was made in the Palace central heating, which was inefficient and fuel-hungry at the best of times, and the building became an even more uncomfortable icebox in the depths of winter. The Queen, who always liked to 'sleep warm', with heavy blankets and a hot-water bottle sometimes even in summer, told her maids to pile on more bedclothes.

(One of the Queen's other eccentricities was her unpunctuality. A favourite family anecdote recalled how she had always managed to arrive late for dinner with her father-in-law, George V. Eventually, after yet another of her inevitable apologies, the old King, who was also one of her admirers, had replied with a smile: 'You're not late, my dear. We must have sat down two minutes early!' In marked contrast, she was never to be late for an appointment throughout the whole of the war.)

In peacetime the King was a moderately heavy cigarette-smoker – usually around twenty-five cigarettes a day; but, although he found it tiresome, he cut his wartime ration down to ten. As tobacco supplies dwindled, a daily pack of ten cigarettes came to be regarded by most nicotine addicts as an extreme luxury, but smoking was the only personal indulgence over which the King's determination faltered. He argued that he would be less efficient at his work if he were totally deprived.

There was, however, no lack of determination by either of Their Majesties about the need to keep the family together in Britain. The government had prepared a contingency plan for sending the two princesses to Canada, safely beyond the reach of any German bomber; but from the Palace the Queen gave a succinct and now famous answer: 'They can't go without me. I won't leave the King – and the King will never leave.'

Scotland seemed to offer a relatively safe haven (although, as things turned out, it was to suffer air attacks); but that also meant only very occasional family reunions, and the home finally chosen for the princesses was Windsor Castle. This was well within reach of the Luftwaffe, but its deep cellars were reinforced to serve as air-raid shelters. Moreover, the King and Queen decided from the outset to make Buckingham Palace their weekday war base and to spend what little free weekend time there might be at Windsor.

On 14 September in that first year of war, George VI was faced at the Palace with a personally delicate encounter. He returned from a tour of the London docks to find his brother, the Duke of Windsor, waiting upon him alone.

The two brothers had not met since that night in December 1936 when the one had left his former kingdom and the other had become its sovereign. Now the Duke had come with his Duchess from their home in France – brought across the English Channel in the destroyer *Kelly*, under Lord Louis Mountbatten's command – to offer his services to the King.

For an hour the brothers talked in private. George VI congratulated the Duke on looking so well and inquired courteously after his wife – the Duchess had stayed behind at her London hotel; but no word was spoken about the past. The Duke made it clear that he would be grateful for an active wartime job. However, the best the King could offer was to send him back to Paris as a member of the British Military Mission to France, with the rank of major-general. His Royal Highness accepted and the brothers parted with an exchange of good wishes.

Resolving that problem was a minor matter compared with the King's increasing worries about the future of his government. Neville Chamberlain was coming under growing criticism not only from the official Labour opposition in the House of Commons but from many of his own Conservative MPs. The King was bewildered and angered by much of the Westminster gossip that filtered through to the Palace. His strong personal admiration for the Prime Minister blinkered him to Chamberlain's vacillations and lack of forthright command.

The Parliamentary rumblings continued into early 1940, throughout the period of military stalemate on land – the so-called Phoney War, which was by no means phoney in the North Atlantic, where German U-boats were busy sinking Allied merchant ships. Then, on 7 May, the abscess of discontent and frustration erupted at last. Chamberlain's impotent leadership was denounced in a House of Commons debate which reached its emotional peak with the quotation from Oliver Cromwell flung at the Prime Minister by one of his own party's MPs, Leopold Amery: 'You have sat too long here for any good you have been doing. Depart, I say, and let us have done with you. In the name of God, go!'

Chamberlain called at the Palace that same evening to report to the King; astonishingly, he was in a buoyant mood. Despite the scene in the House, he said, he still had friends at Westminster, and he was confident he would succeed in his aim of constructing a united coalition government. George was consumed with indignation at the Westminster 'back-stabbing'.

For two more days the King waited restlessly, listening to every radio news bulletin, reading and re-reading his personal copy of *The Times* – specially printed for the Palace every day on rag paper instead of the poorer-quality newsprint. Like Neville Chamberlain himself, he could not face the unpalatable fact that the Prime Minister's time had surely run out.

10 May was a day of shattering news. In the morning the King learned that the Germans had launched their *Blitzkrieg* – lightning war – against France and the Low Countries, and in the late afternoon Chamberlain came to the Palace to offer his resignation. His downfall had come with the Labour Opposition's declaration that, although it was ready to serve in a coalition, it would not do so under Chamberlain's premiership.

It was a bleak hour for both men. Chamberlain, now crumpled in spirit, once again chewed on the bones of his betrayed hopes for peace; the King wondered aloud at the 'grossly unfair' treatment meted out to such a dedicated public servant. He deeply regretted that he had no choice but to accept Chamberlain's resignation, but he expressed the opinion that the fifty-nine-year-old Foreign Secretary, Lord Halifax, should take over as prime minister. To his sovereign's further disappointment, Chamberlain explained that Halifax did not feel it would be appropriate for a modern war to be directed by a peer of the realm.

The King knew precisely what that meant – and the prospect gave him no pleasure at all. For the only other contender in the leadership stakes was that maverick politician, currently First Lord of the Admiralty, Winston Churchill. And he had not endeared himself to His Majesty by striving for the overthrow of Stanley Baldwin at the time of the abdication. Whatever his personal feelings, however, his constitutional duty was beyond question, and immediately after the end of the melancholy audience with Chamberlain he dictated a summons to Churchill to attend at the Palace at six o'clock. It took the motor-cycle courier less than five minutes to deliver the message to the Admiralty building at the eastern end of the Mall. No crowds were gathered around the Palace when, at a few minutes before six, Churchill's black Admiralty car drove into the forecourt. The paunchy figure with the aggressively up-thrust jaw who heaved himself heavily

(Above) Green Drawing Room: used as an area for assembling deputations before they are received in the Throne Room. The white and gold pilasters support a gilded frieze composed of wreaths of laurel. Note the mirrored doors and the carved female figures supporting the clusters of lights.

(Below) Chinese Room: a reminder, with its tapestries, screens and jade, of the once-great popularity of Oriental art among sovereigns – and the well-to-do generally.

Objets d'art *from the Royal Collection, all acquired by George IV. (Above left) Sèvres pot-pourri vase in the form of a ship, dated 1758.*

(Above right) A Parisian clock, in gilt and patinated bronze, illustrating the rape of Europa (Zeus in the form of a bull).

(Below left) A late 18th-century French astronomical clock of white marble enriched with bronze mounts finely chased and gilt.

(Below right) Early 18th-century Japanese lacquer bowl, with gilt bronze mounts made in France in the mid-18th century.

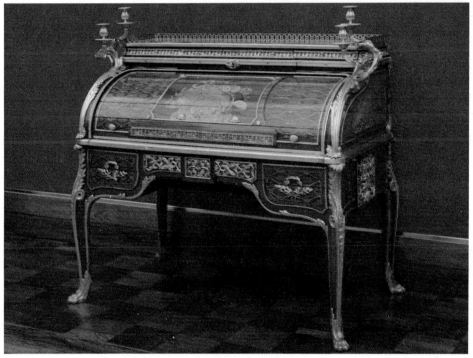

(Above) Marble fountain nymph by Antonio Canova (1757–1822).

(Below) French roll-top desk, second half of the 18th-century, made of oak veneered with purplewood and incorporating marquetry panels on a ground of harewood.

(Left) Late 18th-century French cabinet, made of oak veneered in ebony and inset with plaques of pietra dura. *The cabinet supports three soft-paste Sèvres vases.*

(Right) Late 18th-century French cylinder-top desk, made of oak and pine. The cylinder-top is inlaid with an armorial trophy incorporating the arms of Louis XVI's youngest brother, the Comte d'Artois (who ascended the French throne in 1824 as Charles X).

from the rear seat was greeted by a solitary Palace official and at once conducted upstairs to the King's private sitting room.

In his history of the Second World War, Churchill described the historic interview in these words: 'His Majesty received me most graciously and bade me sit down. He looked at me searchingly and quizzically, and then said, "I suppose you don't know why I have sent for you?" Adopting his mood, I replied, "Sir, I simply couldn't imagine why." He laughed and said, "I want to ask you to form a Government." I said I would certainly do so.'

Despite the pleasantries, George VI was still brooding over his regret that the man in whom he was placing such momentous trust was not Lord Halifax. He was not alone in that preference; it was shared by, among others, Clement Attlee, the Labour Party leader. How differently things might have turned out if Halifax had indeed been the man called to the Palace that evening is now a matter for idle speculation. But in the years ahead the King was to admit that his own judgment had been at fault and to say of Churchill: 'I could not have had a better Prime Minister.'

In western Europe, meanwhile, the Nazi invaders continued their advance. One small, unexpected domestic result was that Buckingham Palace found itself turned into a temporary reception centre for refugee royals. At five o'clock on the morning of 13 May King George was awakened by one of his private detectives and told, to his initial disbelief, that Queen Wilhelmina of the Netherlands was on the telephone from her palace in the Hague and demanding to speak to him urgently. As he picked up his bedside extension telephone the King was assailed by a cascade of thickly accented and barely decipherable English from the fifty-year-old Queen. Still only half-awake, he managed to take in her two most urgent requests: would he please, please, send fighter aircraft to help defend her country, and please look after her daughter, Princess Juliana, and the Princess's husband, Prince Bernhard, who were on their way to London with their two small children? To both questions the astonished King replied that he would do his best.

Later that morning Juliana, Bernhard and family duly arrived, to be followed a few hours later by Wilhelmina herself and her government. Despite opening their dykes and flooding their borders with Germany, the Dutch had been unable to hold off the Nazis and Holland was entering its long and bitter ordeal of occupation.

George VI and Queen Elizabeth had never previously met the Dutch royal family, but without hesitation they made them as comfortable as the wartime Palace allowed until they were found permanent settlements for their exile. Had there been no invasion, Juliana's nine-month-old daughter, Princess Irene, would have been christened in Amsterdam, and Wilhelmina was deeply touched when Queen Elizabeth insisted on putting the Buckingham Palace chapel at the refugees' disposal. For the only time in history the rites of the Dutch Reformed Church were performed within the Palace walls.

To the Palace, too, came the tall, gaunt-faced King Haakon of Norway, whose country had been overrun and who, at sixty-seven, had been forced to seek primitive shelter in the woods of Lapland before escaping to Britain. He was full of lugubrious forebodings that the Nazis would attempt a parachute raid on Buckingham Palace and pluck up all its royal incumbents as hostages. He hovered listlessly around the Palace, still shocked by the speed of events – a British expedition's attempt to protect Norway had ended disastrously and a nation of

A crater ten feet deep and lumps of torn-out masonry mark the attempt by Hitler's Luftwaffe to destroy Buckingham Palace.

George and Elizabeth had spent much time surveying the ruins of other bombed homes, especially in the badly-hit East End of London. The bombing of the Palace therefore helped to strengthen the links between the royal family and the people, and Elizabeth said: 'I'm glad we've been bombed. It makes me feel I can look the East End in the face.'

three million people had been subjugated by a German invasion force of around
eighty thousand men.

On the European mainland the *Blitzkrieg* moved swiftly to its climax. King
Leopold of the Belgians surrendered, France was hammered into capitulation, and
Britain, with the satisfaction of at least having rescued most of her expeditionary
force at Dunkirk, alone remained in the war against Hitler. Paradoxically, a feeling
of relief swept through Britain. It was quite spontaneously echoed by George VI
when he summed up popular feeling in a letter to his mother, Queen Mary:
'Personally I feel happier now that we have no allies to be polite to and to pamper.'

Such a curious, insular reaction mystified many foreigners. An officer of the
Polish army-in-exile, passing a group of chattering, smiling people clustered for no
apparent reason outside the Palace, remarked to a fellow-countryman: 'The British
are either very brave – or very unimaginative!'

*The Palace bombing des-
troyed the chapel, and many
of the rooms remained windowless until after the war.
At the time the narrow
escape of the King and
Queen was kept secret.*

In fact, the British were beginning to create a unity among themselves that was
unique in their history and owed very little to authority. By general consent they
chose to adopt the King and Queen and Churchill as their idols, and Buckingham
Palace and 10 Downing Street as the national shrines to which all looked trustingly
for eventual deliverance from their enemies. Such a faith was simple, and to many
no doubt naive, but it was deep-rooted. The widely held belief that the Crown's
fundamental virtue is that its wearers stand 'above politics' was largely forged
during the war.

Ironically, the most unlikely underwriter of such popular sentiments about the
special bond between the inhabitants of the Palace and 'the people' was the hated
German Luftwaffe itself. On 9 September 1940, during the height of the bombing
blitz on London, a stray delayed-action bomb fell on the north side of the Palace,
outside the Regency Room. It exploded in the early hours of the next morning,
blowing out every window on that side of the building.

The King and Queen were away from London at the time – but on 13 September
they were in the Palace, upstairs in a small sitting-room (their usual room was now
windowless), talking to Sir Alexander Hardinge, His Majesty's private secretary,
when suddenly they heard the roar of a diving aircraft and through the open
windows saw two bombs falling, followed by the shuddering crunch of
explosions from the quadrangle only thirty yards away. With only brief glances at
each other's startled faces, and no word exchanged, they hurried into the outside
corridor, away from the hazards of splintering glass. The building trembled under
further blasts. Altogether six bombs were dropped, one of which wrecked the
Palace chapel. The bomber had dived straight along the course of the Mall, below
heavy cloud, and it was obvious that the Palace was a deliberately selected target.

A plumbers' workshop beneath the chapel was badly damaged in the raid, and
three of the four men working there were injured. After ensuring that the
wounded men were being cared for, Their Majesties toured the servants' quarters.
They found all other members of the staff safe and, the King noted in his diary,
'quite calm through it all'.

News of the royal couple's narrow escape was suppressed until after the war,
but the evidence that the Palace was as much at risk as the thousands of already
destroyed or damaged ordinary homes gave long-suffering Londoners a great
morale boost. Thinking of some of her recent tours with her husband around the
heavily pounded areas of east London, Queen Elizabeth commented, 'I'm glad
we've been bombed. It makes me feel I can look the East End in the face.' And out

of the Palace 'incident' (as bombings were called in officialese), enterprising songwriters concocted a jaunty number that soon became a dance-hall and radio favourite – *The King Is Still in London*. ''Cos', the lyrics added proudly, 'that's where he wants to be.'

During the war Buckingham Palace was bombed a total of nine times by a variety of aerial missiles, but apart from the wrecking of the chapel there was no other major destruction. Repairs, including even the replacement of glass in windows, were not put in hand until after the war. Meanwhile the family's former home, 145 Piccadilly, was completely destroyed.

After the Battle of Britain and the end of the first campaign of air raids on London and other cities, Britain braced herself for the expected German invasion. While that threat lasted, King George went about his daily duties armed, and Queen Elizabeth undertook regular target practice in the Palace grounds with a .303 rifle and a .38 revolver, and later an automatic pistol presented to her by Churchill. Afterwards, Churchill said he felt sure that, had the invasion come, Their Majesties would have followed his advice to the nation that anyone facing death from enemy troops should try to 'take one with you'.

When they were not at the Palace the King and Queen travelled thousands of miles, criss-crossing Britain in a special ten-coach train, touring streets and factories by day and resting in their sleeping-car at night. At the remote sidings where the train halted overnight, Post Office engineers plugged in direct telephone lines so that the King could talk to his ministers in London and members of his household at the Palace.

Each time they returned to Buckingham Palace, the Queen, in particular, made a

Wartime investitures at the Palace were somewhat less formal than those of peacetime. Here, in May 1945, King George is about to present the Victoria Cross to Sergeant John Hinton, of the New Zealand Forces. The war had been over for five days in Europe but was to continue in the Far East for another three months.

point of sitting down to read through some of the most notable of the daily letters from the King's subjects. One that she long remembered was from a young woman who wrote: 'Your Majesty, I appeal to you as one Scottish lassie to another. I am in love with a Polish soldier but he doesn't want to marry me. But, Your Majesty, it is most imperative that he should marry me as soon as possible, and I beg of you to help me.'

The letter was sent from the Palace to the Polish ambassador, who in turn passed it on to the commanding officer of a Polish army camp in Scotland. A few weeks later the Queen received a further letter from the Scots girl: 'Your Majesty, I am now the happiest woman in the world. My Polish soldier married me, and I owe it all to you.'

Not all the palace correspondence had such a heart-warming flavour. Despite gaining two new allies – Russia, after Germany's invasion in June 1941, and the United States after the attack on Pearl Harbour and the opening of the war with Japan – Britain passed through a dismal period of ill fortune, and, although many letters reminded Their Majesties of the old quip that 'Britain always loses every battle – except the last one', others gave expression to a swelling undercurrent of uneasiness about the future.

The King shared the public concern. Members of the household noticed that he often looked unusually tired and distracted. He was particularly depressed over the whispered criticism of Churchill that began to buzz around the lobbies of the House of Commons. At their weekly private luncheon, on 17 February 1942, the Prime Minister himself raised the matter, telling the King bitterly that he felt like a man who was 'hunting the tiger with angry wasps about him'.

Most assuredly, there was much cause for the King and his chief Minister to feel downcast. Singapore, Britain's supposedly impregnable fortress in the Far East, had surrendered to the Japanese after the greatest military defeat in the nation's history. Nearer home, in north Africa, Tobruk had fallen, with the loss of thirty thousand prisoners. King, Prime Minister and people yearned for a victory.

On 1 July the King awoke to find the summer weather was beginning to break, with heavy clouds hanging over the Palace and stretching across to Westminster. The louring day fitted King George's mood. He was too uneasy to tackle very much work, for in the Commons Churchill was facing the bitterest moment of his wartime leadership. Unbelievable though it seemed to the nation generally, one of his own party's senior members, Sir John Wardlaw-Milne, had tabled a motion of 'no confidence in the central direction of the war'.

For all the unprecedented authority over the people that Parliament had acquired, Britain was still a democracy, and even at the height of a world war could openly discuss the possible sacking of its national leader. The King could not help wondering what Hitler and Stalin would make of such 'degenerate' behaviour; and, despite their own worries, a great many ordinary British people were angered by the prospect of Churchill's being made a scapegoat.

Churchill relied on his greatest Parliamentary asset – his brilliant oratory. And he was particularly stung by the south Wales Labour MP Aneurin Bevan, himself no mean orator, who silenced the House with his indictment that 'the Prime Minister wins every debate in this Chamber but loses every battle'. Everything hung on the way the motion was handled; and to his great glee Churchill was saved by a ludicrous blunder committed by the chief assailant himself, Wardlaw-Milne. To the astonishment and derision of members he declared that it 'might be a good idea' if Churchill were deprived of overall power and the Duke of Gloucester appointed Commander-in-Chief of the British Army, 'without, of course, administrative duties'. The pricked balloon collapsed, and the House dismissed the censure motion by four hundred and seventy-five votes to twenty-five, with some thirty abstentions.

The King was as delighted as Churchill himself. There was no personal reflection on his brother, the Duke, in the reaction of the House. The King knew better than Wardlaw-Milne that, for all their sense of frustration, his subjects could not contemplate the replacement of an elected leader by a royal Prince – and Gloucester would never have been so misguided as to accept such an appointment.

In any case, the pessimists had spoken too soon and good fortune was soon to smother their mutterings. For the King the first hints of change came in an engaging little incident after a Palace dinner-party. Churchill was called away to the telephone and returned loudly humming the popular song 'Roll out the Barrel'. He had just been told of the progress of the Eighth Army's offensive at El Alamein in the Western Desert – an offensive that was to end in total British victory; and even though he could not say much in front of the other guests he could never resist a touch of drama.

It was an appropriate moment for good cheer, since the chief guest at the dinner was Eleanor Roosevelt, wife of the United States President, Franklin D. Roosevelt, whose support for Britain had been unflagging even before his own country became directly involved in the war. Mrs Roosevelt was impressed by the personalities of Their Majesties but astonished at conditions in the Palace. During her visit she was accommodated in the Queen's own bedroom on the first floor, where the bomb-shattered windows had been boarded up and the only daylight came through small, central cut-outs in the boards, covered with transparent material.

'Buckingham Palace is an enormous place and without heating', she wrote in her diary. 'I don't see how they keep the dampness out. The rooms were cold except for the smaller sitting-room with an open fire. In every room there was a little electric heater.' Her most vivid impression, however, was of Palace meals, with the royal servants, in their wartime blue battle-dress, entering the private dining-room solemnly bearing silver salvers in the middle of which lay ridiculously tiny morsels of food. It struck her as even more incongruous that those dismal scraps should be served on to gold plates; but, as she was told, apart from the gold and silver this was standard British feeding – 'on the ration'. A woman of radical views and by no means enthusiastic about monarchical systems, she saw the acceptance at the Palace of national austerity as one of many indications that (as she put it) the royals were doing 'an extraordinarily outstanding job for their people'.

Like their President's wife, the thousands of American soldiers who flooded into Britain were fascinated by the image of the Palace. Few of those who passed through London could resist, as *Time* magazine reported, going to 'gawk through the iron fence at Buckingham Palace in the hope of seeing the King'. One of *Time*'s ever-vigilant correspondents noted down the following snatch of dialogue outside the railings: 'Says a cockney, also gawking, ''He's a decent bloke, you know. Works hard. I wouldn't have his job.'' Says G.I. Joe, ''Yeah, not much chance for promotion.'''

Equally a source of wonder to the magazine was the continuing 'Englishness' of the King's life at the Palace, as evidenced by the fact that 'like every Briton who can manage it, he has his cup of morning tea, a black Indian blend, in bed at about eight o'clock. From 11 a.m. to 1 p.m. he sees people. In a typical week he saw five admirals, two air marshals, two British generals and two American. . . . The war has given him a new and tempered toughness, a new confidence, an easier manner. As Duke of York he was shy, hesitant in public, agonised by his stuttering. Now he walks with dignity. He is still only 5 ft 8in tall and slightly built. But he seems a bigger man.'

George VI took a close personal interest in relations between his people and the American servicemen, particularly in the earliest days of the allied forces' build-up in Britain. Secretly there were official apprehensions about possible conflict, mainly because American troops were better paid and better fed than their British comrades-in-arms. But the King was genuinely warmed by the good-natured acceptance of each other by the two nationalities in his overcrowded, traditionally insular kingdom.

Some of the American top brass whom he met were occasionally embarrassed by the swiftly spreading legend of their men's remarkable sexual prowess. But the King still had the capacity to laugh – he had a particularly shrill laugh, which could be heard well outside his private rooms – and he collapsed with mirth on being told the war's most famous story about Americans in Britain, which in one of its many versions ran as follows: A G.I., surveying the battered taxi he had flagged down in Piccadilly Circus, asked the driver, 'You know what we'd do with a wreck like this back in the States?' 'Well,' mused the driver, 'you'd do what you do with everything – either chew it or screw it.'

The top-rank Russian command was represented only once at the Palace – in the person of Vyacheslav Molotov, the Soviet Foreign Minister, who in 1939 had signed the notorious Soviet-German pact on behalf of Stalin. Not unexpectedly, the conversation – translated by Ivan Maisky, the Soviet ambassador to Britain – was a trifle heavy-footed, and George VI summed up Molotov as a 'small, quiet man with a feeble voice, but really a tyrant. He was quite polite.'

Far greater pleasure in the realm of Anglo-Soviet affairs was given to the King by a suggestion from Churchill that he should command the forging of a Sword of Honour to be presented to the people of the Russian city of Stalingrad to commemorate their heroic and victorious stand against their German attackers. George VI spent many hours, between other duties at the Palace, mulling over a series of draft designs. He finally decided to commission a magnificent, two-edged convex blade made of the finest Sheffield steel, and himself wrote the inscription to be engraved upon it: 'To the steel-hearted citizens of Stalingrad, the gift of King George VI, in token of the homage of the British people.' After the death of Stalin and the unveiling in the Soviet Union of his 'crimes' against state and Communist Party, the name of Stalingrad was changed to Volgograd – but the sword was never returned to Britain for an amendment to the inscription. Today, so far as is known in the West, the gift, with its embarrassing place-name, is locked away from public view.

Awards and medals of all kinds were of absorbing interest to the King, and in the early days of the war, while the first air raids hammered London, he had sat night after night at his study desk working out the designs for the decorations he was to call the George Cross and the George Medal – the highest awards after the Victoria Cross.

'I felt sure a special medal would be needed to award civilians for work in air raids and the cross for bravery and outstanding deeds in this sphere,' he wrote to his mother, Queen Mary, who had been sent to spend the war years at Badminton, the Duke of Beaufort's home in Gloucestershire.

In 1942 he took the unusual and imaginative step of decorating a whole people – the 270,000 men and women of the island of Malta, who received the George Cross for the courage and fortitude with which they had endured ceaseless bombing and attempts to starve them into surrender by the sinking of supply ships.

By D-Day – the date of Allied invasion of occupied Europe – the King had made a number of visits to his troops overseas, causing varying degrees of anxiety to Churchill and Queen Elizabeth. (Characteristically, for he was a man with a tidy mind, he had called his lawyers to the Palace before the first of the journeys to ensure that all his personal papers were in order – 'in case something should happen to me'.) Yet no prospective overseas venture caused such turmoil as his plan to be personally involved in the D-Day Normandy beach landings. It touched off a singular little drama, not without its touches of humour, in which the monarch and his Prime Minister sparred around each other with the trepidation of two amateur boxers waiting to see who would make the first lunge.

George VI prepared the way with a certain gleeful, boyish cunning. At one of his regular Tuesday Palace lunches with Churchill, on 30 May 1944, the King casually inquired as to where his Prime Minister expected to be when the assault on the Continent was launched. Churchill, busily washing down his minuscule portion of cold meat with a Scotch-and-water, failed to notice the trap set for him, and replied equally casually that he intended to be on board one of the guardian warships. 'In that case,' said the King, 'I shall go along as well.' He was pleasantly surprised when, instead of the anticipated protests, Churchill merely muttered his assent.

Next day, however, alarm bells began ringing in advisers' minds, and none more loudly than those in the mind of Sir Alan Lascelles, who, after Alexander Hardinge's retirement through ill-health, had taken over as the King's private secretary. He immediately fastened upon the obvious and appalling hazards that had gone unconsidered at the previous day's lunch. How, at the most crucial moment in the greatest war in history, could the nation possibly accept the risk of having both its sovereign and its Prime Minister killed on the same day, perhaps even at the same moment? And what a mind-bending responsibility would be placed on the commander of the ship in which the two foremost men in the land would be sailing!

The role of the monarch's private secretary at that time was considerably wider than today, and one of far-reaching influence. He was, in all senses, a private confidant, effectively the only person outside the royal family who could directly and personally warn the King against unwise decisions. Hardinge, for instance, had even gone as far as to tell Edward VIII, on the eve of the abdication crisis, that he should ship Mrs Simpson out of the country 'without further delay'.

Lascelles now waded in with both feet and declared that neither the King nor Churchill should proceed further with their reckless proposal. In an earlier age, no doubt, such an importunate royal servant would have lost his head. Lascelles kept his, and so did George VI. He pondered over what had been said, realised the wisdom of it, and wrote to 'My Dear Winston' pressing him to take the same sensible view. When King and Prime Minister next met, together with Lascelles, Churchill somewhat petulantly declared that if the King really wanted to go he

Britain had been at war for two thousand days and nights. But now, on VE (Victory in Europe) night, a vast and thankful throng surges around the Palace – the natural focal point of the nation in times of crisis or great rejoicing.

would need to have the Cabinet's approval – 'and that I should not feel able to recommend'.

Well, that, the King said, he quite understood; but in any case he had already made it clear in his letter that neither of them should go. Even more querulously, Churchill replied that despite the King's advice he still intended to go.

Lascelles, listening askance to the verbal skirmishing, tried desperately from the ringside to signal the knockout moment to his fighter. 'I was thinking, sir,' he murmured, 'that it is not going to make things easier for you if you have to find a new Prime Minister in the middle of Overlord [code-name for the Normandy landings].'

Briskly side-stepping that blow, Churchill snapped, 'Oh, that's all arranged for and, anyhow, I don't think the risk is one hundred to one.' (In the event of the deaths of himself and his colleague, Anthony Eden, Churchill had nominated as his successor the little-known and colourless member of his war cabinet, Sir John Anderson: a typically foxy move to ensure that the Churchillian era would not be outshone by a dynamic successor.)

Steadfastly determined not to see his man out-pointed, Lascelles suddenly remembered that none of His Majesty's ministers could leave the kingdom without royal permission. To which the Prime Minister replied that anyone aboard a British warship would legally be on British territory.

The encounter ended in stalemate, and 'selfish' was the word which the King used to describe Churchill in his diary. But the squabble simmered on over the next few days with a series of letters – 'My Dear Winston . . . . George R.I.' from the Palace, and 'Sir . . . . Your Majesty's humble and devoted Servant and

Winston Churchill with Queen Elizabeth and Princess Elizabeth on the balcony on VE Day. The Princess is wearing the uniform of the Auxiliary Territorial Service (ATS) in which she served, in the final war months, as 'Second Subaltern No: 230873 Elizabeth Alexandra Mary Windsor'.

VJ (Victory over Japan) Day, 15 August 1945. A few hours earlier, at midnight, Clement Attlee, the new Prime Minister, had broadcast the news of Japan's surrender. 'The last of our enemies is laid low,' he said. 'Long live the King!'

Subject, Winston S. Churchill' from 10 Downing Street. It terminated, as it was bound to, with surrender by Churchill – but not without a final flick from the old lion's tail. As Prime Minister, he wrote to the Palace, he ought to be allowed to go wherever he thought it necessary for the performance of his duties. However, he had decided to 'defer' to the King's 'wishes and indeed commands' since those so clearly arose from His Majesty's concern about his Prime Minister's personal safety. For that royal motive he was 'deeply grateful'.

King George was somewhat mollified by being allowed to visit the invasion beaches ten days after D-Day; but he returned to London to find it suffering under a new and even more sinister form of air attack – from V1 flying bombs, the first of the 'secret weapons' which Hitler hoped could still win him the war.

The blast from the explosive warheads of these small robot aircraft, nicknamed 'doodlebugs' by Londoners, blew out more windows at the Palace. Throughout the capital and southern England people became unhappily familiar with the crackling–gargling noise of the V1 motor, which cut out abruptly at the end of its pre-arranged fuel limit and caused the robot to fall as a bomb. The King and Queen quickly learned, along with everyone else in the bombardment areas, that if you heard the motor stop immediately overhead you were safe – the glide path of the winged beast would carry it to ground some way off. But the effect of blast was severe, and at the peak of the so-called 'vengeance' campaign V1s were destroying or damaging seventeen thousand houses a day. And, while they and the raids by their successors, the V2 rockets, lasted, the King and Churchill ate their Tuesday working lunches in the Palace air-raid shelter.

London was still a target area in March 1945 when the King wrote to President and Mrs Roosevelt inviting them to 'be our guests at Buckingham Palace' during their projected trip to Britain a few months later. The invitation was not, however, to be taken up. On 12 April President Roosevelt died suddenly at his cottage – the 'Little White House' – in Warm Springs, Georgia, leaving both King George and Churchill with the feeling that they had lost one of the best foreign friends Britain had ever had the good fortune to possess.

In Europe the last rotten timbers of the Nazi empire were fast collapsing. On 4 May Churchill telephoned the Palace to tell King George that the Germans in the Netherlands, Denmark and north-west Germany had surrendered. The final capitulation of the enemy to the Western Allies and Russia was signed at Rheims in north-east France on 7 May, and all fighting officially ceased next day. Britain had been at war for two thousand days and nights.

Among newspaper clippings in a file on his desk, the King came across one which recorded readers' answers to the question: 'What shall we do with Hitler?' His favourite entry was: 'Let Hitler live with my in-laws for a month.' His subjects, he noted, had not lost their sense of humour. And the problem of a post-war Hitler was now entirely academic. The Führer, who had lived long enough to kill so many millions, had ended by killing himself in his concrete bunker under the ruins of Berlin.

Tuesday 8 May was designated as VE (for Victory in Europe) Day, and it seemed as though the whole of London had turned out of doors and headed for the Palace. The seething mass of people chanted, 'We want the King,' and went wild with glee when the King and Queen appeared on the balcony with the two princesses and Winston Churchill. Eight times altogether the royal family came out – the last time at midnight, smiling into the lights which, after all the years of the hideous blackout, had been switched on again. Overhead, Royal Air Force bombers dropped coloured flares; searchlights probed the skies, no longer seeking enemies but adding to the gaiety of the celebrations.

During the evening, between his balcony appearances, the King broadcast a call to his people to retain their wartime unity for the forthcoming tasks of peace – to build a world, he said, such as those who had not returned to welcome victory 'would have desired, for their children and for ours'.

At a little before eleven he gave his permission for the princesses, escorted by a group of young officers, to join the crowds who were determined to make a night of it in London's West End. In common with most of the revellers, his daughters were drawn to look at the capital's lights – unbelievable phenomena, especially to young people who could hardly remember what fully lighted streets and buildings had looked like. From the distant eastern end of the Mall the floodlit Palace itself seemed to be shimmering like a moon between the trees.

The all-night crowds were orderly and good-humoured – no one in them appeared to have spotted the Princesses – and there was a complete absence of the tempestuous scenes which had greeted the end of World War One. A brilliant cartoon by Zec in the *Daily Mirror* aptly captured the prevailing mood of King and country. It showed a wounded soldier offering the world a garland labelled 'Victory and Peace in Europe' and saying: 'Here you are – don't lose it again.'

That same mood, of soberly balanced relief, was evinced by the crowds that gathered again outside the Palace on 15 August to mark VJ (for Victory over Japan) Day. And for the King the celebrations were tinged with regret. He could not bring Churchill out to greet the crowds with him, for Churchill was no longer Prime Minister. The change – one which bore the deepest significance – had officially

Two shy but strong-willed men: King George and Clement Attlee, the first post-war Prime Minister, outside the Palace. The Labour Party had won a landslide victory in the 1945 General Election, and the King respected Attlee for his total personal integrity.

come three weeks before, on 26 July.

A couple of minutes before 7.30 on the evening of that day, a modest Austin Six saloon car, driven by a handsome, middle-aged woman, swung through the main Palace gates. It stopped with a violent lurch in the inner courtyard (the driver never was able to achieve a rapport with automobiles) and from the front passenger seat emerged a small, crumpled man with an undersized soft hat perched squarely on his bald head.

At first glance he might easily have been taken for a slightly nervous bank manager come to discuss investments with a highly placed if not entirely satisfied customer. But, nervous as he certainly was, he was no bank manager. This Palace visitor was fifty-two-year-old Clement Richard Attlee, leader of the British Labour Party, which for the first time since its foundation in 1900 had gained an overwhelming Parliamentary majority. Chauffeured by his wife Violet, he was answering the royal summons to attend and receive his commission to form Britain's new, post-war government.

The obvious friendliness with which George VI greeted Attlee in the first-floor sitting-room would have astonished those people still stunned by what they saw as a lurch towards a corporate state – in which, almost certainly, the monarchy would be swept away, along with the House of Lords. Even the King, who had got to know Attlee during the war (when the Labour leader acted as Deputy Prime Minister during Churchill's absences overseas), was uneasy about the future; he, too, was bewildered by the unexpected and dramatic swing to the left.

Paradoxically, though, he was not as astonished as Attlee, who had hoped for the summons to the Palace but never really expected it. And it was in keeping with his deceptively 'ordinary' suburban appearance that he should have received it in the most prosaic circumstances – while having tea with his family in a station hotel in the run-down London district of Paddington.

Attlee, like Churchill and the King, had favoured the idea of keeping the wartime coalition in office until the defeat of Japan. The Labour leader had feared that a rush to the polls immediately after Germany's surrender would put his party at a disadvantage: voting registers would be out-of-date, and many of the men serving overseas would have insufficient opportunity to study the contending political programmes.

A majority of the Labour Party, however, was not prepared to wait for perhaps another eighteen months to two years – no one, of course, knew of the prospect of a swift, nuclear end to the war with Japan; and Attlee was obliged to tell Churchill that Labour would not sustain the national government beyond October 1945. But Churchill could see no hope for the effectiveness of a government lingering on under a death sentence. On 23 May he went to the Palace to resign, was re-commissioned by King George to form a temporary 'caretaker' administration, and called a general election for 5 July.

The Conservatives went into the election campaign with what, in political jargon, is called 'cautious optimism'. After all, they had the great warrior, Winston, as their personal standard-bearer, and the nation's indebtedness alone was surely worth at least a fifty-seat majority. And, as George VI could see every morning from his special copy of *The Times*, Churchill was greeted at the hustings as an all-conquering hero. Everywhere the people shouted 'Good Old Winnie!'

In contrast, Attlee's tour of the more decisive constituencies was subdued. He was naturally less well-known to the mass of voters, and he was certainly far less flamboyant. Effervescent oratory was not his style. The form of his speeches was more suited to the memoranda of committee rooms than to the public platform. Yet, for all that, it was the content of those speeches, with their promises of far-reaching social reform, about which people talked. They went to see Churchill, but to hear Attlee.

Voting papers were sent out to the battlefields and, from far-away Burma to devastated Europe, servicemen marked their crosses and dropped their ballots into mobile, sealed boxes. Uniquely, for a British general election, there was a delay of twenty-one days, from polling day until 26 July when all the service votes were delivered to the UK and counted. (King George was amused by gossip that the Russians thought Attlee a Simple Simon. What authority, they wondered, could possibly have voting papers in its possession for weeks and not make the 'corrections' necessary to guarantee its party's victory?)

The result was a shattering surprise. Out of 619 seats in the House of Commons, Labour had secured 393, giving it an absolute majority over all other parties of 167. Altogether the Conservatives lost 176 members, most of whom had been at Westminster since the early or middle 1930s. It was a bemused and dejected Winston Churchill who met the King at the Palace on the night of the results and took his official leave as Prime Minister. Neither man could adjust to events. Churchill was deeply wounded at having been so brusquely dismissed; and, for the only time in his reign, King George spoke reproachfully of his people. He called them 'very ungrateful'.

The reasons behind the extraordinary landslide were not as simple as they seemed that night at the Palace. There were widespread public attitudes that went deeper than anything to do with wilful 'dismissal' or ingratitude. It soon became clear that Churchill's personal prestige stood as high as ever; but his party's bill had been mounting up for years. Too many people, and especially, so it seemed, most servicemen, were not prepared to hand back power to men whom they blamed for much of the ill-conduct of British affairs before the war. There was no way, under the party political system, that Churchill could be given special dispensation, and although he retained his own Commons seat he was brought down as leader in the fall of lesser men.

Labour's programme appeared as revolutionary to George VI as it did to the party's opponents – nationalisation of basic industries, including coal, railways and steel, a national health service, a vastly new and expanding welfare state. Yet he closely followed the example set by his father when dealing with the first, minority Labour government. The new leaders had to be 'given a chance'.

As time passed, mutual respect between King and Prime Minister was consolidated. Attlee had long been an admirer of the monarch, largely because of his conscientious attention to duty; and King George was warmed by the PM's integrity and total absence of pomposity and self-aggrandisement. Once, when someone mentioned Attlee's modesty, Churchill growled: 'He has much to be modest about!' But that was simply sour grapes. What the King saw was a man of iron-willed determination who was born to be a political team leader. Yet, despite the personal respect between them, George VI could never quite understand Attlee's reformist zeal, and there were times at their weekly meetings when he felt moved to issue mild warnings about the dangers of too rapid economic and social changes. On those occasions Attlee, scratching his head just above his left ear as he invariably did at tricky moments, muttered that in Britain changes deferred

George VI broadcasts to his people at home and abroad. His stammer made it an ordeal for him to face a microphone but his struggle to overcome the impediment won him many admirers.

meant changes abandoned. The one consolation for the King was that there were people in the Labour Party who thought Attlee too slow a mover, and the Prime Minister was just as dogged in brushing their protests aside.

To his surprise the King found himself enjoying the stimulation of talks with what his mother called his 'Socialist men', with heavy emphasis on the offending word. He developed a special affection for the Foreign Secretary, the bluff, bulging ex-trade union leader Ernest Bevin. 'Mr Bevin says . . . ' the King would relate with admiration after a Palace session in which, amidst a clatter of dropped Hs, the Foreign Secretary had expounded on world events with what seemed like earthy and sound common sense. Bevin was particularly quick to recognise the implications of the Soviet Union's post-war imperialism.

Of all Palace audiences of the period there were few so memorable as that given to Aneurin Bevan, that same fire-eating Welsh socialist who had been a prickly critic of the wartime coalition and who had jousted with Churchill during the famous no-confidence debate. Bevan, who had gone to the Palace primarily to talk about his work as Labour's Minister of Health, recalled that as a young man he, too, had suffered from a serious stammer. He courteously inquired if he might be permitted to express his admiration for the way the King had dealt with his own disability. George VI was so touched that for a moment he could barely mumble his thanks; but sudden inspiration enabled him to wisecrack, 'Now tell me, Mr Bevan, how are you liking the responsibility of running a government department instead of criticising it?' Bevan laughed as loudly as the King. However, it was not so very long before the mercurial Welshman resigned from the government and returned to the role of backbench chastiser in which he felt less restricted.

The King never succeeded – as, indeed, few others did – in discovering much about the private man underneath the Prime Minister's apparent unflappability. He heard that on the rare occasions when he was obliged to sack a minister (and that was nearly always only to replace an older with a younger man) Attlee would scarcely raise his head from his customary doodling of complex little designs on his note-pad. But he would add, as the saddened man left the room, 'By the way, my regards to your wife.'

George VI did once wonder aloud, at a private Palace audience, how the Prime Minister spent his limited spare time. But he was completely stumped for an adequate comment when it emerged that Attlee was working his way through the complete works of Edward Gibbon, the eighteenth-century author of the magnificent but somewhat daunting Decline and Fall of the Roman Empire.

Britain itself sometimes seemed to the King to be embarking upon a decline. The war had left the country bankrupt and dependent on loans, and its industrial plant had been worked until it was almost ready to fall apart. Clothes rationing was finally ended in 1949, but restrictions on petrol remained in force until 1950 and food rationing dragged on for nine weary peacetime years – until 1954. All the national emphasis was on 'austerity' and self-denial: not a pulse-quickening banner under which to march towards a new, victorious future, but essential while the economy made a slow and laborious recovery from its war wounds.

Buckingham Palace itself was in a shabby and forlorn state. In addition to boarded-up windows and the ruined chapel, the garden entrance, originally used exclusively by members of the royal family, was wrecked, and a more detailed survey disclosed some other, previously overlooked, structural damage. The balcony, on which the family had greeted the cheering crowds on VE and VJ Days, was found to be badly cracked by bomb blast.

Like other householders – or, more strictly speaking in his case, as a tenant, since the Palace was State property – the King had to take his place in the queue for domestic repairs. Rehousing and rebuilding were two of the most formidable of all problems, and were still to be far from solved thirty-five years later. A diffident royal inquiry addressed to the Minister of Works, George Tomlinson, as to when the Palace might have its windows restored brought the answer: 'It'll come your turn, sir!'

Months passed and nothing happened until one day Tomlinson arrived at the Palace accompanied by a team of workmen. 'Ah, George,' said the King, 'I see it's come our turn.'

In most large cities and towns, and notably in London, there had grown up a substantial black market, operated in part by professional criminals but more widely by a new race of petty thieves and opportunists popularly known as 'spivs'. Money could procure almost anything that was officially designated as being in short supply – food, clothes, petrol-ration coupons, spirits. And it was largely as a gesture of disapproval of that anti-social 'black economy' that George VI for a long time put a ban on formal evening courts at the Palace. However legitimately the guests might have come by the petrol for their limousines, or their dazzling bejewelled gowns, the King was anxious to avoid any impression that national austerity was only for lesser mortals.

There had been no replacement of furniture or fittings in the private apartments and there were tattered patches of carpet in the King's study over which the less regular visitors stumbled. The building now had the musty air that Edward VIII had imagined he could detect, and the most the antediluvian central heating system could deliver was a faint gasp of warmth that was immediately lost among the high ceilings. The Palace was almost the last place to wish to be in during the ghastly winter of 1946–7 – one of the worst British winters on record.

Towns were isolated by blizzards, and coal supplies, which were already perilously low, could not be moved over snow-blocked railway tracks and roads to the power stations. On 11 December 1946 electricity was cut off from the Palace for nearly two hours – power blackouts hit the whole of the country, and for one period of forty-five minutes there was no current flowing anywhere in England, Scotland or Wales. But worse was to come. Temperatures in the early months of 1947 dropped to as low as −30°F. The Thames froze at Windsor and the sea at Folkestone on the south-east coast of England, and water-pipes burst at the Palace. In line with other domestic consumers in London, the south-east, the midlands and the north-west, Buckingham Palace was allowed no power each day from nine in the morning until noon and from two in the afternoon until four. Power-line cuts lasted until 5 May, and from then until 30 September all homes, including royal residences, were prohibited from using either electricity or gas for heating, on pain of a £100 fine or three months' imprisonment.

The King and Queen and the princesses were spared most of the personal suffering of what was summed up in the headlines as the Great Freeze: they left in February for a tour of South Africa and did not return until late April. But the effects of the freeze made the Palace even less welcoming to come back to, and the King especially was relieved to be able to snatch some rest at Sandringham. The Lodge there had not been used by the royals during the war – it had been thought to be too vulnerable to bomber attacks – and George VI had developed a bad case of homesickness. He said of Sandringham: 'It's the place I love better than anywhere else in the world.' Royal servants at Sandringham, Windsor and Balmoral felt rather sorry for their colleagues at Buckingham Palace. It was all very well to enjoy the glamour of working at the great national royal residence, they said, but all that discomfort in that mouldy old museum!

The Palace, however, was about to emerge from its gloom and dress itself up for a shining occasion: a royal wedding – of all events the unbeatable heartwarmer. On the evening of 9 July 1947 a young naval officer, Lieutenant Mountbatten, drove himself to the private entrance in his MG sports car, dined with the King and Queen alone – Princess Elizabeth was absent at a private dinner-party in a Park Lane hotel – and stayed overnight. Next morning the following statement appeared in the *Court Circular*:

It is with the greatest pleasure that the King and Queen announce the betrothal of their dearly beloved daughter, the Princess Elizabeth, to Lieutenant Philip Mountbatten, RN, son of the late Prince Andrew of Greece and Princess Andrew (Princess Alice of Battenberg), to which union the King has gladly given his consent.

Elizabeth and Philip had first met in 1939 at the Royal Navy's Dartmouth College, where he was a cadet captain of eighteen and she a thirteen-year-old girl, dutifully trailing along behind her parents on an official visit. Soon after the war it was evident to the Queen that Elizabeth was in love with the handsome young officer who had by then become a regular visitor to the Palace.

Immediately upon the announcement of the engagement, Palace staff launched a flurry of scrubbing, dusting and marble-polishing in preparation for the wedding, fixed for 20 November. Out of protective packing-cases deep-lined with straw and old newspapers came crystal chandeliers, delicate glassware and priceless pictures. The Queen personally supervised the re-hanging of the royal collection of paintings – and, wisely, she reduced the numbers in many of the rooms, thus avoiding the clutter that in pre-war days had swamped some of the best works. She selected fewer than fifty pictures to be hung in the long first-floor picture gallery, and the visual result was far more satisfying than it had been with the previous assembly of one hundred and twenty-two.

Most of the walls and ceilings in the state rooms could have been improved by a lick of paint, but the Queen merely smiled and shrugged her shoulders when word came back from the Ministry of Works that paint too was 'in short supply'. The more valuable furnishings were brought back from their wartime storage places. But other furniture, which had remained at the Palace in locked rooms, seemed little the worse for its six-year burial under dust-sheets. The cleaning ladies – traditionally known in the Palace as the 'daily women' – removed several tons of dust, although they did find that many of the establishment's decrepit vacuum-cleaners had become far more adept at blowing than at sucking. Royal domestic appliances were, rather like Britain's heavy industries, not as young as they had been. The fact that some of them still worked at all was due to the ingenuity of mechanics who had improvised unobtainable spare parts out of bits of old metal and pieces of wire.

The dark, satanic kitchens hardly looked the most likely places for the preparation of exotic banquets, but the King and Queen made a very happy decision in bringing in a Yorkshire-born master of the culinary arts, Mr Ronald

Aubrey, as *chef de cuisine*. Before the war he had been the royals' private chef at Royal Lodge, Windsor; he had his own skilful way with traditional English dishes, which the Queen much preferred to the French cooking normally regarded as a standard requirement at royal palaces.

In time Aubrey reorganised the kitchens and had the walls painted in bright colours; he installed the latest electric cookers when supplies of them, and the power with which to run them, ceased to be so short. Poultry, game, fresh vegetables and fruit from the royal farms at Sandringham and Windsor were used to supplement the post-war food rations, and it was Queen Elizabeth herself who chose each day's menu in consultation with Mr Aubrey.

There was some talk at first of holding the royal wedding at Windsor Castle, where a simpler ceremony, without an elaborate procession, might be more in keeping with the country's cost-conscious mood. George VI, however, was very much against the idea. He rightly sensed that the war-weary public was hungry for a show and would not take kindly to the use of Windsor, for all its historic associations, as a substitute for Westminster Abbey. Besides, everyone knew that the bride at whom the crowds would stare was almost certain – barring tragedy – to be Queen one day, and the rightful places on the biggest occasions for sovereigns, present or future, were the capital city, the Abbey and Buckingham Palace.

On the eve of the wedding Philip was created Duke of Edinburgh, Baron Greenwich and Earl of Merioneth and presented with the Order of the Garter, which had also been bestowed on his bride-to-be a week earlier. It was, the King said, 'a great deal to give a man all at once, but I know Philip understands his new responsibilities on his marriage to Lilibet'.

In bright, wintry sunshine the day itself fulfilled all the crowds' expectations. The bride was sixty seconds late at the Abbey – her bridal bouquet was temporarily mislaid, and royal staff heard a few choice words from the King before it was discovered stored away in a Palace cupboard. But it was the dazzling sight of the married couple driving back to the home of the bride's parents that made the day for the chilled spectators in the streets. Among the vast collection of foreign royal guests, who were also greeted with enthusiasm, were many who no longer had thrones to go back to. But that, in its own way, served to give extra point to the survival of Britain and its House of Windsor.

From the Palace that night the King wrote to his honeymooning daughter: 'Your leaving has left a great blank in our lives but do remember that your old home is still yours and do come back to it as much and as often as possible.'

In letters to his daughters George VI invariably signed himself 'Papa', but his official signature was 'George R.I.' (Rex Imperator, or King-Emperor). That, however, was soon to be shortened to 'George R.' India, the jewel in the crown of the British Empire, was moving towards independence. Partly under pressure from President Franklin D. Roosevelt, the British government had, in 1942, promised India that she would be granted dominion status once the war was won. But the powerful Indian Congress Party had demanded total British withdrawal, a series of rebellions had been bloodily suppressed and two Congress leaders, Mahatma Gandhi and Pandit Nehru, had been thrown into jail. It was not a glorious hour in British history.

Behind the basic problem of future status lurked the frightening danger of conflict between India's Muslims and Hindus, and in June 1945 George VI had invited leaders of both groups to a meeting at Buckingham Palace. The outcome left him deeply depressed. Nothing, it seemed, could ward off the threat of civil war in the sub-continent.

In a brilliant flash of inspiration Clement Attlee decided to invite Lord Louis Mountbatten to accept the appointment of last Viceroy of India, to oversee the transference of power which, for all its likely perils, had become inevitable. However, the proposal was not without some delicate facets. Mountbatten, who had been the South-East Asia Supreme Commander during the war against Japan, was also the King's cousin and close confidant – and Philip's 'Uncle Dickie'. In the midst of the war, Churchill had said of the Indian problem: 'I have not become the King's First Minister in order to preside over the liquidation of the British Empire.' Yet now that was exactly what the King's own relative was being asked to do. If the whole business ended in a shambles the Throne itself might seem to be implicated.

Fully aware though he was of such a hazard, George VI did not hesitate in endorsing Attlee's invitation and pressing Mountbatten to accept. Under his cousin's guidance the formal transfer of power took place in August 1947. But it unavoidably meant the partition of the former Indian Empire into two in-dependent nations – the predominantly Hindu dominion of India and the Muslim state of Pakistan. As the King had feared, the division led to mass migration from one state to the other, and in the brief period of three weeks around 200,000 people were massacred in bloody religious riots. The consolation for George VI and his government was that, but for Lord Mountbatten's negotiating skill and the respect in which he was widely held by both sides, the end of the British Raj would undoubtedly have been far more bloody.

It was a matter of satisfaction for Mountbatten and the King that India and Pakistan decided to remain within the British Commonwealth, and in April 1949 George VI welcomed their Prime Ministers, together with those from the rest of the Commonwealth, to an audience in the White Drawing Room at the Palace. The last paragraph of a statement drawn up by the Commonwealth Prime Ministers and read to the King that day at the Palace stated: 'Accordingly the United Kingdom, Canada, Australia, New Zealand, South Africa, India, Pakistan and Ceylon hereby declare that they remain united as free and equal members of the Commonwealth of Nations, freely co-operating in the pursuit of peace, liberty and progress.' In his reply the King declared: 'I wish that certain other countries, who are not privileged to belong to our British Commonwealth, could show an equal degree of commonsense and good temper when they meet us round the Conference table.'

George VI intended to put his personal seal on that 'commonsensical' association of nations by a visit to Australia and New Zealand, but illness forced him to defer the plan – it would only be a postponement, he hoped. Diagnosis showed that he was suffering from the early development of arteriosclerosis (hardening of the arteries), but he forbade anyone to allow the alarming details to reach Princess Elizabeth, who was then expecting her first child.

The baby, Charles Philip Arthur George, future Prince of Wales, was born at Buckingham Palace on the evening of 14 November 1948. For the first time since the days of James II the King vetoed the custom of having a state official present at all royal births – a practice designed to ensure that there was no subversive attempt to switch babies and place a usurper in the cot. Instead he telephoned the Home Secretary after the infant boy had arrived. King George had never forgotten

They heard that the King was ill and, on Sunday, 23 September 1951, they flock-ed to the Palace to show their sympathy and concern. The bulletin, which can be seen hanging in a frame on the railings, reads: 'The King underwent an oper-ation for lung resection this morning. Whilst anxiety must remain for some days, His Majesty's immediate post-operative condition is satisfactory.' The an-nouncement was signed by eight doctors.

the farcical caper that had taken place when his youngest daughter, Margaret Rose, was born at Glamis Castle, his wife's Scottish family home, in August 1930. R. J. Clynes, the sixty-one-year-old Home Secretary in Ramsay MacDonald's Labour government, had spent sixteen days at nearby Airlie Castle waiting for the summons to attend the royal birth. Just after eight on the night of 21 August Mr Clynes received an urgent telephone call telling him to hurry to Glamis or he would be too late to do his official duty. A police car rushed him through rain-soaked Scottish lanes, and he stumbled into the castle to find the expectant father, then Duke of York, pacing nervously up and down the billiard room. The two men were still there when, at 9.22 p.m., a smiling doctor announced that Elizabeth, Duchess of York, had been safely delivered of a daughter. Mr Clynes declared himself content. It was quite sufficient, he said, to have been 'in the presence of the birth' without needing to observe it. The pointlessness of the custom and the irritation of having a minister around at a very personal moment stuck in the Duke's mind and persuaded him as King, eighteen years later, to put an end to it once and for all.

At least his illness did not prevent the King from enjoying the new addition to his family – nor, a few months before, had it stopped him from participating in the public and private celebrations of his and the Queen's Silver Wedding. But, without unduly dwelling upon the subject, the royal couple recognised that an uncertain future lay immediately ahead of them.

It was characteristic of George VI that at the onset of his illness his thoughts turned for a moment from the Palace, where his workaday duties lay, to Sandringham, from which his heart was seldom absent. He took half an hour off from official paperwork in his study to write, in his own hand, a report on his ailment to George Middleton, his local Sandringham doctor. He felt it would be both improper and discourteous to leave Dr Middleton to find out about his patient's condition from a public announcement issued in London.

The King's medical advisers in the capital observed his development with growing concern and eventually concluded that surgery was imperative in order to relieve the strain on the arteries in the monarch's right leg. A first-floor sitting-room looking on to the Mall was converted into an operating theatre.

Any moment of surgery must always impose a heavy strain on a sovereign's doctors and consultants; even among the most experienced and distinguished practitioners the fear of some totally unforeseeable accident or inexplicable misjudgment is awesomely oppressive. But, as a good constitutional monarch must, George VI had tutored himself in the difficult art of trying to understand the problems of those who served him. He could see that the gowned and masked figures around him would benefit from encouragement and, screwing up his eyes against the concentrated glare of the theatre lights in the seconds before the anaesthetic was administered, he declared: 'I am not in the least worried.'

He made a good post-operative recovery; and, for the onerous responsibilities undertaken, he rewarded his principal surgeon, Professor James Learmouth of Edinburgh – and did so with a nicely turned touch of humour. As Learmouth completed his final examination at the Palace, the King bade him kindly to pass over the royal dressing-gown and slippers and, having done that, to kneel. Raising himself with an effort from his couch, the King announced with mock severity, 'You used a knife on me and now I'm going to use one on you!' He produced a sword which, until that moment, he had kept concealed, touched Professor Learmouth on the shoulders and dubbed him Sir James.

Although the surgery succeeded in its immediate purpose, nobody at the Palace could fail to notice that the King's general health was showing a slow but steady decline. Touchingly enough, it was when he was at his smiling ease with his two grandchildren, Prince Charles and Princess Anne (who had been born on 15 August 1950), that the deterioration was most evident. The creasing of the cheeks in a smile emphasised his gaunt features, and his eyes reflected a persistent and debilitating fatigue.

Influenza took hold, and official Palace bulletins spoke vaguely of an area of 'catarrhal inflammation'. Queen Elizabeth suspected that the King's condition was more serious than that, and so too did the doctors. On 16 September 1951, again at the Palace, a small section of tissue from the King's left lung was removed and sent for laboratory analysis. The result confirmed the worst apprehensions: George VI was suffering from cancer and, even with the removal of the entire left lung, which the doctors now advised, his life-expectancy could be counted in no more than months.

The full facts were put to Queen Elizabeth, but she firmly decided that the King should not be told. She herself gently explained to her husband that there was a 'bronchial complication', and, as always, his confidence in her was total. Whatever he might have suspected – and there is no evidence that he ever suspected the truth – he received the news calmly, if only in an attempt not to add to her burdens. Yet privately he was depressed, overcome by the chilling loneliness that most people experience when they are faced with a major operation. He told a close friend, 'If it's going to get me well again I don't mind, but the very idea of the surgeon's knife again is hell!'

More Palace bulletins follow. 24 September: 'The King has had a restful night. His Majesty's condition this morning continues to be as satisfactory as can be expected.' 7 p.m., 24 September: 'The King has gained strength during the day.' 7.15 p.m., 25 September: 'The King has had a comfortable day and has been able to take some nourishment.'

As the King waited, bracing himself for the fresh ordeal, his attention was drawn once more, and for the last time, to his elder brother, the Duke of Windsor, who was on a brief visit to Britain. In the kingdom that had once been so briefly his, the Duke was by then an almost forgotten man. He had spent the greater part of the war years as Governor of the Bahamas. For a while he had personally knitted socks for British troops, attended to the minor and humdrum ceremonies of his distant outpost, and brooded nostalgically of his homeland while sipping afternoon tea from water boiled in his favourite kettle, which he nicknamed 'Kettley'. He and his Duchess were about to embark on their arid years of aimless wanderings around the world from one uninspiring high-society resort to another. George VI did not meet his brother on this occasion but, as a small mark of friendship, sent him three brace of grouse.

On 23 September 1951 George VI presented himself for the third time in the Palace's temporary operating theatre and the offending lung was successfully removed. Throughout the following days the doctors remained anxious, for there was a high risk that the strain imposed upon the King's system, and the state of his arteries, might induce a coronary thrombosis. To everyone's relief, however, the patient made good progress. He was even able to crack a joke, in pseudo-cockney, about 'all this trouble with me blowers!'

Within a few weeks the King was able to leave his bed for a short time each day, and quickly began to take a more cheerful view of his prospects. On 30 January the following year he was sufficiently recovered to enjoy one of the happiest and most relaxed evenings of his life since the war: a visit, with the Queen, Princess Elizabeth and the Duke of Edinburgh, to the Drury Lane Theatre to watch a performance of the musical *South Pacific*.

11 a.m., 26 September: 'The King has had a restful night but His Majesty's general condition this morning is good and progress is maintained.'

11.15 on the morning of 29 September 'Six days have now elapsed since the operation on the King. This has been a period free of complications. His Majesty is gaining strength daily.'

Despite his recovery from the immediate effects of the 1951 operation, the King's health slowly declined. For millions of subjects this photograph, taken in January 1952, was the most conclusive evidence that George VI had become a very sick man. On the tarmac at Heathrow Airport he chats with Princess Margaret (left) and his wife, Queen Elizabeth. All three are awaiting the departure of the aircraft that Princess Elizabeth and Prince Philip have just boarded for a flight to Kenya.

The next morning, Princess Elizabeth and her husband flew out of London Airport to east Africa on the first leg of an official tour that was to take them on to Australia and New Zealand — to undertake that visit which the King had been obliged to cancel for himself. Press photographers captured a memorable shot of the royal father waving to his daughter and son-in-law, and all his subjects could see how pale and haggard he had become. King, Queen and Princess Margaret waved until the departing aircraft had vanished in the clouds. Then the royal parents took their leave of London and the Palace and went off to see the New Year in at Sandringham. As ever, the tranquillity of the Norfolk countryside seemed to work wonders for the King, and the Queen was especially happy at his contentment.

The King's final farewell as Princess Elizabeth's aircraft taxis to the runway. He was never to see his elder daughter again. He died a month later, in his sleep on the night of 5/6 February 1952. The Princess learned in Kenya that she had become Queen Elizabeth II.

Following the cortège of the brother to whom he surrendered his throne, the Duke of Windsor (formerly Edward VIII) walks down Whitehall beside his nephew, the Duke of Kent. At the far left is the Duke of Gloucester.

He spent part of the day on 5 February out shooting hares, and later listened to the radio broadcast of the reception given to Elizabeth and Philip in Kenya. At midnight a watchman making his rounds of the gardens saw the King closing his bedroom window. Throughout the night the house was silent. The next morning, 6 February 1952, the King's valet, James MacDonald, took the usual cup of tea to his master's bedroom. There was no movement from the bed; the King, it appeared, was sleeping peacefully. MacDonald opened the curtains and once more approached the bed. Then he could see that the sleep into which George VI had fallen was the one from which he would not awake.

Queen Elizabeth was told at once, and those around her forever afterwards remembered the dignity and self-control with which she entered the bedroom and gazed upon the King's lifeless body. They were deeply impressed, too, by the fact that in those first few minutes of her personal grief she did not forget her immediate and wider responsibilities.

'We must tell Elizabeth,' she said, and then paused as though encompassing the full meaning of her words. 'Yes,' she repeated, 'we must tell Elizabeth – we must tell the Queen.'

The new Queen, Elizabeth II.

7

ELIZABETH II AND PHILIP

A SUMMARY

SOMETIME DURING THE NIGHT OF 5/6 February 1952, Princess Elizabeth became Queen and inherited Buckingham Palace for the span of her lifetime; but precisely when these things happened she would never know. Not that such ignorance mattered. Under the hereditary system the last intake of breath by the dying sovereign coincides absolutely with the next intake by the living sovereign. Hence the ancient cry: 'The King is dead – long live the King!'

Prince Philip knew before the new Queen herself that the Crown had passed to her. In the soggy heat of the African afternoon of 6 February he was aroused from a post-luncheon siesta by his equerry, Commander Michael Parker. The Reuter news agency in London had alerted its worldwide subscribers with a flash – a top-priority message – breaking the news that George VI was dead. As yet, Parker noted, no official confirmation had been received from the British government, but the accuracy of the Reuter report could not be doubted.

Meanwhile Elizabeth, unaware of the momentous event, was resting in another part of Treetops, the Kenyan lodge cunningly and comfortably built into a massive wild fig-tree, thirty feet above ground and overlooking the Sagana river. Together, she and Philip had been relishing their brief stop-over in Kenya.

Eventually she appeared, home movie camera in hand, absorbed with plans to see more of the surrounding dramatic landscape and to add to her collection of close-ups of the colourful wildlife. For an hour Philip walked her around the gardens of the lodge, saying very little but keeping her well out of earshot of the telephone whose ominous ringing must soon be expected. Even as her husband he dared give no hint of the news of her accession without official confirmation. But, when at last he was summoned back alone to the lodge, he knew for certain, merely by the expression on his equerry's face, that he was liegeman to a Queen.

All their adult lives sovereigns-to-be must prepare themselves for the inevitable moment, but for Elizabeth that moment was especially traumatic – not to have known just when she had become the Queen, not to have taken leave of her father (to whom she was so close) in the hoped-for traditional manner at the royal bedside. It is, however, an unwritten rule that royals should not give vent to deep personal emotions in public, and despite all her inner feelings Elizabeth neither broke nor even bent that rule. Asked by what name she wished to be known, she firmly made her famous reply: 'My own name, of course – what else?' And when the first official documents of her reign were brought to her she hesitated only momentarily before inscribing herself 'Elizabeth R.'.

Among the telegrams handed to her was one from Winston Churchill, now back as Prime Minister, expressing the nation's sorrow at the late King's death and ending: 'The Cabinet in all things awaits Your Majesty's commands.' In the strictest terms of a constitutional monarchy that statement may not have had a great deal of meaning – but it was impressively Churchillian.

At London's Heathrow Airport, where Churchill and other ministers were lined up to greet their Queen on her return, observers made a mental note of the fact that the relationship between Elizabeth and Philip had undergone a perceptible shift from that of husband and wife to that of Queen and consort. It was Elizabeth who left the aircraft first and went alone to receive the condolences and expressions of loyalty from her ministers and from Clement Attlee, leader of the Opposition. Philip followed, but now as the husband who must walk behind the Queen.

Early days at Buckingham Palace were easy neither for the Queen nor for Philip. It had long been their intention that, when the day came for Elizabeth to ascend the Throne, they would continue to live in their own private residence, Clarence House, and use the Palace solely as a work-place and for ceremonial occasions. (They, too, had that characteristic royal aversion to the idea of calling the Palace home.) But Winston Churchill (the same Prime Minister who had 'awaited Her Majesty's commands') would have none of it. Employing the most felicitous words, of which he was so incomparably a master, he insisted that the people expected their sovereign to be seen to be living and working at the Palace – and that the people's will must prevail.

Elizabeth at least had all her attention absorbed by her royal duties, but Philip was uncertain and unhappy about his place in the scheme of things. He was not even officially the consort, as Victoria's beloved Albert had been, and it gradually became clear to him that if he were to have a function he would need to devise one for himself: something that, in time, he was to achieve brilliantly enough. At first, however, Palace officials were at a loss as to how to help him shape his employment, and he railed against some of their sillier proposals. Among others, ex-King Peter of Yugoslavia, husband of Philip's cousin, Queen Alexandra, detected signs of strain in Philip, and said of him: 'It was as if a volcano had been

Elizabeth on the way to her crowning, with her husband beside her, seemed to many to epitomise the times — youthful, vibrant and optimistic. The miseries of war were beginning to fade and hopes for the nation's future were high.

Gazing up towards the Palace balcony after the Coronation at the Abbey, the crowds saw what seemed to be the ideal royal family. Only the two small children, Prince Charles and Princess Anne, appear slightly bemused by all the fuss.

The Coronation was the first major event to be broadcast by post-war television. In their NAAFI in West Berlin, British soldiers and members of the Women's Royal Army Corps wait for the transmission to begin.

The first garden party of the new reign is over, and the royals make their way back into the Palace. The Queen Mother follows the Queen and behind her stroll Princess Margaret and the Duke and Duchess of Gloucester.

stoppered up. I don't know how long he can last – bottled up like that.' In the end it was Philip's own toughly independent temperament that persuaded him to stop attending to pointless advice. As privately as possible he took to driving in an unmarked car from Buckingham Palace to the House of Commons to listen to some of the major debates. He began making visits to factories and coalmines, building up his own personal research about industry and the nation's economy.

There were times in the formative years when he found himself obliged to recognise the gulf between private interests and public demands – as, for example, in the case of his three surviving sisters, married to German princes, who were suffering the privations and hardships of a defeated and shattered Germany. Out of a natural and brotherly sense of compassion he proposed to send them gifts of food and other necessities; but official word was crisply passed along to the Palace requiring him to abandon his generous impulses lest news of them should leak out and affront a public opinion which was not yet in the mood to forgive recent enemies.

Practical involvement in the work at the Palace really began for Philip when the Queen appointed him chairman of the commission set up to supervise her Coronation. He went to work with all his bustling energy and showed himself anxious to overlook no detail, however small. He even went to the extent of standing on the Palace balcony and, to the fascination of the staff, tilting his head backwards and forwards as if acknowledging unseen crowds. Only later did it emerge that he was not undergoing some kind of mystical transformation but proving that the weight of the crown would make it impossible for the Queen to look upwards and follow the Royal Air Force fighters in their fly-past after the Coronation ceremony.

His own decision to learn to fly did not, as some people at the Palace seemed at first to believe, spring from a romantic desire to be technically in the fashion. The real reason was much more in keeping with his personal pride: since he would at times be required to wear the uniform of a Marshal of the Royal Air Force, he thought it only right that the wings on his tunic should have been genuinely earned.

The deficiencies of the Palace, which were many and varied when they moved in, irritated Philip more than Elizabeth. Despite their earlier modernisation by George VI's chef, Philip condemned the kitchens as 'bloody awful'. One of their worst aspects was their distance from the private apartments, which resulted in meals starting out as hot but arriving as tepid, congealed messes. Breakfast, the one meal of the day by which the very modestly eating Queen and her husband set great store, was especially dismal, and for a time Philip took matters into his own hands and cooked the morning bacon and eggs in his own electric frying-pan. Yet his plans for new and more conveniently sited kitchens were later vetoed on the grounds of cost.

As the Queen sometimes noticed with a certain baffled wonder, electronics became a subject of frequent and enthusiastic discussion – on Philip's part. Since Britain had been one of the major pioneers of the new magic, it seemed fitting, he thought, that some of its benefits should be available in Buckingham Palace, of all places. As a result, electronically operated doors and windows were installed in some of the rooms, and the private sitting-room acquired what was then a very advanced gadget – a remote-controlled television set. Officialdom watched the developments with wary eyes and saw to it that they did not spread too far and wide. It would never do for the Palace to become over-modernised. Royals had to try to live with the fact that the Palace was what it was: a museum with restricted living quarters for distinguished tenants.

Yet, although Philip took a special interest in the running of the Palace, the division of duties between himself and the Queen did not extend to work on state papers. Normally only the sovereign (and to a lesser extent her heir) sees the contents of the official despatch-boxes sent daily to the Palace, but Ministers at one time suggested that Philip might usefully look at them too. The Queen turned the proposal down. In many royal relationships – that between Victoria and Albert, for example – such a decision could have been construed as a slight by a top-level working wife to her important if necessarily subordinate husband. On closer examination, however, it can be seen as a wise and far-sighted judgment, and it would appear, on the evidence of some of those close to the royal couple, to have worked without causing disharmony.

Essential matters of state can be conducted only by the sovereign and her ministers, and, while she can and obviously does discuss major problems privately with her husband, she could never constitutionally offer his views in place of her own. No one has ever envisaged a king telling his prime minister, 'My wife has read the papers and she is concerned about the government's attitude . . . .' Equally, it would be unacceptable to any Minister to be told, 'I understand the reasons behind this but my husband is not very happy about them.' In firmly deciding to keep her boxes to herself Queen Elizabeth proved to be more percipient than those who sought to advise her otherwise.

But although Philip was officially excluded from work on state papers, one of his most important contributions to royal duties in the early Palace days was in

Group Captain Peter Town-send and Princess Mar-garet sightseeing in Kimber-ley during the 1947 royal tour of South Africa. The Princess had already fallen in love with the RAF war-time fighter pilot who was now equerry to her father, George VI.

helping to improve the Queen's public image. Her voice and style on radio and television, as well as at public ceremonies, had the stamp of the typical, cosseted English upper-class lady, whose particular mannerisms are among the nation's least attractive. Satirists of the so-called 'swinging sixties' capitalised on one especially grating introductory phrase, which invariably sounded like 'Mae husband and aay'. Critics, Philip had pointed out, would be only too ready to 'wail and gnash their teeth' over anything that sounded prissy or precious. And once, when the Queen was showing signs of tension just before the recording of a television speech, he is alleged to have whispered to the programme producer, 'Tell the Queen to remember the wailing and gnashing of teeth!'

The results of his guidance have been notable, and in helping the Queen to appear more natural and relaxed he can claim credit, along with others, for masterminding a highly successful public-relations campaign. Of course, ex-perience has been of great benefit to the Queen, and the ultimate accolade for the combined efforts of herself and Philip was bestowed by an audience which burst into gleeful applause when Elizabeth, with a commendable sense of humour, made self-mocking use of a deliberately exaggerated version of 'Mae husband and aay'.

Public relations at the Palace, conducted with very considerable subtlety and skill, play an essential part in the presentation of modern royalty. Occasionally, however, royalty takes a heavy knock, and no blow has been potentially more hazardous than the famous Princess Margaret – Peter Townsend affair of the 1950s. To the new generation grown up since then it may seem a curious fuss about little, but its real villain – the scapegoat lurking unseen in the wings – was deemed to be the very man who had been instrumental in placing the crown on the head of the Queen's father and therefore upon her own head: the unfortunate Duke of Windsor, whose own marriage plans had proved so unacceptable.

Group Captain Peter Townsend (with the Distinguished Service Order, Distinguished Flying Cross and eleven German fighter aircraft shot down in the Second World War to his credit) had been equerry to George VI, and first met Princess Margaret, then aged thirteen, at Buckingham Palace. His wartime marriage, like many another of those years, had ended in divorce, with himself as the petitioner or, in the much-quoted semi-legal jargon, the 'innocent party'. By 1953, when he was thirty-eight and she was twenty-three, romance had ripened, the church was privately emitting disapproving coughs, the Palace was showing signs of alarm and the British press was repeating its Edward VIII – Mrs Simpson performance by keeping quiet. Only when newspapers in the United States had given the affair excited coverage did there arrive at the Palace an edition of a British Sunday newspaper, much given to dwelling on the frailties of mankind, which thundered: 'It is quite unthinkable that a Royal princess, third in line of succession to the Throne, should even contemplate a marriage with a man who has been through the divorce court.'

The melancholy end of a thwarted love affair. A dispirited Princess Margaret drives through London on the morning of 31 October 1955 a few hours before issuing her public statement: 'I have decided not to marry Group Captain Peter Townsend . . . I have reached this decision entirely alone.'

Crowds outside the Mansion House, in the City of London, shouted 'Good luck, Margaret'; but Dr Geoffrey Fisher, Archbishop of Canterbury, hurried to the Palace for a two-hour consultation with the Queen and Philip; and, when Sunday came round again, another, more heavyweight newspaper declared: 'The Princess's marriage could lead to a controversy capable of splitting Church and State more profoundly than anything for 300 years.' Churchill took a similar view, and on his advice Elizabeth explained to her sister at a painful Palace session that, under the 1772 Royal Marriage Act, Margaret could not marry without the Queen's consent until she was twenty-five, two years hence. Consent was out of the question, since the Church of England did not permit marriage between divorced people and the Queen was temporal head of the church – 'Defender of the Faith'.

An excuse was found to pack Peter Townsend off to a sinecure job in Brussels for a couple of years in the hope that the love affair would cool down. It did not do so, and Anthony Eden, successor to Churchill as Prime Minister, tried a new and tougher tack. If Margaret insisted on becoming Townsend's wife she would forfeit the £15,000 a year which would otherwise be hers when she entered upon an approved marriage, she would be denied a religious ceremony, and like Uncle David and his Duchess she and her husband would be kicked out of the United Kingdom, at least for a few years. The Queen Mother was given the unenviable task of communicating Eden's ultimatum to her daughter.

Despite all the outward pretence to to the contrary, the real power of the government in a constitutional monarchy was clearly evident. The general public, having an instinctive and sentimental love for lovers, was all for Margaret and Peter. Out of 70,142 readers voting in a poll arranged by the *Daily Mirror*, 67,907 were for the marriage and only 2,235 against. But, whatever popular opinion might appear to be, Eden and his Cabinet were determined to make no concessions. In a national crisis – and that was how they saw the matter – royals of whatever rank would do as they were told.

In the evening of Monday, 31 October, Margaret issued the following statement:

I have decided not to marry Group Captain Peter Townsend. Mindful of the Church's

After the Christmas holidays Prince Charles leaves Newbury (Berkshire) railway station on his way to board the bus taking him and his fellow pupils back to Cheam School for the start of the spring term, 1958.

teaching that Christian marriage is indissoluble, and conscious of the Commonwealth, I have resolved to put these considerations before any other. I have reached this decision entirely alone, and in doing so I have been strengthened by the unfailing support and devotion of Group Captain Townsend. I am deeply grateful for the concern of all those who have constantly prayed for my happiness.

Very few people believed that the decision was spontaneously Margaret's, but neither did they blame her personally for the humbugging statement. Sometimes royals must be called upon to pay a high price for their privileged position, and it was unfortunate for Margaret that, in her case, the price was a little bit too steep.

The irony for the thwarted Princess was that, many years later, her separation from Lord Snowdon, the man she eventually married, provided a few days' excited gossip but no hint of a national upheaval. The subsequent divorce caused only a minor ripple of interest. For governments, churches and palaces, as for all institutions, times change, and yesterday's unthinkable is today's unexceptionable.

One of the longer-term legacies of the Townsend episode was a new, although not particularly welcome, realisation at the Palace of the growing and tenacious demands for information by the modern communications media. Piquantly enough, it is the Queen, once the apprentice in public relations, who has managed better with the press and broadcasting than Philip, formerly her PR tutor. Like her mother, Elizabeth has accepted the endless and sometimes tedious presence of press photographers and TV cameramen, and responded graciously. Philip soon became first wearied and then often angry – thus incurring the justifiable resentment of technicians undertaking jobs to which others have assigned them. A man who hovers frequently on the brink of irascibility and rudeness, he once startled guests at a reception by barking at a TV sound-recordist who was manoeuvring a microphone in his direction; 'Why don't you stick that thing!'

Yet, with the support of Palace aides, the Queen and Philip have succeeded in protecting themselves from intrusion into most aspects of their private lives. One of their best-kept secrets, for example, was the fact that for many years (until her death in 1969) Philip's mother, Princess Andrew of Greece, lived at Buckingham Palace. No member of the household, none of the staff, ever talked to outsiders about the lonely figure occasionally to be seen, almost wraith-like, passing through the corridors in the grey nun's habit of the Christian Sisterhood of Martha and Mary, which she had founded in 1949. Although quite deaf in her later years, she could lip-read in English, Greek, French and German; but when a visitor, intrigued by such remarkable abilities, diffidently inquired further about her, Philip abruptly put a stop to the questioning with the admonition, 'My mother's life is her own business.'

It was, however, the Queen rather than Philip who intervened with the press over the undue and persistent publicity given to Prince Charles when he was sent in 1957 to his father's preparatory school, Cheam, in Berkshire. She summoned a group of newspaper editors to a conference at the Palace and instructed her private secretary, Sir Michael Adeane, to confront them with the problems that, on their instructions, their journalists and photographers were causing. He spelled out the decision they were forcing upon the Queen: unless Charles was allowed to live a normal schoolboy's life among other boys of his own age he would have to be brought back to the Palace and educated by private tutors. The press would then bear responsibility for having frustrated an important experiment in the democratisation of the heir's education. Fleet Street's editors digested the message, and the invasion of Cheam School was called off.

Charles settled down well enough for his first Cheam report to say of him: 'Passionately keen on and promising at games. Academically a good average.' The one sport from which he was banned was boxing. His parents, after consulting advisers at the Palace, decided it would present too many obvious dangers for a boy destined to be the future King.

Since it was considered democratic to send Charles to Cheam, and subsequently to Gordonstoun (the Scottish Highlands school founded in 1935 by Kurt Hahn and also attended by his father), it was thought equally important by the Queen and Philip that he should complete his education at university. So it was that on 22 December 1965 six advisers sat down to a working dinner at the Palace with the royal parents: Harold Wilson, the Prime Minister; Dr Michael Ramsey, Archbishop of Canterbury; Earl Mountbatten; the Dean of Windsor; Sir Charles Wilson, chairman of the Committee of University Vice-Chancellors; and Sir Michael Adeane, the Queen's Private Secretary. By consensus the six men recommended Cambridge as the university for Charles and Trinity as his college. Charles began by reading archaeology and anthropology, but switched to history. After his three years as an undergraduate he went down from Cambridge with second-class honours – the first heir to the Throne to take a degree. Confirmed anti-monarchists were surprised that the Prince had not been awarded a 'first'; they had counted on a conspiracy between the Palace and the university to enhance his academic stature. In fact, at the time they are marked, examination scripts at Cambridge bear candidates' numbers which can only subsequently be keyed to names.

Following in father's foot-steps. On his first day at Gordonstoun School in Scotland (May 1962), Prince Charles greets his house-master, Mr Whitby. The Duke of Edinburgh and Mr Robert Chew, headmaster (left), look on. In his day, too, the Duke had been a pupil at the school.

The Palace has found itself increasingly involved during the present Queen's reign in matters of national politics (although not of party politics). As the uncertainties of the outside world made Britain's international position more delicate, the Queen's household was set to the task of helping to arrange overseas tours that would either consolidate the Commonwealth or stimulate trade – or both.

Apart from one brief period, from the late 1950s to the early 1960s, Britain staggered from one economic crisis to the next. Optimistically responding to promises, the realm's electorate gave its support in turn to socialist and Conservative policies, and still the crises appeared with the regularity of the rising sun. It was not what people had dreamed of as a 'new Elizabethan age' – but at least the Crown and the Palace seemed constant and secure.

They may not have been so totally secure in those months of 1956 when Britain, in partnership with France, embarked on the disastrous invasion of Egypt. The nation and the Commonwealth were deeply and bitterly split, the Anglo-French leaders were condemned as aggressors by the United Nations and the 'special relationship' between the kingdom and the United States almost came to an abrupt end. In Britain the man at the centre of the affair was the Prime Minister, Sir Anthony Eden, whose obsessive desire to topple Gamal Abdel Nasser, the Egyptian dictator, may have been due to ill-health. No one knows for certain what was said at the regular Tuesday Palace meetings between Eden and the Queen. But it has been suggested that she was opposed to the whole reckless venture – as a result of which Britain was later accused of deception and falsehood. She had the right, under the constitution, to warn the Prime Minister of the perilous course upon which he was launched, and it seems likely that she did so, although confirmation will have to await that distant time when the archives of the reign are opened to historians.

Had the adventure not been called off in time (mainly because of United States pressure) the constitutional consequences could well have been the gravest in the modern history of the Crown. As it was, Suez (to use the one word that encapsulates the near-tragedy) remains the darkest period of the reign.

There have been other duties required by governments which Palace officials and the Queen have found privately distasteful but towards which they have been obliged to present brave public faces. None has been more trying than the reception at the Palace, during his 1971 visit to Britain, of Emperor Hirohito of Japan, in whose name appalling atrocities were committed against British servicemen during the Second World War. Quite apart from what they had learned from the official records, the royal couple could not help being influenced in their personal views of Hirohito by Philip's 'Uncle Dickie', Lord Mountbatten, who had fought the Emperor's men as Supreme Commander, South-East Asia. He could not bring himself to embrace forgiveness, and boycotted the state banquet. For once on a state occasion the crowds stayed off the streets as a mark of disapproval, but the Palace officials who helped the Queen to formulate her speech for the banquet spoke delicately but unmistakably for the people. In their words Her Majesty told the Emperor: 'We cannot pretend that the past did not exist. We cannot pretend that the relations between our two peoples have always been peaceful and friendly.'

The reception given by the Japanese to the Queen when she paid a reciprocal visit to Tokyo in 1975 greatly pleased her subjects, however, and the unhappy

Royal weddings are always a 'hit' with the British. Just married, Princess Anne and Captain Mark Philips make the regulation Palace balcony appearance. With them are Anne's page and bridesmaid, Prince Edward and Lady Sarah Armstrong-Jones.

The 25th anniversary of the Queen's coronation, 1978. Elizabeth and Philip have watched an evening fireworks display from the Palace and now they respond to the cheers of the crowd.

past was finally laid to rest. The only irony was that the interchange of visits, originally seen in London as trade-promoting exercises, turned out to be a greater boon to Japan than to Britain.

Throughout all the years of the reign the Palace has witnessed a realm undergoing revolutionary changes. The Queen now presides over a multi-racial society, and she has played her honourable part in trying to encourage harmony among all her peoples. Political attitudes have become increasingly polarised and industrial relations endowed with greater bitterness. Occasionally Prince Philip, in the phrasing of some of his exhortations to industry, has appeared to become involved, and the Queen has needed to tread with extra-special caution to remain aloof from national bouts of fisticuffs.

People no longer display as reverent an interest in every royal person as their grandparents did. Some royals are more popular than others, and in several straw polls Princess Anne and Princess Margaret, for example, have not shown very high ratings. Wisely, the Queen and her husband, encouraged by advice at the Palace, have kept Prince Andrew and Prince Edward out of the public spotlight while they complete the process of growing up.

From time to time the suggestion is made that Queen Elizabeth might abdicate before the natural completion of her reign so that Prince Charles may not, like Edward VII, come to the Throne too late in life. The idea does not, so far, have any real support at the Palace. Influential forces there are highly sensitive about the word 'abdication' – even when applied to circumstances very different from the last time it haunted the royals.

The Queen's Diadem.

8

THE PALACE TODAY

THE HOUSEHOLD AND THE STAFF

BUCKINGHAM PALACE TODAY BELONGS TO THE NATION. A 'tied cottage' in Prince Philip's words, it is one of three state-owned royal residences occupied by the Queen and her husband. The other two are Windsor Castle and Holyroodhouse in Edinburgh. (Sandringham and Balmoral are the Queen's private residences.)

The building is now some forty times larger than when George III bought it and wished it to be known as 'Queen's House', and its rooms total around six hundred, depending on how many closets and storage places are included in the calculation. While opinions may differ about its architectural status, it has a certain solid dignity, and a magnificent setting, at the end of the broad, thrusting Mall and fronted by leafy St James's Park. Its façade greatly benefited from being given a thorough clean in 1970 – for the first time since the 1930s – and the warm gleam of its Portland stone has been resurrected.

Behind that stone frontage is not so much a mansion but more of an institution – part work-place, part official reception centre, part museum and part living-quarters for the sovereign, her husband and the Heir to the Throne.

Examples of the famous gold plate of the Palace as it was displayed on state occasions during the Victorian and Edwardian reigns. When functions were held in the State Dining Room the draped table, on which the pieces were massed, was placed in a mirrored alcove where its brilliance was reflected in the light of many candles.

It has its roots in the past, with its vast state apartments recalling long-gone casts of opulent courtiers, bewigged and powdered under shimmering candle-light, but lives very much in the present, with busy offices filled with the patter of electric typewriters and teleprinters. It has (at last) a modern central-heating system, up-to-date kitchens, cost-accounting, and footmen who only occasionally exchange their black tail coats for scarlet livery. In many respects it is reminiscent of the Hollywood of the golden years – permanent sets ready-made for glamour and magic, yet behind it all a hard-working and efficient industry, with the best hand-picked technicians in control.

As befits a royal institution, the Palace has a complex hierarchy, divided basically into two tiers – the household and the staff. As a general guide, members of the household may be thought of as the 'executives': they have direct personal contact with the Queen. The staff are the general employees filling a wide variety of clerical and manual jobs.

Altogether about four hundred people are required to run the Palace, but, although the list of members of the household appears formidably long, many of the people on it hold purely honorary posts and are called upon only on special occasions. The Poet Laureate, Sir John Betjeman, is a member of the household, for example, and so, too, is Malcolm Williamson, Master of the Queen's Musick. Neither is specifically required to produce a poem or a cantata for an appropriate royal event, but is welcome to do so as and when his creative abilities move him. The Poet Laureate receives an honorarium (which has not altered in value for three centuries) of £97 a year, which once used to be made up partly in cash and partly in sack – a white wine imported from Spain and the Canary Islands – possibly on the assumption that all self-respecting seventeenth-century poets were robust drinkers. Questioned as to exactly what the Laureateship entailed, one poet upon whom the honour fell, Cecil Day-Lewis, shook his head in despair and replied, 'God knows – I've never dared ask!'

Over the ages three household titles have evolved for the most senior appointments at the Palace: Lord Chamberlain, Lord Steward and Master of the Horse. Their holders are, respectively, responsible for duties 'above stairs', 'below stairs' and 'out of doors'. Evolution was, however, not always a smooth process. In the mid-nineteenth century there were frequent 'demarcation disputes' between these three senior royal servants. The cleaning of the insides of the windows was the responsibility of the Lord Chamberlain, but the cleaning of the outside glass was the responsibility of the Commission of Woods and Forests. The Lord Steward's men were required to lay the Palace fires, the Lord Chamberlain's minions to light them. When, as often happened, the various departments failed to synchronise their duties, the unfortunate royals sat shivering and gazing disconsolately at windows through which they could not clearly see for one side of grime. The planning of work in these modern time-and-motion-study days is less eccentric.

Let us look in more detail at today's top men and their Palace functions:

The Lord Chamberlain – currently Lord Maclean, twenty-seventh Chief of the Clan Maclean, a former Chief Scout of the Commonwealth, aged sixty-four – is the most senior of the senior officers, responsible for most household appointments and for all forms of ceremonial at court.

The Queen's own personal flag (as distinct from the royal standard which is an emblem of the kingdom). The initial 'E' is topped by the royal crown within a chaplet of roses – all is in gold on a field of blue, and the flag is also edged in gold.

The Lord Chamberlain's bailiwick extends, indeed, far beyond the Palace walls. He exercises authority over the Constable and Governor of Windsor Castle, the Superintendent of State Apartments at St James's Palace, the Keeper of the Jewel House at the Tower of London and a variety of keepers of other royal objects – paintings, books, manuscripts and swans. Some of the swans on the River Thames between London Bridge and the famous rowing centre, Henley, belong to two of the City of London's ancient Livery Companies – the Dyers and Vintners – and the rest are royal property. Once every year, at the time of 'swan-upping', the cygnets on the river are counted. The Vintners' swans are marked with two little notches, one on each side of the beak, and the Dyers' with one notch on the right side of the beak. The Queen's swans are not marked, but both hers and those belonging to the Livery Companies are pinioned so as to prevent them flying away from the River Thames.

Up to a hundred or so years ago the great privilege of owning swans had a distinctly material basis: they provided a valuable source of fresh food in the difficult winter months from October to January. Now, in this advanced age of successful food storage, swan-upping is retained largely as a quaint and colourful custom.

Selected shops and manufacturers whose goods or services have been in regular and substantial demand by the royal household for at least three consecutive years are permitted to use the much-envied 'By Appointment' label, and it is the Lord Chamberlain who issues them with the warrant to do so. He is also responsible for the organisation of royal weddings and funerals – but not for the funeral of the sovereign, which, by tradition, is supervised by the Earl Marshal, the Duke of Norfolk, the Premier Duke of the kingdom.

Upon appointment each Lord Chamberlain is presented with a wand of office which, in years past, he would ceremonially break in two at the conclusion of the sovereign's funeral service. Since the art of breaking a wand neatly and cleanly without loss of dignity may not be within the command of all men, a present-day holder of the office is given a rod designed to unscrew into two equal-length parts.

Lord Maclean's predecessor, Lord Cobbold, a former Governor of the Bank of England, quietly made a number of changes to give the household a less inbred, closed look when he took office in 1963. Although an Old Etonian himself, he sought to loosen the 'old-school-tie' influence in household appointments, and only one of the first five 'executives' he engaged had been at Eton College. Commenting on the changes, he said with satisfaction (though not, some might argue, with complete accuracy): 'We've entirely got rid of the idea that here it's all huntin', shootin' and fishin' people.'

Second in command to Lord Maclean is the Comptroller, Lieutenant-Colonel Sir Eric Penn, a very tall, graciously-mannered man who came to the Palace from the Grenadier Guards and who has been a personal friend of the Queen since her days as Princess Elizabeth. Much of his work, too, involves ceremonial duties, as well as helping to advise on household appointments and caring for the Queen's art collection. Until the archaic system was abolished in 1968, Sir Eric also had the task – which he personally abhorred – of advising the Lord Chamberlain on his function as censor of theatrical stage plays. More in sorrow than by choice he found himself in the early 1960s obliged to object to the blue language and bawdy gestures of Joan Littlewood's classic stage production of *Fings Ain't What They Used To Be*.

The Lord Steward, at present the Duke of Northumberland, nominally has control of all Palace functions 'below stairs', but his post is largely honorary and the professional executive is his subordinate, the Master of the Household – at the time of writing Vice-Admiral Sir Peter Ashmore, a former Chief of Allied Staff at NATO Naval Headquarters. He has a deputy and sixteen officials and clerks, and supervises a catering staff of forty-five, as well as fifty-eight housemaids and fifty-three pages and footmen.

Within their domain, the Lord Steward and the Master have control over the court post office and the Palace police; they are responsible for security and for the 'Court Circular', the Palace's daily record of the royal family's public activities which appears every weekday morning in *The Times* and the *Daily Telegraph*.

Their jurisdiction also covers the quaintly named Board of Green Cloth, which holds the right to license certain premises in the neighbourhood of the Palace where alcohol may be served. In the distant past the licensing provision extended to a radius of twelve miles, having been instituted as a means of stamping out any public 'brawling, duelling, drunkenness, etc.' that might be offensive to the royal personage. Green Cloth licences still apply to three public houses around the corner from the Palace – the Silver Cross, the Old Shades and the Clarence – as well as the premises of the Royal Society, the National Gallery and eleven clubs. Nowadays, as Prince Charles is especially wont to complain, the incessant clamour of traffic outside the Palace is more of an assault upon royal nerves than any well-regulated set-to with rapiers in the Mall might be.

Sir Peter Ashmore, too, is a personal friend of the Queen – she attended his wedding in 1952 – and was an equerry to her father, George VI. In a sense he is the general manager for all internal and domestic services not only at Buckingham Palace but at all the royal palaces.

The Deputy Master of the Household and Equerry (Lieutenant-Colonel B.A.

The royal mews at the Palace are open to the public, who have the chance to inspect some of the coaches, horses and harness.

Harness in the royal mews is regularly polished to a gleaming brightness. Adjoining the mews is a large covered riding school where the Queen rehearses each year for the Trooping the Colour ceremony.

Stewart-Wilson) shares, with a second equerry (at the time of writing, Lieutenant-Commander Robert Guy) the duties of accompanying the Queen on many of her public engagements at home and abroad. Another of the Palace's Old Etonians, Robert Guy was educated for his service career at the Royal Military Academy at Sandhurst and took up his post in 1976 in succession to Lord Plunket, who in turn had succeeded Group Captain Peter Townsend, Princess Margaret's friend. (When Lord Plunket was appointed there was, inevitably, a flurry of rumours that he himself might marry Margaret.)

The Master of the Horse is, again, basically an honorary post. It is held today by the Earl of Westmorland, but its practical duties are undertaken by the Crown Equerry, who is invariably a retired officer of the armed forces; the present incumbent is Lieutenant-Colonel Sir John Mansel Miller.

Much though the title may evoke visions of stables and harness, the Crown Equerry's province embraces all that is out of doors at the Palace. It is populated by four officials and clerks, eleven chauffeurs and thirty-nine grooms and coachmen. The Palace also has ten gardeners and one hundred maintenance men (mostly building staff and engineers, who also undertake work at Kensington Palace) but all these workers are directly employed by the Department of the Environment.

The Crown Equerry is responsible for the Queen's travelling arrangements by car or carriage. He is involved in the organisation of every state spectacular that includes horses, and responsible for the regular training of the Queen's horse for the ceremony of Trooping the Colour, held on the first or second Saturday in June on what is designated for confusion's sake as the Queen's Official Birthday. (Her actual birthday happens to be 21 April – but in the British climate that is not a day to be relied upon for a successful open-air occasion; and, in any case, it is outside the main tourist season.)

Trooping the Colour, which has been an annual event since 1805 except for wartime interruptions, is staged on Horse Guards Parade, on the west side of Whitehall, and it is the only time when the Queen, an accomplished horsewoman, is seen riding side-saddle. For two or three weeks beforehand she rehearses in the Palace riding school, which adjoins the Royal Mews and is part of the Crown Equerry's province. In this fine school, seventy-five yards long, the royal horses are continually trained to accustom themselves to the noise and flurry of state occasions. From time to time bands play as they are exercised, and stable-lads stand by, cheering wildly and waving miniature Union Jacks – all as part of a well-considered preparation for the days when the horses will encounter the real thing on the streets of London.

Her Majesty still keeps in touch with her former, colourful Master of the Horse – the eighty-year-old Duke of Beaufort, who held the post for forty-three years, from 1936 to 1979. He paid £300 for his red, gold-laced Master's tunic in 1936 and it was so well made that he never needed to replace it and has handed it on to his successor. He has been called 'the greatest foxhunter of our time', and when the Queen visits his seventeenth-century home, Badminton, for her favourite horse trials he always makes sure she is served the speciality of his table – fresh salmon. He is universally addressed as 'Master': not, however, in honour of his former service at the Palace but because he is Master of the Beaufort Hounds, a service his family has rendered for ten generations.

The most important household member in close daily contact with the Queen is

Trooping the Colour, 1979. The Queen leaves the Palace, on her horse Burmese, for the ceremony which is always held on the Horse Guards Parade, Whitehall. It is the only occasion on which the Queen, an accomplished horsewoman, is seen riding side-saddle.

her private secretary, a personal royal appointment. This is an onerous post – an amalgam, as we have seen in earlier pages, of royal servant and confidant.

The private secretary is Her Majesty's principal official adviser on all problems – constitutional, political or domestic – that she may encounter. He is also concerned with correspondence between the Queen and her ministers at home and throughout the Commonwealth, advising on material for her speeches and planning her day-to-day engagements.

The present private secretary is the Right Honourable Sir Philip Moore, fifty-nine, son of an Indian civil servant, who gained a scholarship from Cheltenham College to Oxford where he won a double Blue in hockey and rugby. His hobbies are golf, tennis, fishing, cricket and shooting, and during his four years' service as British Deputy High Commissioner in Singapore he and his wife, Joan, raised diplomatic eyebrows with their enthusiasm for the pop music of the Rolling Stones.

All major decisions about royal activities and work at the palace are made by the Queen in consultation with Sir Philip, who is responsible for sifting invitations and proposals for the Queen's programme each July and December when royal engagements for the following six months are planned.

Sir Philip came to his job in 1978, having succeeded one of the most notable of modern private secretaries, Lieutenant-Colonel Sir Martin Charteris, whose work had a decisive effect on relations between the sovereign and her people. Sir Martin was formerly secretary to the Queen when she was Princess Elizabeth, and following her accession he served as her assistant private secretary for twenty years. (On his retirement he became Provost of Eton, thus reinforcing in a rather unusual way that apparently indissoluble link between the Palace and the College.)

He was largely responsible for the flashes of humour and light-heartedness which the Queen began to introduce into her public speeches (when the occasions were appropriate) and which contributed very considerably towards enhancing her personal appeal. A man whose usual urbane appearance belies an inner high-spiritedness, he sometimes shocked vigilant observers of royal events by surreptitiously indulging in the antiquated habit of snuff-taking. Such observers would have been even more surprised had they known that his silver snuffbox was a gift from Her Majesty.

In a time when protocol was much more starchy than it is today, Sir Martin beavered away at his self-appointed task of trying to make royal appearances more adventurous and less rigidly formal. During the planning of the Queen's visit to New York in 1957 he found that his two bosses, Sir Michael Adeane, then Private Secretary, and Her Majesty herself, were opposed to a royal walk through a supermarket and a royal ascent of the Empire State Building. They both dismissed such ventures as 'too gimmicky' but Sir Martin, at the risk of incurring a double package of icy displeasure, persisted and finally won his point. The resulting inclusion of the two items in the itinerary delighted New Yorkers.

Within the private secretary's office a post of great importance and influence is that of the press secretary, at present held by forty-one-year-old Michael Shea. The role of the press secretary is among the most curious ever devised at the Palace, for unlike his counterparts in commerce, show business and politics he does not disseminate news designed to promote his royal employer. Instead, he and his staff spend much of their time warding off inquiries aimed at eliciting personal and sometimes highly intimate details of royal life and living.

Despite what, at first sight, might seem to be something of a negative assignment, Michael Shea and his team are held in high regard by the British media. Strangely enough, the reason tells one a good deal about the place of the Palace in national life. For, although its purpose may not be laid down in any job specification, the press section treads with remarkable skill a path between courteous and helpful assistance with 'permitted' facts and the protection of the royal mystery which is a crucial factor (however irksome to investigative reporters) in preserving the Crown as an institution standing above, and free from, the murkiness of the political cockpit.

A press secretary at the Palace is a modern innovation, and Mr Shea is only the sixth to hold the office since the Second World War. He is a one-time deputy director of the British Information Services in New York, and author of political thrillers under the pseudonym 'Michael Sinclair'. Among his predecessors the best remembered (although not with affection by the press) is Sir Richard Colville, an ex-naval commander and friend of George V, whose routine response to most seekers after knowledge at the Palace was 'No comment'. But much of today's notable improvement in press-palace relationships is owed to reforms pursued by Bill Heseltine, Sir Richard's successor and now deputy private secretary to Her Majesty.

Heseltine, an Australian, is one of the few senior men at the Palace who was educated at a grammar school, as distinct from a public school. For four years he was private secretary to one of the Queen's favourite Australians, Sir Robert

Menzies, then Prime Minister in Canberra, and was therefore a natural candidate when Her Majesty decided she wanted a new and young recruit from the Commonwealth to join her household.

He helped to usher in an era, already well advanced in Scandinavia but new to Britain, in which members of the Royal Family began to grant interviews to selected newspapers and television. And one invention during his four-year tenure of office was the royal 'walkabout' in which, for the first time, her ordinary, non-privileged subjects came within close-up distance of the Queen on her tours.

Bill Heseltine also played an influential part in Palace negotiations with the BBC and Independent Television for the making of the highly successful 1969 TV film, *Royal Family*, which gave viewers in Britain and abroad the first inside glimpse of the royals at home.

Press secretary and assistant press secretary have direct access to the Queen, and those press questions which they sometimes feel bound to refer personally to her are usually answered promptly – even when, on occasion, the Queen feels bound to say that she has nothing to say! Inevitably there are times when press officials, caught on the hop by probing inquiries, may be reduced to intelligent guessing – not always with happy results. Something like that happened in the winter of 1979 during the furore over the public unmasking of Anthony Blunt, the spy for the Russians who had been Adviser for the Queen's Pictures and Drawings. Asked if the Queen had been told, during Blunt's time in her employment, that he had been uncovered by the security authorities and given immunity from prosecution (in return for his 'assistance') a member of the press secretariat replied that almost certainly she must have been. Later that day the Palace was obliged to announce that the answer was 'unauthorised'.

A burnt-out spy is an unusual kind of problem for the Palace; gossip and heavy hints about royal romances are the ingredients upon which nervous anxiety flourishes. Officials at 'Buck House' (as some of the snobbier would-be hangers-on will persist in calling the place) still feel a touch of perspiration on their brows at the recollection of those days in late 1972 when Princess Anne began to be seen in the company of young Lieutenant Mark Phillips.

Robin Ludlow, the then press secretary, who genuinely believed that the newspaper stories of love-in-the-air were unfounded, did his dutiful best to persuade Fleet Street that it was devoting time, ink and paper to a non-starter. To his understandable anguish, it eventually emerged that the newspapers were right and whoever had encouraged the laying-down of a Palace smokescreen was wrong.

Even the Queen's beloved corgis are considered newsworthy, and reporters felt especially rewarded, some years ago, when they learned that one of the Queen's favourite bitches, Heather, had suffered the amputation of a leg after what the Palace described as 'undue playfulness' between the royal pets. The high point of the news item was that Heather insisted upon hopping around the Palace on three legs as though no ill had befallen her. She died three years later – but from old age, the Palace said, and not from the effects of her injury.

The most senior members of the royal family rarely carry anything as vulgar or mundane as money around with them, nor do they often sign cheques. Payment of Palace and royal bills is undertaken by the three household members of the Privy Purse Office, assisted by a total staff of twenty-three officials, clerks and others and including six chartered accountants. The men at the top are Major Sir Rennie Maudslay, Keeper of the Privy Purse and Treasurer to the Queen, the deputy and the assistant. Sir Rennie personally signs most of the cheques on Her Majesty's behalf, and, despite the ever-present problem of cash-flow, his office has the reputation – much admired by purveyors of food, wine, power supplies, telephones and a multitude of other goods and services – for paying on the nail.

Most of the Queen's own private banking business is handled by Coutts and Company, one of London's oldest banks, first set up in the Strand, near Trafalgar Square, in 1692, and still in the Strand – although in new, awesomely impressive twenty-first-century premises. Not unnaturally, Coutts do not tell inquirers who in their organisation looks after the Queen's account or whether she ever drops in to see if everything is in the black. It is certain, however, that Queen Elizabeth has no need to channel all her income to Coutts in order that they may pay off her debts, as they did for her distant predecessor, George IV.

Although it is unlikely, despite the anti-sex-discrimination laws, that a woman will be seen in any of the top household posts now held by men, there is at the Palace someone approaching the feminine equivalent of the Lord Chamberlain: the Mistress of the Robes, currently the Duchess of Grafton. Her principal tasks are to accompany the Queen on main state occasions and some overseas visits and to supervise the rota of the nine ladies-in-waiting who attend upon Her Majesty at other public functions. Their titles illustrate their nominal place in the hierarchy – there are two regular Ladies of the Bedchamber and one Extra Lady and four Women of the Bedchamber and two Extra Women – but they are all truly upper-crust and combine the duties of personal companion and general helpmeet to the sovereign. The four Women, who also assist the Queen with her private correspondence, work a kind of shift system – two weeks on duty, six weeks off.

Ladies-in-waiting live at home and no longer at the Palace; each receives an honorarium (currently around £1,000 a year) to cover clothes and expenses and takes her meals in the Household Dining-Room.

The presence of the Church of England is very strongly felt at the Palace – as is only to be expected, for after all Her Majesty is 'Head of the Church and Defender of the Faith'. Ever since Henry VIII broke away from the jurisdiction of Rome, various Parliamentary Acts have dug trenches and put up bastions against the possibility of Roman Catholicism finding its way to the throne. At the beginning of her reign the Queen was obliged to pronounce: 'I, Elizabeth the Second, do solemnly and sincerely, in the presence of God, testify and declare that I am a faithful Protestant, and that I will, according to the true intent of the enactments which secure the Protestant succession to the throne of my realm, uphold and maintain the said enactments to the best of my powers according to the law.'

Despite that declaration, religious intolerance is no longer any more an aspect of royalty than it is representative of the overwhelming majority of people in the United Kingdom. And it is a fact that the Norfolks, whose Dukes have long been responsible for arranging the coronations and funerals of Britain's sovereigns (conducted according to the rites of the Church of England), are a Catholic family.

The Queen's ecclesiastical household is substantial in number – thirty-six chaplains, four extra-chaplains, and a dean (the Bishop of London), a Sub-Dean and eleven priests and organists of the Chapels Royal (the Queen's private chapels at Buckingham Palace, Windsor Castle, Windsor Great Park, Hampton Court Palace, the Tower of London and Sandringham).

The Music Room: renowned for its noble bay of five great windows looking out onto the gardens. Domed ceilings are a feature of many of the state apartments of the Palace.

Queen's eye-view: the Palace as the royal family see it from the 'rear', or garden, side. On a hot summer's day, under the shade of the trees, the Queen could well imagine herself to be deep in the countryside, although Trafalgar Square is no more than three minutes' car drive away.

Centre Room: from the public's point of view this is undoubtedly the most famous room in the Palace; from here, and through the open French window, members of the royal family step on to the balcony to greet the crowds. The décor of the room is Oriental.

Viewed at a glance, the endless list of names and titles in the Queen's household appears to cover almost every aspect of service required for life at the very top. There are, for example, thirteen physicians, surgeons and oculists – and a coroner. And there are serried ranks of Lords-in-Waiting and Gentlemen Ushers who, among other duties, assist in keeping the throng at bay during crowded state occasions at the Palace. Prince Philip has his own household and so, also, do Prince Charles and Princess Anne.

The staff at the Palace (the 'downstairs' as distinct from the 'upstairs' household) now number around 330 male and female full-time workers and around 100 part-timers. Surprisingly, Palace pages are not young cherubs but men senior in rank to footmen and under-butlers. Pages wear blue coats and black trousers with gilt-buttoned blue waistcoats and, on special state occasions, change into black-and-gold braid livery with fine white wool-cloth breeches, stockings and black pumps with buckles. Footmen and under-butlers wear black tail coats and trousers with scarlet waistcoats trimmed with very narrow gold braid. On special occasions they appear in scarlet livery decorated with gold braid, scarlet plush knee-breeches, pink stockings and black buckle shoes.

In the past most of the staff had a pretty thin time of it, with discomfort and sub-standard food offsetting the prestige of the job. Even up to the time of Elizabeth II's accession, maids and footmen lived in dormitories reminiscent of the bed-and-board accommodation for shop assistants described in H. G. Wells's *Kipps*.

Today's circumstances are vastly improved. Each living-in page, footman and maid has a comfortable bed-sitter equipped with washbasin, easy chairs, wardrobe, writing table and chest-of-drawers. The chefs are accommodated in an annexe close to their kitchens, and chauffeurs and grooms have flats above the

The royal yacht Britannia *enters Nassau harbour in the Bahamas. The yacht was designed to be easily convertible to a hospital ship, and she is used by the Royal Navy for special duties when not engaged on royal tours.*

stables and garages in the Royal Mews. Staff have their own self-service canteen where drinks are available at reduced prices, a shop and a small sick bay.

Most members of the staff belong to the Civil Service Union – which has its own Palace branch – and, although wages now run in line with equivalent civil-service grades, financial rewards for the general run of the Queen's servants have never been notably high. Strikes at the Palace are unknown – consultation between household and staff is regarded as very good – but minor grievances do sometimes bubble over, as happened in March 1979 in the Royal Mews. The Palace coachmen complained that they were earning too little, and threatened to put the brake on ceremonial processions unless their wages were lined up with those of the chauffeurs who drove the royal limousines and had recently been granted an extra £12.60 a week, putting their basic weekly earnings up to £63. In a rare declaration to an intrigued outside world, a spokesman from among the stable workers said: 'We don't object to them [the chauffeurs] getting the money, but we're adamant we should get the same. It's a damn sight easier turning the ignition key of a Rolls-Royce and driving it around Hyde Park Corner than taking a coach-and-four on the same journey.' However, the stable staff were told that the chauffeurs had been given their rise in compensation for a longer working week and basic pay remained unchanged at £55 a week for a coachman and £33 for a stable-lad, although some adjustments have since been made in line with the upsurge in inflation.

In July 1978 ten full-time gardeners walked out in a pay protest on the day of a royal garden party for seven thousand international guests. Some of them were earning as little as £30 a week, but as a Palace official pointed out: 'These gardeners are employed by the Department of the Environment and not by Her Majesty.' And, anyway, she added, 'The gardens are looking simply super.'

The closest the Palace has come to embarrassing industrial action was when some employees threatened to stage a sit-in at their canteen unless something was done about increasing the frequency of hot meals. Swiftly, eggs and chips appeared on the menu as a supplement to cold meat dishes, and the harmony which prevails so well at the royal palaces was restored.

A good many royal servants take on additional outside jobs to bolster their incomes, but working for the Queen does have its benefits – in kind. For, as one staffer put it: 'Many of us are given good accommodation at low cost – and, when all is said and done, there is total job security.' Few members of the staff are ever fired, and then only for serious breaches of discipline.

Among the Palace staff there is one very special and particularly highly regarded lady – Miss Margaret MacDonald, officially the Queen's dresser and known to all members of the royal family as 'Bobo'. Apart from early and brief employment as a Scottish hotel chambermaid, Miss MacDonald has spent the whole of her life in royal service.

The Queen Mother, then Duchess of York, first engaged her as a nurserymaid in 1926, when Princess Elizabeth was four months old. Now in her late sixties, she is treated almost as an extra member of the family – a kind of surrogate mother, who has played the part of guide, comforter and helper to the Queen throughout some of the most significant years of Her Majesty's life and reign. She lives comfortably in her own well-appointed suite immediately above the Queen's private apartments, and while other members of the staff eat in their canteen she dines in her rooms.

One man who is seldom far from the Queen's side when she leaves the Palace is her royal bodyguard, Commander Michael Trestrail, forty-nine and from good Cornish working-class stock. His father, Jack, was the most popular greengrocer in the little town of Redruth, ten miles from the port of Falmouth. Invariably discreet, as rightly becomes a policeman attached to the Palace, he is however known to have said that the only one of his duties to which he has a strong aversion is attending the annual Royal Ascot horse-race meeting. But whether this is due to comments from his police colleagues about his having to don the obligatory morning suit and topper, with lime-green carnation, or to the tensions created for any bodyguard by the crowds which press around the Queen, is not clear. Although he is not by inclination a betting man, he is reported to indulge in a minor flutter at Ascot, and on one occasion confessed philosophically to have ended up losing £2.

Details of security at the Palace and of the royal family are well-guarded secrets, for obvious reasons, but there has been a tightening-up since the recent wave of international terrorism developed and especially since the Provisional IRA leaders made it clear that they included British royals among those whom they chose to call their 'legitimate targets'. Neither the Queen nor Prince Philip has shown any signs of being deterred by threats from continuing to carry out public engagements; but the royal family felt the chill of mindless brutality touch them in the summer of 1979 with the IRA murder of Earl Mountbatten.

The annual wage and salary bill at the Palace currently runs at around £1,500,000; other costs, including maintenance, account for a further £1,000,000, and the rates due to Westminster City Council, in whose borough the Palace

A view of the Queen's sitting room in the royal yacht Britannia.

stands, came to £101,609 in the 1979–80 financial year. The payroll charges are met out of the Queen's Civil List, her annual expenses allowance from the government,* which in March 1980 was fixed at £2,716,300. Maintenance and other costs of royal residences are borne directly by government departments, and the present total for Buckingham Palace, St James's Palace, and Windsor Castle is £3,300,000 a year. Letters, telegrams and telephones are paid for by the Post Office Corporation.

The government also pays for the Royal Yacht *Britannia* (£2,150,000 in 1979) and the Queen's Flight (£1,800,000). A refit for *Britannia*, estimated to cost around £5,000,000 and put in hand at Portsmouth in September 1979, was described by Mr Charles Irving, Conservative MP for Cheltenham, as 'nothing short of a national scandal'. He hastened to emphasise, however, that he blamed the Defence Ministry for the apparent 'extravagance', and not the royal family 'because they have nothing to do with it'.

The fact is often overlooked, however, that the Royal Yacht, built in 1954, is a ship of the fleet – the oldest still in commission – and is used by the Royal Navy for special duties when not engaged on royal tours. She is also designed to be quickly converted into a hospital ship with up to four hundred beds. From 1974 to 1979 *Britannia*'s total running costs amounted to £12,750,000, but that included £1,379,000 for a refit in 1976 and for her fuel-oil and pay for 277 officers and ratings.

The Queen's Flight could not be described as over-lavish jet-age luxury – it consists of two Wessex helicopters and three fifteen-year-old propeller-driven Andovers. The aircraft are also available to senior members of the government and senior officers of the armed forces on duty.

In 1980–81 annuities being paid to other members of the royal family include £244,000 for the Queen Mother, £135,000 for Prince Philip, £85,000 for Princess Anne, £82,000 for Princess Margaret, and £20,000 for Prince Andrew. On the Queen's direct orders, Prince Andrew at present personally receives only £4,500 a year; the balance of £15,500 is retained by the royal trustees.

The amount allocated to the Civil List in 1980 represented an overall nineteen per cent increase compared with 1979, except that Princess Anne's individual allowance rose by thirty per cent. The Palace explained that in 1979 the Princess had overspent by 'several thousands of pounds in pursuance of official duties' – an explanation that brought cries of rage from Labour Opposition MPs, who were particularly incensed to learn that a major factor in her expenses was the upkeep of Gatcombe Park, the eighteenth-century, thirty-room mansion in Gloucestershire bought by the Queen for Anne and her husband, Captain Mark Phillips, for a reputed £500,000. The house is now designated as an official residence and partially maintained from the Civil List.

For the present, and certainly while he remains a bachelor, Prince Charles receives no state allowance. He is financed instead from the profits of the Duchy of Cornwall, which has been the fiefdom of the heir to the Throne since Edward III instituted it in 1337 for the benefit of his eldest son, the Black Prince. The yearly profit from the Duchy, which owns 131,744 acres of land in seven English counties – Cornwall (including the Scilly Isles), Devon, Dorset, Gloucestershire, London,

---

* Royal family accounts are audited by the Treasury to ensure that the money is spent as expenses for official duties: Civil List allowances are not salaries.

One of the three propeller-driven Hawker Siddeley Andovers that make up the Queen's Flight. The aircraft are also available to senior members of the government and senior officers of the armed forces on duty.

Prince Charles, sporting a moustache which, only the day before, had been part of a full beard, arrives at Westminster Abbey, in May 1975, for his installation by the Queen as Great Master of the Most Honourable Order of the Bath.

Somerset and Wiltshire — has in recent times averaged about £250,000. Prince Charles surrenders half of each year's 'take' to the Treasury in lieu of income tax. Most of the £125,000 he retains goes to pay his staff and meet the expenses of his own household.

Since 1975 the Queen has supplemented her Civil List with money from her own private resources, and in 1979, for example, she also provided £218,200 towards the expenses of the Dukes of Gloucester and Kent, of Princess Alexandra, and of Princess Alice, the Countess of Athlone. She also meets all the expenses of entertaining at Buckingham Palace.

The guessing game of 'How much is she really worth?' has never produced anything approaching a definitive answer, and the secrecy surrounding the facts of her private fortune remains impenetrable. She receives the net income of the Duchy of Lancaster, which owns agricultural estates and properties in nine towns, including parts of London, and which in 1979 amounted to £625,000. Although she pays no income tax on those earnings, income from the Crown Estates — some 250,000 acres throughout Britain — goes to the government; again in 1979, it contributed a very healthy and welcome addition to the Treasury's coffers of £6,500,000. (Revenues from the Crown Estates did belong to the Crown until George III handed them over to the government in exchange for a regular Treasury stipend.)

At the Palace, and at Windsor, the Queen presides over the priceless royal collections of pictures, books and manuscripts, jewels and stamps (the stamp collection was started by her grandfather, George V); but she retains these only for her lifetime and is not free to dispose of them.

So far the only direct, official reference to the Queen's private wealth ever made — and that a negative rather than a positive statement — came from Lord Cobbold (then Lord Chamberlain) when he gave evidence in 1971 to the House of Commons Select Committee on the Civil List. He declared:

A showcase of some of the Queen's art treasures in the Palace, with the Diadem as the centrepiece.

Her Majesty has been much concerned by the astronomical figures which have been bandied about in some quarters suggesting that the value of these funds may now run into £50 or £100 million or more. She feels that these ideas can only arise from confusion about the status of the Royal Collections, which are in no sense at her private disposal. She wishes me to assure the Committee that these suggestions are wildly exaggerated.

There can be little doubt that the Queen is one of the wealthiest women in the world, but it is unlikely that she is ahead of one of her fellow-royals, ex-Queen Juliana of the Netherlands. When Juliana handed over her throne to her daughter, Beatrix, on 30 April 1980 it was said that her holding in the Dutch half of Shell Oil was alone worth £50,000,000. And that was but one item in an extensive 'portfolio'. Those who have for long cited Elizabeth II as the richest woman on earth might do well, therefore, to delete her name and substitute Juliana's.

In his book *The Court of St James* Christopher Hibbert calculated that altogether, and including money spent on foreign tours, the office of the head of state cost the nation in 1979 some £14,000,000 a year. Despite its size, he thought the amount 'relatively' paltry when compared with expenditure elsewhere; for example, well over half as much again is spent by the British National Health Service on anti-depressant drugs.

As for Buckingham Palace – a 'labour-intensive' institution – the basic economic problem is that, even with comparatively modest staff costs, it is increasingly expensive to run; its maintenance bills, too, quite naturally mount with its age. It is doubtful, however, if one could find another major establishment as well and as carefully operated financially. The approach to expenditure is one of ultra-caution. 'You could say we are parsimonious,' a Palace spokesman recently remarked. When the newly elected Thatcher administration embarked on its series of stringent public-spending cuts, household officials immediately began to make another of their frequent checks on Palace costs. In the winter of 1979–80 the central heating of the building was reduced by five degrees, and pages and footmen were instructed to switch off any lights left burning in unoccupied rooms or on temporarily deserted desks.

For her private use the Queen still makes do with a twelve-year-old Rover car, and it is no secret that some of the royal dresses originally ordered for overseas tours are remodelled for extended life at home. Indeed, much of what otherwise might be regarded as slightly eccentric parsimony at the Palace undoubtedly stems from the Queen herself. She has a strong dislike for personal ostentation – probably derived, as some Palace-observers believe, from the wartime example of her parents, who strove, as far as their special position allowed, to accept the shortages and austerity willingly borne by their subjects. And maybe there is even a hint of nostalgia in that. For, as one courtier put it: 'Like most people who experienced it, the Queen looks back with pride on the wartime unity of Britain. Something as apparently trivial as fussiness over the household accounts could be an indication of a need to want to go on sharing, in some way, with people's troubles – if you allow Britain's present economic difficulties as "trouble".'

It is probably such attitudes at the top which account for the fact that, whatever else it may be, the Palace is not a centre of lavish living: certainly not for royals – who could, if they chose, behave with the private extravagance that characterises many of the international jet set.

The Queen at home.

9

THE QUEEN AT THE PALACE

ROYALTY IN RESIDENCE

NOWADAYS, THE QUEEN AND PRINCE PHILIP are almost always in residence at Buckingham Palace – except for absence on overseas tours, of course – during most of the autumn and winter. They spend Christmas at Windsor and the New Year at Sandringham, Easter at Windsor, a few days in July at Holyroodhouse, and August and September at Balmoral. Tourists who go to look at the Palace will know that the Queen is at home when they see the royal standard flying from the flagpole set on the roof. (After dark, the standard is floodlit until midnight.)

The Queen and her husband have their private apartments on the first floor of the Palace, overlooking Constitution Hill. Prince Charles, the Prince of Wales, has his suite on the floor above his parents. All the rooms are comfortable, but certainly by no means as opulent as those, for example, of many of the wealthiest heads of multinational corporations or of many oil-rich sheikhs.

At eight o'clock each morning the Queen is aroused with a cup of tea, brought to her either by 'Bobo' or one of the other dressers, and copies of *The Times* and the *Daily Telegraph* are placed on her bedside table. (Later she will see a summary of royal stories in other papers compiled by members of the press secretariat.) When she has bathed and dressed she joins Prince Philip – whose suite adjoins hers – in the private dining-room for breakfast.

The room is dominated by an oval-shaped mahogany table and three sideboards to match. Very rarely are servants in attendance; the Queen and Philip help themselves to their bacon and eggs from dishes which have earlier been delivered to the dining-room and placed on hotplates. During most of the meal the royal couple listen to the morning's radio news, but the set is switched off for the final fifteen minutes of breakfast-time while they are serenaded by bagpipes played by the Royal Pipe Major on the terrace. Bagpipes for breakfast may not be to everyone's taste – and particularly not, it seems, to Prince Philip's – but the tradition was started by Queen Victoria, and to abandon it might very well look like a snub to the Scots.

Almost everywhere the Queen goes in the Palace, she is accompanied by a scurry of corgis, and she likes to feed them herself – beginning in the dining-room in the morning, when she puts down their bowls of doggie food on white plastic sheets. Like any devoted pet-lover she chatters to each animal, and her voice can be unexpectedly harsh when she has occasion to reprimand one or another.

The day's work, in their respective studies, begins for the Queen and Prince Philip at around nine-thirty. Her study is also a sitting-room, with a marble fireplace, a settee and matching armchairs and, against the large window, her desk, on which papers and other documents overflow. The desk could be that of any high-grade company executive, with a display of family photographs, an ornamented silver ink-stand and an adjustable lamp. By the Queen's left elbow stands a small bracket clock and, just behind it, a spray of flowers in a blue vase. One of the two telephones is fitted with a scrambler device for the most confidential of conversations with her ministers. There are no ashtrays on the desk, for Her Majesty, like Philip and Prince Charles, is a non-smoker. At night the study is lighted by Waterford glass chandeliers.

Prince Philip's study provides a wealth of evidence of his interest in electronics. There is a variety of press-button gadgets that, among other operations, control the opening and closing of the curtains, and the large television-set. During his lifetime the room was used by George VI; but Philip has made a number of alterations – including the lowering of the ceiling, which has greatly improved the study's proportions, and made it much warmer in winter.

Almost always the first visitors of the day to the Queen at work are her private secretary, the deputy or assistant. Together they run over the day's main business and go through the principal items of correspondence selected from the scores that arrive every day from organisations and private individuals at home and abroad. Many of the official letters from public bodies of various types invite visits by Her Majesty, and a host of complex factors are taken into account before she reaches a final decision: whether the invitations are to areas she has not visited for some time; whether there are special regional problems, such as heavy unemployment, and where the royal presence would be felt as a morale-booster; whether an institution is concerned with matters of particular social interest, such as the care of handicapped people or the sick and elderly, or with some new industrial development. Out of all the invitations that flow in during a year the Queen will, on average, accept perhaps one in fifty or sixty – which still invariably gives her a tightly packed engagement diary. And, among other routine events, the Queen regularly attends eight special annual 'occasions': the Royal Maundy Ceremony, on the Thursday before Easter Sunday; the Chelsea Flower Show; the Derby; Royal Ascot; the Garter Ceremony at St George's Chapel, Windsor; the Braemar

Gathering in Scotland; the State Opening of Parliament; and the Remembrance Day ceremony at the Cenotaph in Whitehall.

A large proportion of the letters from her private subjects pose personal problems and seek to secure the sovereign's aid. Many are passed on to the appropriate government departments for their consideration but all receive an acknowledgement from the Palace. Children's letters are usually handled by the ladies-in-waiting, whose knack of drafting warmly worded, captivating replies has become legendary. (In the matter of all types of correspondence, indeed, Palace officials show a far greater understanding of the need for well-chosen phrases than the general run of civil servants.)'

On a table next to the Queen's desk stand the red despatch-boxes containing secret government papers and sent every day to the Palace (or wherever the Queen happens to be) from 10 Downing Street and the Whitehall ministries. The boxes hold copies of the Cabinet minutes, and information on foreign affairs compiled by the Foreign and Commonwealth Office.

It has long been a well-known fact that the Queen is scrupulously conscientious about 'doing the boxes', and reads and remembers the smallest details. She has conditioned herself to be a fast reader, and in the earlier days of her reign would often catch out officials and ministers who erroneously assumed that she could not have noted everything set before her. On his retirement as Prime Minister, Sir Harold Wilson said the best advice he could offer his successor was to 'do his homework before his audience [with the Queen] and read all his telegrams and Cabinet committee papers in time, and not leave them to the week-end, or he will feel like an unprepared schoolboy'.

Although the Queen has her own copies of *Hansard*, the daily printed verbatim report of Parliamentary proceedings (named after Luke Hansard, who began printing the *House of Commons Journal* in 1774), she also receives each evening a special six-hundred-word summary of the day's business. This, by custom, is prepared for her by the Vice-Chamberlain, a junior government minister and member of the household (currently Anthony Berry, MP for Southgate) appointed by the Prime Minister.

The daily tasks of correspondence, the boxes and reading the Parliamentary report are supplemented, as needed, by a visit to the Queen by the Master of the Household, who comes to the study to discuss practical management affairs, and by a visit of the Keeper of the Privy Purse, who presents and analyses the household accounts.

The latter half of each morning is set aside for the Queen's reception, in the Audience Room, or the 1844 Room, of distinguished visitors, who are likely to range from an ambassador of a foreign government, come to present his letters of credence to the Court of St James's,* to a church or industrial leader or a senior officer of the armed forces. Found at the end of the royal apartments, the Audience Room is close to the Gift Room, which contains a collection of gifts of various sorts, most of them reserved by the Queen as personal family presents. Opposite is a door opening on to the small room, furnished with comfortably padded dog-baskets, where the corgis take their nightly rest.

Newly appointed ambassadors are brought to the Palace in one of the royal

---

* St James's remains the official title of the royal court even though ambassadors are no longer received at St James's Palace.

landaus – with others provided for the principal members of their staff – and accompanied by the Marshal of the Diplomatic Corps, Lord Michael Fitzalan Howard. They enter the Palace by way of the Grand Entrance. Occasionally these ceremonies can be rather strained affairs, depending upon the quality of the ambassador's English (or French, which the Queen speaks well) and on how 'friendly' his country and Britain are at the time. Experience has enabled Her Majesty to make most visitors feel at ease but there are times when even she is disconcerted by the stultifying effect which the awesome surroundings appear to have on some people. A classic occasion, recorded for posterity in the television film 'Royal Family', was the reception of the then American Ambassador, Walter Annenberg, who, having been thrown into a tizzy by the royal question as to where he and his wife were living, uttered the memorable reply: 'We're in the embassy residence, subject of course to some of the discomfiture as a result of a need for elements of refurbishing, rehabilitation.'

Among others to whom audiences are granted are bishops, British ambassadors on their way to overseas posts, and civil servants newly appointed as heads of government departments or retiring from the service. All of them expect the Queen to show a reasonable amount of knowledge about their particular spheres of work, and her close reading of official documents almost unfailingly stands her in good stead. She rarely needs to ask for a specific briefing on any notable. Since she is one of the most widely travelled of the world's heads of state, she finds it second nature to be able to introduce a good deal of 'local colour' and assessments of international leaders into her conversations on foreign affairs.

Despite the inevitable moments of tension on ceremonial occasions, every effort is made to help visitors to the Palace to feel relaxed. Before they arrive a footman circulates through the corridors, freshening the air by swinging a censer filled with smouldering lavender; and the imperturbable manner in which Palace officials explain ceremonial procedure to each arrival makes the whole process appear less forbidding. Yet, all the same, visitors are expected to pay careful attention to the traditional niceties – the forward steps towards the sovereign, the pause and the bow. As Lord Cobbold, the former Lord Chamberlain, put it: 'All ceremony is ridiculous if it isn't perfect. The whole thing is to keep the trappings and the mystery – and not look ridiculous. People like it and it retains some sort of dignity. As long as it doesn't get out of balance it isn't a bad thing.'

Inevitably, even royalty has to effect some compromises between the medieval and the modern, as an observant guest in the 1970s might have glimpsed. For example, at a state banquet in the Ball Room he would particularly have noted the footmen in their gold-braided scarlet, and remembered the strange sight of the Lord Chamberlain and Lord Steward entering the room backwards, their faces always towards the Queen and members of the royal family coming in procession from the Music Room. But later, if he were conveniently placed, he would have been intrigued to see the flash of red and green lights, concealed in flowers near the Queen's place at the table and operated by a steward, summoning the footmen to bring on or clear away the dishes.

Every Tuesday evening, unless one or other is away on state business or Parliament is in recess, the Queen receives her prime minister for a general discussion on government matters and policies. This is one of the principal occasions when the sovereign may, if she wishes (and according to the Walter Bagehot doctrine), offer advice or warnings. It is said that Clement Attlee, the first post-war Labour Prime Minister, and George VI – two shy men – would often sit silently for long periods staring tongue-tied into mid-distance. Now for the first time there are two women at the head of affairs in Britain – Elizabeth II and Mrs Margaret Thatcher – and it is intriguing to speculate on whether they sometimes take the opportunity to put aside the weighty problems of economic and world upheaval and indulge in cosy talk. No one knows, because the Tuesday meetings are always conducted in strict privacy with none but the Queen and Prime Minister present.

It has been suggested that by some discreet means (whether telephonic or telepathic is not clear) the Prime Minister is 'made aware' of what the Queen will be wearing that evening in order to avoid that real or imagined feminine catastrophe of a clash in colour or style of dress. But this is probably no more than another of the many pieces of dreamed-up gossip that surround the Palace and its people.

From time to time the Queen holds a meeting at the Palace (or, indeed, wherever she may happen to be) of her Privy Council – an event that highlights the curious and rigid formality which is a deep-rooted aspect of the sovereign's most important state duties. The Privy Council traces its ancestry back to Norman times, when kings surrounded themselves with a council of royal chief officials – the *Curia Regis* – which they could use as a sounding-board or as an ally in the application of their divine right. In Tudor times the Council became an all-powerful arm of government and developed, as all unrestrained forms of government must, into a tyranny. Those whose politics were considered dangerous found themselves arraigned before the Privy Council's notorious Court of Star Chamber. Later the Council's powers were reduced – and so was the number of members regularly consulted, for as Lord Macaulay, the historian, said: 'Every large collection of human beings, however well-educated, has a strong tendency to become a mob.' At the Restoration, therefore, Charles II sought advice from just a handful of Privy Councillors who formed a kind of committee of the main body. As the committee met in the King's small study, known as the royal closet, it came to be called the 'Cabinet'.

The Cabinet remains the centre of power, but today the activities of the Privy Council itself are limited to formalities – to receiving the Queen's approval, which she must voice in person, on such matters as Proclamations or Orders-in-Council, which give effect to Cabinet decisions, and to making appointments to Crown offices. It is all done in the Queen's name because every government of the United Kingdom is formally Her Majesty's Government, just as the opposition is Her Majesty's Opposition. And a meeting of the Privy Council is still officially described, with all the proper air of pomp and circumstance, as 'The Queen's Most Excellent Majesty in Council'.

Only on very special occasions is a full Council summoned – and for that the Queen must be truly grateful, for a complete roll-call of Privy Councillors today would produce more than three hundred names. The reason for the swollen size is that, in addition to members who have held high ecclesiastical or judicial office, all cabinet ministers are automatically honoured with the appointment, which they retain for the rest of their lives – unless 'advised' to resign as a result of some criminal or other heinous behaviour. (The most recent resignation of a Privy Councillor was that of John Stonehouse, a former Cabinet Minister jailed for theft and forgery in 1976.) Newly appointed Councillors are required to swear an oath to preserve the Queen's secrets – hence the confidential nature of Cabinet business – and to kiss hands with the Queen. Spotting Privy Councillors is easy: they are always referred to as 'the Right Honourable'.

In practice, now, the regular Council meetings are attended by three or four ministers (headed by the Lord President of the Council, who is also a member of the government) and the Clerk of the Council. This small group of officials forms the 'acting Council'.

At Buckingham Palace, meetings of the Privy Council are held in the 1844 Room. The Lord President is always summoned in first, and alone, to present the Queen with a résumé of the business due to be transacted. After some five or ten minutes the other Councillors are called to the royal presence by the rasp of a buzzer. As they file in they see Her Majesty standing in front of a round table with the Lord President on her right. In turn they shake the sovereign's hand and stand in line alongside the table – for, even though chairs are set in place, no one ever sits during a Privy Council meeting.

The Lord President reads out a summary of Orders-in-Council, official appointments and other decrees and documents requiring the Royal Assent, and in response to each the Queen pronounces the one word 'Approved'. On those occasions when appointments of county High Sheriffs must be made, a list of names is presented to the Queen on a roll of vellum and, against those selected, she stabs a tiny hole with the point of a brass bodkin – a tradition said to date back to an occasion when Elizabeth I, having mislaid her pen, pricked the names with her sewing-needle. The Queen does not actually put her personal signature to Acts of Parliament. A group of peers known as the Lords Commissioners, usually three, are appointed to apply the Royal Assent. In theory the sovereign has the power to refuse assent – called the Royal Veto – but the last to exercise such power was Queen Anne, in 1707.

If neither the Queen nor her Councillors have other urgent business to attend to, the meeting ends with a brief period of social conversation. The Queen is properly addressed as 'Ma'am'; but, according to a former Lord President, Richard Crossman, one Councillor, George Brown (now Lord George-Brown), amazed his colleagues by calling her 'My dear'. There is, however, no indication that she was outraged or even mildly annoyed – possibly because of the particular Privy Councillor's well-known natural warmth and exuberance.

Some fourteen times a year – six each in spring and autumn and eight in summer – the Queen holds investitures at the Palace at which she dispenses the honours awarded to her subjects in the New Year and (royal) Birthday lists. Only a few of the honours are in her personal gift – appointments to the Order of the Garter, the Order of the Thistle (a Scottish award), the Order of Merit (founded in 1902 by Edward VII), and the Royal Victorian Order and Royal Victorian Chain. The rest go to those selected by the government – around one thousand a year, out of a total of more than five thousand possibles. Anyone can suggest a name (except his or her own) simply by writing to the Prime Minister at 10 Downing Street, and every name is considered. The Queen is shown the provisional list, and unless she raises any objections – and, in view of the government's 'advice', she rarely does – those chosen are then told that they will be 'recommended' to the sovereign, provided they are willing to accept the proposed award. Most people are only too anxious to agree; on average each year a couple of dozen decline, usually because of personal objections to the honours system.

At one time the lower degrees of honours – OBEs and MBEs (Officers and Members of the Order of the British Empire) and BEMs (British Empire Medals) were generally regarded as suitable specifically to reward long and worthy service in local politics, municipal government, education, charitable trusts, trade unions and so on. More recently, however, the range of people chosen has been widened to embrace sportsmen, artists, journalists and pop stars.

On the morning of an investiture the recipients arrive at the Grand Entrance of the Palace at ten o'clock and are conducted up the Grand Staircase – lined by dismounted members of the Household Cavalry, which is composed of the British army's two senior regiments, The Life Guards and the Blues and Royals (Royal Horse Guards and 1st Dragoons) – and through the East Gallery to the Ball Room. In an annexe on the Ball Room's south side they are briefed on procedure by officials of the Central Chancery of the Orders of Knighthood (which organises the event and is part of the Lord Chamberlain's office) and to each jacket or dress is fixed a small hook on which the Queen will hang the appropriate medal. Meanwhile, the recipients' admiring relatives and friends – their admission tickets restricted to two for each honoured subject – wait in the Ball Room itself. In the gallery a Guards' or Royal Marines' orchestra plays selections of melodies from popular stage and screen musicals.

At eleven precisely the Queen enters with a posse of household officials and, smiling, walks to the west end of the Ball Room and to a dais set beneath a crimson velvet, gold-embroidered canopy. The orchestra strikes up the national anthem and at its conclusion the Queen bids the visitors to be seated. The seventy-five-minute ceremony begins.

As their names are called, the recipients emerge from the annexe, at the Queen's right-hand side of the dais, and approach the royal presence. First come the new knights, who bow and kneel at a footstool before the Queen. She takes up a long, slender sword and deftly and briefly touches the blade upon each shoulder of the kneeling figure. She does not, contrary to popular belief, utter the words 'Arise, Sir So-and-So.' The knights are followed by the rest of the morning's lucky ones, in descending order of award; in many cases the Queen will crown their own glorious day with a few chatty words, mostly about the particular merit that has brought them to the Palace. When an extra-special smile and an almost imperceptible nod indicate that the hallowed moment is over, the recipient takes three backward paces, bows again and leaves the Ball Room through a passage on the left of the dais, leading to the West Gallery. He or she is then free to stride proudly back along the Cross Gallery and the East Gallery and into the eastern end of the Ball Room to watch the rest of the proceedings seated on a white-and-gold chair.

Her Majesty stands throughout the ceremony, and what impresses most of those who have collected royal awards is that the smile which seems, from a distance, just that little bit too artificially turned on appears authentically personal and warm when viewed eye-to-eye. It is that remarkable ability to seem to show interest in a succession of fleeting faces, during what must sometimes be a tedious routine chore, that gives Elizabeth II (and the Queen Mother, for that matter) her particular charisma.

Far less decorous affairs than investitures are the annual Garden Parties held in the Palace grounds on three weekday afternoons (Tuesdays or Thursdays) in July. Queen Victoria started them in order to extend her contacts with the upper social set of her time. Today their main purpose is to reward those who have made some mark in their community or industry, or in commerce, with the privilege of being entertained to tea by the Queen in her own backyard. They are not exactly cosy get-togethers, however, for as many as nine thousand people may be invited on any one day. And it has been estimated that every party costs the Queen around £2 a head for tea and cakes and a further £3,000 for bandstands, tents, toilets and ambulance facilities (to cope with any fainting cases or sudden ill-health – not with any untoward effects from the food supplied by mass-catering companies).

At four o'clock twenty Yeomen of the Guard appear by the terrace beyond the garden windows of the Bow Room, and there is much shuffling and scuffling as the guests form two vast ranks facing expectantly towards the Palace. Soon afterwards the Queen and Prince Philip and other members of the family emerge, and there is a highly welcome hush while the national anthem is heard. Its final notes signal the start of the pushing and shoving and unseemly scrummage that so often characterises the garden parties.

The Queen and her husband progress along two separate pathways through the crowds, and, since there are no roped-off areas or barriers, fifty Gentlemen Ushers protect the royals from being overwhelmed. Nearly all these courtiers are ex-Service officers, tall and with impressive martial bearing, who keep their backs to the crowd and maintain an effective degree of order without appearing the least bit aggressive or discourteous. Her Majesty, followed by an equerry and one or two ladies-in-waiting, walks alongside the Lord Chamberlain, who conceals within his hand-held grey top-hat a list of particular notables with whom the Queen is expected to exchange a few moments of social chit-chat. At each pause in her stroll along the line, those at the back of the crowd press forward to catch the momentous exchange of words.

Elizabeth and Philip no doubt feel a certain sense of relief when there is a fairly full turn-out of the royal family – including, maybe, the Queen Mother, Prince Charles, Princess Margaret and Princess Anne – for then the pressures on them are somewhat eased. But for most of the guests a close view of the Queen is the whole purpose of the event. At one party the mayor of a London borough, standing on a green garden chair for a better view, summed up his afternoon: 'Our mayors are invited every year and, as we never get re-elected, this is my first and last garden party. But I've just seen her – and that's it! I'm off now.'

The Queen takes tea in the royal tent, the diplomats in theirs, and the crowds pile into the two-hundred-yard-long general tent. Democratically enough, the tea served in all three tents is the same, but there is no question of any 'general' tea-drinker gate-crashing the royal tent, whose area is clearly marked off with white chalk lines on the grass and chairs and which can be approached only by those bearing special tickets. After tea long lines form outside the ladies' and gents' toilets, discreetly placed under the trees and with proper plumbing. And all the time two bands provide a continuous supply of festive music – one band under an awning on the Constitution Hill side of the grounds, the other near the lake on the south side.

Royal garden parties are not all that much beloved of working Londoners, who fume about the traffic snarl-up caused by the guests' cars. Too often, too, it rains in July, and sodden feet and bedraggled dresses are the prices paid for an event which the Queen and Prince Philip must, very understandably, be happy to see over and done with.

Genuinely closer contacts with people outside the court are always difficult for any royals to make, but a move was launched in May 1956 for periodic, informal lunches at the Palace. Some are still held, although now less frequently. The purpose was to bring together groups of people, always eight at a time, whose varied interests and backgrounds would make for stimulating conversation and also give the royal couple extended insights into life and work beyond the Palace walls. Actors, authors, newspaper editors, sportsmen, musicians and popular entertainers have formed a cross-section of guests.

When such informal luncheons are held, guests assemble at twelve-thirty for sherry or martinis in the Bow Room, where a helpful equerry makes the introductions between those who may not have met before. After about five minutes the Queen enters and the guests are introduced to her by the Master of the Household. Some guests will have been 'recommended' by her household officials and others personally chosen by her or Prince Philip.

Lunch, at one, is taken in the adjoining 1844 Room. The dining-table is oval and the Queen sits halfway along one side, with the guests ranged around her. If either Philip or Prince Charles is present, he sits facing the Queen. Since none of the three 'first' members of the royal family are great eaters or drinkers, the menu will be one of plain fare – a starter, an English roast and a simple sweet, followed by biscuits and cheese or fresh fruit, and coffee. Two wines will be served – a hock and a claret – and, at the end of the meal, brandy or liqueurs.

When such luncheons first became regular features at the Palace many guests had mixed feelings about the likely benefits to the Queen. There was a tendency, they felt, for everyone to feel obliged to make some contribution, however unproductive, to the table-talk, and for there to be a certain rivalry as to who could make the most lasting impression and capture the royal ears. The Queen's great attribute at social occasions is her ability – honed by a lifetime's experience – to ensure that each person is given a chance to be noticed. At the same time, the effort required of any member of the family on such occasions is prodigious, and few people can feel completely at ease. Her Majesty tends to show greater interest in 'inside' gossip about professions and careers than in earnest dissertations.

At the end of one informal luncheon, signalled, as the moment always is, by the Queen's glance towards the steward who will draw back her chair, one guest at least felt a sense of relief, not for himself so much as for his sovereign. He said afterwards, 'Her skill as a hostess was impeccable, and she has an acute sense of humour. But I couldn't help feeling that she probably would have been happier enjoying a quiet, private meal without having to keep the conversational ball rolling all the time.' Some other guests, however, have found the luncheons entertaining and instructive and have been impressed by Her Majesty's breadth of interest. ('She didn't mention horses once,' said one, bearing in mind the Queen's reputation for being an excessively 'horsy' woman.)

Once every year, in late October or early November, the Queen leaves the Palace to perform one of her most important constitutional duties – the opening of the new session of Parliament. With all the trappings and archaic ceremony that attends it, this colourful event is an amalgam of many facets of the Crown in the United Kingdom. It is a reminder of the long history of the monarchy, reaching back now for close on a thousand years, and a reminder, too, of the relationship between the sovereign and her subjects – peers and commoners. And it is within the Palace of Westminster, the home of the two Houses of Parliament, that the only true royal throne in the kingdom stands; the thrones to be seen in Buckingham Palace are throne-chairs used at past coronations.

From the Palace to Parliament the Queen rides in the lumbering Irish State Coach, purchased by Queen Victoria in 1852 and drawn by four greys. She wears a diamond tiara, the Diadem, and the blue collar of the Order of the Garter which Prince Philip, sitting beside her, also wears on his uniform of an Admiral of the Fleet. Resplendent in scarlet and gold, the Master of the Horse rides in a following coach. In front and behind, silvered cuirasses shining like mirrors, trots a Sovereign's Escort of the Household Cavalry. Men of the regiments of Foot Guards line the route that takes the royal couple out of the Palace forecourt, along the Mall and down Whitehall (and, significantly, past the Banqueting Hall where Charles I, the challenger of Parliament, was despatched, headless, into eternity). Even for a Queen this is an awesome occasion, and no doubt Elizabeth recalls those distant history lessons when she first learned that the term 'parliament' is derived from the word 'parley' – for Norman kings would go to Westminster at Pentecost, wearing their crowns, to parley with the lords of the realm at a Great Council.

Her Majesty and her husband are met at the Palace of Westminster by the Lord Great Chamberlain,* the Marquis of Cholmondeley (pronounced 'Chumley') and the Earl Marshal, the Duke of Norfolk. Together, and walking backwards, they lead her to the robing room, where she puts on her ceremonial robe and the Imperial State Crown – removed, for this day, from the Tower of London.

Crowned, and with Prince Philip holding up her right hand, the Queen walks through the Royal Gallery towards the chamber of the House of Lords. Two pages, dressed in scarlet, bear the long crimson train of her robe and immediately in their footsteps tread the Mistress of the Robes and the ladies-in-waiting. Along the way, standing rigidly to attention, are the ranks of the Yeomen of the Guard, and the Gentlemen-at-Arms in tall, plumed helmets, grasping the hafts of their ceremonial axes.

As soon as Her Majesty is seated, the Gentleman Usher of the Black Rod goes to summon the members of the House of Commons to attend in the Lords' chamber. He knocks three times with his wand, and, in line with their traditional right not to admit a royal messenger if they so wish, the door is opened and immediately slammed in Black Rod's face. However, even if the Commons' attendants do not actually say 'Nothing personal, sir', or offer some similar apology, the House accepts this piece of play-acting with good humour, and led by the Prime Minister and Leader of the Opposition, members troop across the lobby to the Lords' chamber.

The scene there is glittering to behold: peers in their robes and coronets, a scattering of peers' wives (there is seldom room to accommodate many) in tiaras and evening gowns, judges in their full-bottomed wigs, bishops and, in a special enclosure, the representatives of foreign governments. And seated on the throne, at the far end of the chamber under a canopy, the Queen, with Prince Philip sitting on her left. Below the throne, further to the left, stands a peer holding the sheathed Sword of State upright and another holding the Cap of Maintenance.

When all are assembled, the Lord Chancellor, who presides over the House of Lords, steps forward, bows, and hands the Queen a printed copy of what is

* This was originally an hereditary Office of State (not to be confused with the Lord Chamberlain of the Household) granted by Henry I to the family of De Vere, Earls of Oxford. The male line, however, died out in the seventeenth century.

formally known as the Gracious Speech. It outlines the main points of government policy for the forthcoming Parliamentary session and is written by Her Majesty's ministers. The Queen adjusts her reading spectacles – one of the very few signs of her advancing years – and begins the recital of ministerial intentions, of which many paragraphs begin 'My Government will . . .' and 'A Bill will be brought before you . . .'.

The Queen's ministers stand listening to their own words with an air of smug self-satisfaction; the opposition leaders wear expressions of contrived neutrality, suitable to the great royal occasion but no doubt concealing inner feelings of outrage, incredulity or (in times when the government wields a decisive voting majority) hopeless resignation. Her Majesty, of course, has spent a large part of her adult lifetime pronouncing contradictory policies from the throne, since the British electorate's sympathies during her reign have swung back and forth between Conservative and socialist. So far (up to 1980) she has been served by no fewer than eight prime ministers, and has nodded sagely a thousand and one times in response to conflicting but cast-iron proposals for making Britain great again.

The ceremony concluded, the royal procession returns to the Palace and the Commons is left to get down to the uninhibited task of defending the Gracious Speech or tearing it into tatters as opposing political allegiances demand.

Even when there are no major state duties to perform, the three senior members of the royal family never spend a whole month within the confines of the Palace. Just one example of the range of events in their diaries is shown in the following list of royal engagements issued from Buckingham Palace for February 1980:

1st: The Prince of Wales visits the headquarters of the General and Municipal Workers' Union at Esher, in Surrey.

2nd: The Prince of Wales visits the British Institute of Management in London.

7th: The Duke of Edinburgh visits the safety vessel *MSV Tharos* near the Piper (oil) platform in the North Sea.

7th/8th: The Duke of Edinburgh, as Honorary Air Commodore, visits RAF Kinloss.

13th: The Duke of Edinburgh, as President of the Royal Society of Arts, presides at a meeting of the Committee for the Environment at Buckingham Palace.
The Queen, accompanied by the Duke of Edinburgh, opens the Vikings Exhibition at the British Museum.
The Prince of Wales, as principal speaker, attends the annual banquet of the British Chamber of Commerce in Bristol.

14th: The Queen and the Duke of Edinburgh give a reception at Buckingham Palace for the winners of the Queen's Award for export and technology.

19th: The Duke of Edinburgh, as President, attends a meeting of the Royal Mint Advisory Committee in London.

20th: The Duke of Edinburgh chairs the selection panel for the Duke of Edinburgh's Design Prize at the Design Centre in London.
The Queen opens the Hope Town Salvation Army Hostel in East London.
The Prince of Wales dines at Britannia Royal Navy College, Dartmouth.

22nd: The Queen, accompanied by the Duke of Edinburgh, opens the Elmsleigh Centre at Staines.

26th: The Queen holds an investiture at Buckingham Palace.
The Duke of Edinburgh opens the 'British Growers Look Ahead' national conference and exhibition of the National Farmers' Union at Harrogate.

From time to time both the Queen and her husband have routine duties to perform for some of the various armed services and other organisations in which they hold senior honorary ranks. For example, and to cite only a few in the total list, Her Majesty is Colonel-in-Chief of the Life Guards, Blues and Royals, Royal Scots Dragoon Guards, Royal Tank Regiment, Grenadier Guards, Coldstream Guards, Irish Guards, Welsh Guards, Canadian Grenadier Guards, 48th Highlanders of Canada, Royal Australian Infantry Corps and Royal New Zealand Infantry Regiment; and, among other things, she is Master of the Merchant Navy and Fishing Fleets and Lord High Admiral of the United Kingdom.

Prince Philip is an Admiral of the Fleet, Field-Marshal and Marshal of the Royal Air Force and holds similar posts in the Australian and New Zealand Royal Navies and Air Forces. He is also Colonel-in-Chief of various British, Canadian, Australian and New Zealand regiments, and so on and so on.

For a man in his position who has no official place in the constitution, Philip has built himself a busy working life. His interests are wide-ranging, but at some time in each week he is almost certain to be found immersed in matters arising from two subjects with which he is deeply concerned: conservation and the protection of wildlife. (He has produced two books – *Birds from Britannia,* a collection of bird photographs taken during voyages in the Royal Yacht, and *Wildlife Crisis*, written in collaboration with the naturalist, the late James Fisher.) He also gives much attention to one of his own most notable creations, the Duke of Edinburgh's Award Scheme, set up to give recognition to young people's efforts in such fields as adventurous enterprises, public service, rescue work and craftsmanship.

In the privacy of his own rooms he now wears spectacles to correct his shortsightedness, but manages sufficiently well without them in public. He used to worry at first about going bald but ceased after realising that popular opinion no longer regards baldness as necessarily unbecoming.

Although he does not carry the formal title of Consort, as did Victoria's Albert, he is the first gentleman of the realm, having been created as such by a royal warrant issued by the Queen soon after her accession, which declared that her husband would henceforth upon all occasions, 'except where otherwise provided by Act of Parliament, have, hold and enjoy Place, Pre-eminence and Precedence next to Her Majesty'.* But he is also the only husband in the realm who has taken an oath of fealty to his wife, in the memorable words of the Coronation ceremony: 'I, Philip, Duke of Edinburgh, do become your liege man of life and limb and earthly worship, and faith and truth will I keep unto you against all manner of folks. So help me God.'

On each 20 November, the anniversary of the royal wedding, there are always flowers for the Queen on the breakfast-table in the private dining-room at the Palace – a remembrance gift from Philip.

With all their tasks to attend to, the Queen, Philip and Prince Charles see little of each other during the Palace working day; Prince Charles, in any case, has his separate establishment and friends, and family meals are rare events. Most of the royals' daytime contacts are confined to brief talks on the intercom system, which was one of Philip's innovations.

When they have no evening engagements, the Queen and her husband usually dine alone, and often, as at breakfast, serve themselves. (As with breakfast, also,

* After the Queen and Philip the next nine personages in the kingdom in order of precedence are Prince Charles, Prince Andrew, Prince Edward, the Archbishop of Canterbury, the Lord High Chancellor, the Archbishop of York, the Prime Minister, the Lord President of the Council and the Speaker of the House of Commons.

the food is taken in heated containers two hundred yards along a corridor from the kitchens and up two floors by lift.) They no longer maintain the once inflexible aristocratic habit of dressing for dinner. If the Queen Mother is to join them for a meal, the Queen makes a point of pretending that it will be served half an hour before its actual time. The Queen Mother has reverted to her lifelong habit of unpunctuality, which she forswore only during the years of the Second World War. But nowadays the rigging of the time usually fails in its purpose, since she is far too astute a woman not to have seen through the ruse, and still arrives late.

In private Philip often prefers a beer with his food, rather than wine, and the Queen, who shares many of her subjects' attachment to superstition, has been known to throw spilled salt over her shoulder.

The pattern of free evenings at home for the royal couple is very much a duplicate of that followed by most people in Britain – communion with the television set. Hardly surprisingly, the Queen enjoys 'horsy' programmes, and Philip is more attracted to wildlife documentaries or current-affairs specials on industry and industrial problems. He is a regular viewer of programmes that deal with new technical and scientific developments.

Both like 'situation' comedy shows (partly, perhaps, because they throw some light on the things that ordinary people find amusing or frustrating in their everyday lives) and historical drama series. *Edward and Mrs Simpson* was avidly followed at the Palace – in particular by Prince Charles, who is understandably fascinated by the life of the man whose abdication was instrumental in ensuring that he would be the heir-apparent. But the Queen and Philip are said to have a distinct aversion to some of the modern 'plotless' television plays. In drama, it seems, they endorse a popular belief in the need for 'a beginning, a middle and a good surprise ending'. Serious conflict about the choice of viewing is hardly likely to emerge behind the closed doors of the private apartments, anyway, since Prince Philip can videotape whatever it was that he or the Queen was unable to see on the night of transmission.

If there is nothing the pair wish to watch on television, the Queen often finishes her favourite crossword puzzle – the one in the *Daily Telegraph* – or she and Philip read; she likes biographies, he is often absorbed in books about the countryside. Even after thirty-three years of marriage, and the endlessly repeated rounds of pageantry in which they have shared, they still find plenty to talk about and even to be amused and surprised at in each other's reactions to the events of the day – even though Prince Philip is allowed to have less first-hand knowledge of state documents than his son Charles, the heir to the Throne.

Evenings finish comparatively early for the royal couple, at around eleven o'clock, and 'Bobo' is usually there to see the Queen to bed. Tomorrow the routine starts again, except when tomorrow is Saturday and the Queen and her husband have escaped from the gloom of the Palace on Friday afternoon and travelled to Windsor for a quiet, free weekend.

Nothing could be further from the truth than that life at the Palace is one endless round of enviable glamour and prodigal living. Elaborate ceremony may be delightfully memorable for once-in-a-lifetime participants, but it is crushingly tedious at times if you are the person always on parade and expected to appear totally fascinated by it all. There is also a certain irony in being mistress of vast and splendid state apartments but confined to living-quarters, comfortable as they are, that occupy just one small area of your Palace.

Yet the Palace is where the people expect the Queen to be. It has taken root in the national consciousness as the centre for the royal family, and is likely to remain so as long as the monarchy survives. One day it may be rebuilt – although nothing is more unlikely at present; yet many people would feel that the Palace was no longer the 'real' Palace if it were torn down and replaced by a modern, more efficiently functional royal headquarters. This may well be a depressing prospect for Prince Charles, who is said to share the age-old royals' antipathy to the place but who one day, excluding some disaster, will inherit the Palace as King.

There are, of course, those who would like to see Buckingham Palace turned entirely into a museum, as the Winter Palace in Leningrad is now a museum. They argue that in a modern democracy the monarchy is an anachronism. Kings and queens no longer govern, nor do they wield any decisive power; it has been suggested that, constitutionally, if the sovereign were to be presented with a Parliamentary bill requiring her execution she would have no choice but to assent to it. In such circumstances why preserve a structure that no longer serves a positive, practical purpose?

The answer almost certainly is that the vast majority of people care little about the practical purposes of the monarchy but a great deal about its deep-rooted and powerful mystique. They look to the sovereign as a symbol, however indefinable, that he or she is at least one institution that stands securely above the rack and turmoil of an uncertain and perilously changing world. And Buckingham Palace enshrines the symbol.

APPENDIX

SELECTED
BIBLIOGRAPHY

INDEX

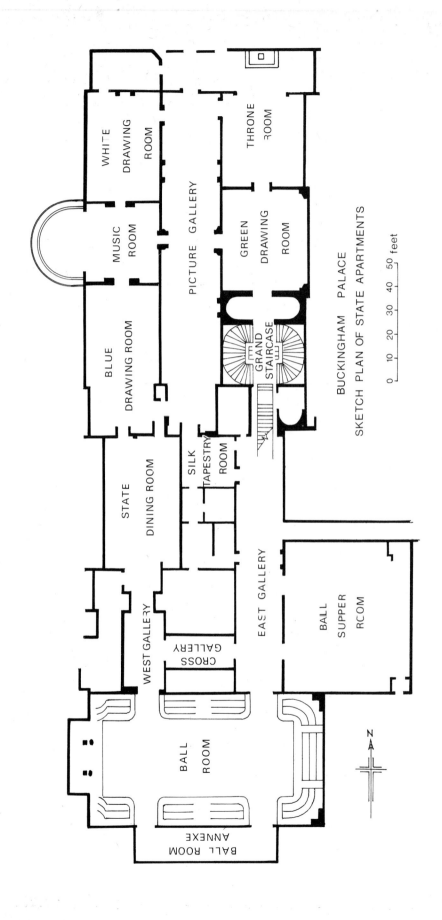

WHITE DRAWING ROOM

MUSIC ROOM

BLUE DRAWING ROOM

STATE DINING ROOM

WEST GALLERY

PICTURE GALLERY

SILK TAPESTRY ROOM

CROSS GALLERY

THRONE ROOM

GREEN DRAWING ROOM

GRAND STAIRCASE

EAST GALLERY

BALL ROOM

BALL SUPPER ROOM

BALL ROOM ANNEXE

BUCKINGHAM PALACE

SKETCH PLAN OF STATE APARTMENTS

0   10   20   30   40   50 feet

N

APPENDIX

THE STATE APARTMENTS

TWO AREAS ONLY OF THE PALACE are open to the general public: the Royal Mews and the Queen's Gallery.

The Royal Mews, where visitors can see the state carriages, horses, harnesses and other regalia, are open on Wednesdays and Thursdays (except during Ascot week in the middle of June) from 2 p.m. until 4 p.m.

Selected items from Her Majesty's collection of art works are on view daily from Tuesday to Saturday between 11 a.m. and 5 p.m. and on Sundays from 2 p.m. to 5 p.m. in the Queen's Gallery, which stands on the site of the former chapel destroyed during the Second World War. Paintings from the collection are rotated from time to time, in order to cover the widest possible range, and among works usually to be seen are those by such masters as Canaletto, van Dyck, Vermeer, Rubens, Lely (who had the distinction of being employed by both Charles I and Cromwell and who became court painter to Charles II), Joshua Reynolds, Gainsborough, Winterhalter (one of Victoria's painters), and Pietro Annigoni, famous for his 1955 portrait of Queen Elizabeth II and who also painted portraits of the Duke of Edinburgh and Princess Margaret.

The Palace's most famous public spectacle, to be seen on most mornings throughout the year, is, of course, the Changing of the Guard.

Seven regiments of the Household Division comprise the Queen's bodyguard: Grenadier Guards, Welsh Guards, Scots Guards, Irish Guards, the Blues and Royals, and the Life Guards.

Although all the regiments are also employed on active service, their guarding of the Palace and the sovereign is basically a ceremonial duty. The hour-long Change begins at eleven o'clock when the Old Guard (the guard about to be relieved) is inspected in the Palace forecourt. Half-an-hour later the New Guard marches in from its barracks to the sound of martial music and, with traditional and colourful ritual, formally takes over its Palace duties. To more music, the Old Guard marches away.

For those who may not be invited to an investiture, a state banquet or a private viewing, the following is a summary of some of the main rooms and other areas of the Palace that form the famous state apartments.

On major state occasions the Palace 'begins' for honoured guests at the Principal Entrance, the archway centrally placed in the east front of the building facing across the forecourt to the Mall. This leads into:

The Grand Hall: a spacious area, slightly smaller at first sight than one might expect of a royal palace but made elegant and impressive by pairs of columns (each pair cut from a single block of veined Carrara marble) and by the white walls and ceiling with their ornamentations in gold. The floor is also of white marble and so is the magnificent mantelpiece – one of the finest in the Palace. Surmounting the mantelpiece and inset in a circular niche is a small bust of the man who inspired the whole building – George IV.

The feature that immediately catches the eye, however, as the visitor looks to the left, facing towards the south end of the Palace, is:

The Grand Staircase. This broad flight of crimson-carpeted marble steps, decorated in white and gold, leads up to a point at which two further flights diverge to left and right. At the conjunction of those two flights stands a marble doorway, flanked by portraits of William IV (on the right) and Queen Adelaide (on the left). Through the doorway the visitor proceeds northwards towards the Green Drawing Room and the Throne Room.

The Green Drawing-Room: 53 feet long by 41 feet wide, this is used for assembling deputations before they are received in the Throne Room. Its walls are decorated with pilasters of white and gold supporting a gilded frieze composed of wreaths of laurel. From the richly ornamented ceiling hang cut-glass lustres with icicle crystals and faceted drops. As in all the state apartments, the oak floor has an inlaid surround typical of English marquetry at its best. Two marble fireplaces, one on each side of the doorway in the western wall which leads into the Picture Gallery, are carved with representations of female figures and surmounted by tall mirrors. Among the furnishing and fittings in the room are a French Empire clock, with the figure of Apollo on one side of the dial, and two fine Italian cabinets. One of these, a gift to George IV, is of ebony and lapis lazuli and the other has a marble front and lapis lazuli columns.

At the north end a marble-framed doorway, topped with a bust of William IV, leads into:

The Throne Room. The central features of this 60-foot-long room are the two thrones of carved and gilt wood set on a three-step dais under a canopy of red velvet with gold fringes. At night seven cut-glass chandeliers illuminate the room and are reflected in the tall, gilt-framed mirror over the marble mantelpiece.

On the walls flanking the thrones are four eighteenth-century wood-carvings in Louis XVI style representing the intermingling of musical instruments, birds, foliage, fruit and arrow-quivers. Each carving gives the impression of a resplendent cascade suspended by the wood-carved version of a silken bow.

The Picture Gallery: this occupies the whole of the central area of the first floor on the west side of the Palace and is 155 feet long by 27 feet wide. Its great glass ceiling is lighted from above, and its walls are lined with many of the finest pictures in the Queen's art collection. (Some of the canvases are 'rotated' between here and the Queen's Gallery, where they can be seen by the public.)

The Picture Gallery separates the Green Drawing-Room and Throne Room, on the east side of the building, from the next three rooms to be described here, which are on the west side.

The White Drawing-Room: 48 feet long, this white-and-gold room is often used by members of the royal family as a centre for assembling before a state function such as a banquet or ball. A huge mirror in one wall is, in fact, a 'secret' door and swings open to admit the royal residents. Over the frieze and cornice are twelve sculptured panels depicting children at play, designed in 1831 by the artist William Pitts. The gold-ornamented ceiling is convex; from its centre is suspended a cut-glass chandelier with an ormolu framework and twenty-four upright candle-shaped lights held in two rings. A number of beautiful candelabra also decorate the room, two pairs of the Louis XIV period being bronze figures holding clusters of lights.

The Music Room: adjoining the White Drawing-Room, this is notable for its vast bay of five great windows, looking out over the palace gardens and lake, topped by a half-dome which is wedded to the room's main dome. In the main dome a series of diamond-shaped panels are decorated, alternately, with representations of the rose, shamrock and thistle. Over the three doorways are sculptured panels showing groups of children representing Harmony, Eloquence and Pleasure. Set into the ceiling, at each corner of the room, are shields bearing the royal arms. The whole area of domes and ceiling is supported by no fewer than eighteen columns in deep blue scagliola – Italian plasterwork which is an almost perfect imitation of stone. At night the room is lighted by two of the most enormous chandeliers in the Palace, one suspended from the smaller dome and the other from the larger dome.

The Blue Drawing-Room: 68 feet long, this was the ballroom until, in 1854, the present Ball Room was added to the south wing of the building. One of the main eye-catching features of this most elegant room is the highly decorated ceiling, into which are let inverted-saucer-shaped domes. Gold-framed mirrors appear, through reflection, to enlarge the room; one of these stands above the marble mantelpiece, to the right of which hangs a portrait of Edward VII and, to the left, one of his Queen, Alexandra. In this room, too, a picture of George Villiers, Duke of Buckingham, with his wife and two children, reminds the visitor of the very early days of the Palace: the painting once hung in the King's Dining-Room of what was then 'Queen's House'.

Among the many memorable objects collected here is an astronomical clock which stands on the mantelpiece and shows the passing of the hours, days, weeks and months and the lunar changes. The general furnishings are of the Regency period.

From the south end a glass-panelled doorway leads into:

The State Dining Room: 74 feet long and 34 feet wide, this was designed by

Edward Blore, successor to John Nash, whose ceiling repeats the decoration of inverted-saucer domes used by Nash in the Blue Drawing-Room.

Above one of the two marble mantelpieces stands a portrait by Sir Thomas Lawrence of the creator of the modern Palace, George IV. The spreading-arm stance of the King, sweeping open his cloak, generates the curious impression of a rather perky rooster. On each side of him hang two Gainsborough portraits of his parents – his father, George III, to the right, and his mother, Queen Charlotte, to the left. The Queen's expression betrays a certain resignation to fate – which, in all the circumstances of her time, is not unduly surprising.

The great dining-table top is of Spanish mahogany and can be extended by leaves, eight feet wide and three feet long, to seat up to sixty guests. The Regency dining-chairs are in gilt with crimson satin brocade upholstery.

At the southern end of the room doors give access to:

The West Gallery: 32 feet long by 16 feet wide, with an arched roof and carvings over the doorways representing the Birth of Venus and Venus with the Armour of Achilles. The walls are draped with Gobelin tapestries from the Louis XV period which depict scenes from Cervantes' story of *Don Quixote*.

The gallery takes the visitor directly into:

The Ball Room: designed for Queen Victoria by James Pennethorne and built between 1853 and 1855. This is the largest of all the state apartments – 133 feet long, 60 feet wide and 45 feet high – and is used for state banquets and investitures as well as state balls.

Immediately upon entering from the West Gallery the visitor sees the two thrones set on a shallow dais and in front of a high, gold-embroidered canopy of crimson velvet. The canopy is formed from the hangings of the imperial Shamiana, or awning, beneath which George V and Queen Mary were seated at the Delhi Durbar in 1911.

At the opposite (eastern) end of the room stands the great organ, with its gilded pipes, and the musicians' gallery. The ceiling is divided into square panels, within each of which is a sunken octagonal decoration. On state occasions the parquetry floor is overlaid with a crimson carpet and at night six great lustre chandeliers give the whole apartment a shimmering glory.

When the room is used for a state banquet the Queen enters, preceded by the Lord Chamberlain and Lord Steward walking backwards, and takes her place at the centre of a huge horseshoe-shaped table, with her guests seated on each side of her in order of precedence. The food is served on gold plates and wine is supped from glasses of English cut crystal which bear the cypher 'E II R'. Two footmen (the term 'waiter' is never used at the Palace) attend upon every eight guests.

There is (as we saw in the earlier account of an investiture) an annexe to the Ball Room, on the south side, and doors at the musicians' gallery end lead into:

The East Gallery: 106 feet long, this directly links the Ball Room to the Grand Staircase. Among its principal features are seven pairs of great doorways, fitted with mirrored doors, and a marble mantelpiece in the east wall carved with winged figures representing the Art of Painting.

To the right of the gallery (as the visitor faces towards the Grand Staircase) two pairs of mirrored doors provide access to:

The Supper Room: 65 feet long, 58 feet wide, 45 feet high. Guests take supper in this domed apartment on the occasion of state balls, observed by the carved busts of George IV, William IV, Queen Victoria and her Albert.

Opposite the southern doorway to the Supper Room is the Cross Gallery, transversely linking the West and East Galleries. Further northwards along the East Gallery the visitor comes to the last of the main set of state apartments:

The Silk Tapestry Room: 26 feet long, 23 feet wide, this small apartment forms, in effect, an annexe to the Picture Gallery (see above) and owes its name to the four panels of seventeenth-century silk tapestries which adorn its walls and represent scenes from the Bible.

Immediately outside the Silk Tapestry Room, the Grand Staircase takes the visitor back down to the ground floor of the Palace. By passing from room to room in the manner which has been described, he has completed an entire circuit of the state apartments. On the ground floor, however, are to be found the so-called semi-state apartments, among which are the following.

The Bow Room: this central apartment is the one room in the Palace known to thousands of 'outsiders', since it is through here that garden-party guests make their way on to the lawns. When opened, its five tall windows in the vast bay form doorways giving access to the terrace. Decorations are white and gold, and graceful columns support the ceiling. The doorway to the room is flanked on each side by black marble mantelpieces with Egyptian-style ormolu mounts.

The 1844 Room: so named after the year in which it accommodated Queen Victoria's guest, Emperor Nicholas of Russia. An elegant, white-and-gold room with a crimson carpet and a ceiling supported by double columns. A special feature among the *objets d'art* is the 'Negress-head' clock – a bronze bust of an African girl in whose left eye appear the hours and in whose right eye appear the minutes of the day.

The Belgian Suite: this group of four rooms (plus the adjoining Carnaervon Room, which serves as a dining-room) is on the north-west corner of the Palace and is used mainly as accommodation for distinguished guests.

Individual rooms in the suite (which was occupied, during his brief reign, by Edward VIII) are: the *Eighteenth-Century Room,* used as a reception room; *the Orleans Bedroom,* furnished with a Louis XVI gilt bed, in which Prince Andrew was born on 19 February 1960; *the Spanish Dressing-Room,* with portraits of the royal family of Spain on the walls; and *the Regency Room,* which is the suite's sitting-room.

Further semi-state apartments are to be found on the east front of the first floor (known at the Palace as the 'principal floor'), including *the Yellow Drawing-Room* and *the Blue Sitting-Room,* but the most notable is:

The Centre Room: 34 feet wide by 26 feet long. It is through the middle french window of this room that the Queen and other members of the royal family emerge on special occasions on to the balcony to acknowledge the crowds gathered outside the Palace. The décor is oriental, with Chinese ornaments and six panels of yellow embroidered silk. The door panels are of gold-and-ivory lacquer, and the pearl-inlaid chairs have coloured dragons as the motif of the satin-brocaded upholstery. Other main features of the room include two marble and ormolu chimneypieces which were originally in the banqueting-room of Brighton Pavilion. Upon the fenders of each of the fireplaces stand two fiery dragons in ormolu, one looking to the left, the other to the right. Ebony cabinets, also from Brighton Pavilion, have door-panels of Japanese gold lacquer with landscape decorations.

Also included in the semi-state apartments is *the Household Dining-Room,* on the ground floor, with windows facing west. Here, in this room with alcoves at each end supported by four white marble pillars, members of the household take their meals – plain food, and no alcohol served.

Among the many corridors which are such notable features of the Palace, one of the most impressive is *the Household Corridor:* 257 feet long, it traverses the whole length of the first floor of the south wing, overlooking the Quadrangle.

The Garden Entrance is on the north front of the Palace and approached by a driveway which passes through a great stone portico on top of which stand the lion and the unicorn. In the centre of the large bay of the Entrance is the garden doorway, used by the Queen and members of the royal family. The stone floor of the Entrance is interlaced with small squares of black Belgian marble. The frieze around the walls is of a honeysuckle pattern.

Gardens: the magnificent gardens, a touch of the countryside in the heart of London, cover 39 acres and have two and a half miles of gravel paths. Special features include a large lake, some 400 feet long and 150 feet across at the widest point, and several species of wildfowl with little grebe and tufted duck among them. There are flamingoes and Japanese cranes, a tennis court, a summer house and a helicopter pad much used by Prince Philip and Prince Charles. Rhododendrons, camellias, magnolias and many other shrubs abound. Among the trees are plane, Indian chestnut, silver maple and a swamp cypress. And in the south-west corner, still flourishing after some 370 years, is a solitary surviving mulberry from that very plantation which was the starting-point of the story of Buckingham Palace.

SELECTED BIBLIOGRAPHY

The earliest years:

FULFORD, Roger. *George the Fourth*, Duckworth, 1949.

GRAEME, Bruce. *The Story of Buckingham Palace*, Hutchinson, 1928.

GREEN, David. *Queen Anne*, Collins, 1970.

HIBBERT, Christopher. *George IV*, Allen Lane, 1973.

LATHAM, K., and MATTHEWS, W., ed. *The Diary of Samuel Pepys*, Bell, 1970.

MACAULAY, T. B. (Lord). *The History of England*, Dent, 1967.

WILSON, J. H. *A Rake and His Times, George Villiers, 2nd Duke of Buckingham*, Frederick Muller, 1954.

ZIEGLER, Philip. *King William IV*, Collins, 1971.

The middle years:

BOLITHO, Hector. *Edward VIII*, Eyre & Spottiswoode, 1937.

COWLES, Virginia. *King Edward VII and His Circle*, Hamish Hamilton, 1956.

CUST, Sir Lionel. *King Edward VII and His Court*, John Murray, 1930.

DONALDSON, Frances. *Edward VIII*, Weidenfeld and Nicolson, 1979.

GORE, John. *King George V, A Personal Memoir*, John Murray, 1941.

HIRD, Frank. *Victoria, The Woman*, Appleton, 1908.

JUDD, Denis. *Life and Times of George V*, Weidenfeld and Nicolson, 1973.

LONGFORD, Elizabeth. *Victoria R.I.*, Weidenfeld and Nicolson, 1964.

MAGNUS, Philip. *King Edward VII*, John Murray, 1964.

NICOLSON, Harold, *King George V, His Life and Reign*, Constable, 1952.

SMITH, H. Clifford. *Buckingham Palace, Its Furniture, Decoration and History*. Country Life, 1931.

SITWELL, Edith. *Victoria of England*, Faber and Faber, 1936.

TOOLEY, Sarah A. *The Personal Life of Queen Victoria*, Hodder and Stoughton, 1896.

WOODHAM-SMITH, Cecil. *Queen Victoria, Her Life and Times* (2 vols), Hamish Hamilton, 1972.

WINDSOR, Duchess of. *The Heart Has Its Reasons*, Michael Joseph, 1956.

WINDSOR, Duke of. *A King's Story*, Cassell, 1951.

The later years:
BARRYMAINE, Norman. *Peter Townsend*, Peter Davies, 1958.
HARDINGE, Lady (Helen). *Loyal to Three Kings*, William Kimber, 1967.
MIDDLETON, Keith. *The Life and Times of George VI*, Weidenfeld and Nicolson, 1974.
NARES, Gordon. *Royal Homes*, Country Life, 1953.
PONSONBY, Sir Frederick. *Recollections of Three Reigns*, Eyre and Spottiswoode, 1951.
SPENCER SHEW, Betty. *Royal Wedding*, Macdonald, 1947.
TALBOT, Godfrey. *Ten Seconds from Now*, Hutchinson, 1973.
WHEELER-BENNETT, Sir John W. *King George VI, His Life and Reign*, Macmillan, 1958.

Elizabeth II:
CHURCHILL, Randolph S. *They Serve the Queen*, Hutchinson, 1953.
CHURCHILL, Winston S. *The Second World War*, Cassell, 1948.
COUNIHAN, Daniel. *Royal Progress*, Cassell, 1977.
FROST, Conrad. *Coronation, June 2, 1953*, Arthur Barker, 1978.
HIBBERT, Christopher. *The Court of St James*, Weidenfeld and Nicolson, 1979.
HOWARD, Philip. *The British Monarchy*, Hamish Hamilton, 1977.
LACEY, Robert. *Majesty*, Hutchinson, 1977.
LAIRD, Dorothy. *How the Queen Reigns*, Hodder and Stoughton, 1959.
LIVERSIDGE, Douglas. *Queen Elizabeth II, The British Monarchy Today*, Arthur Barker, 1974.
MARTIN, Kingsley. *The Crown and the Establishment*, Hutchinson, 1962.
MURRAY-BROWN, Jeremy (Ed.). *The Monarchy and Its Future*, George Allen and Unwin, 1969.
PETRIE, Sir Charles. *The Modern British Monarchy*, Eyre and Spottiswoode, 1961.
SAMPSON, Anthony. *The New Anatomy of Britain*, Hodder and Stoughton, 1971.
WILSON, Mary (and others). *The Queen*, Allen Lane, 1977.
ZIEGLER, Philip. *Crown and People*, Collins, 1978.

INDEX

Numerals in *italics* refer to captions

Buckingham Palace